PROVOKING

FEMINISMS

PROVOKING
FEMINISMS

Edited by **Carolyn Allen and Judith A. Howard**

The University of Chicago Press ■ *Chicago and London*

The essays in this volume originally appeared in various issues of SIGNS: JOURNAL OF
WOMEN IN CULTURE AND SOCIETY. Acknowledgment of the original publication data
can be found on the first page of each essay.

The University of Chicago Press, Chicago 60637
The University of Chicago Press, Ltd., London
© 2000 by The University of Chicago
All rights reserved. Published 2000
Printed in the United States of America
04 03 02 01 00   5 4 3 2 1

Library of Congress Cataloging-in-Publication Data

Provoking feminisms / edited by Carolyn Allen and Judith A. Howard.
     p. cm.
     Includes bibliographical references and index.
     ISBN 0-226-01437-1 (cloth) — ISBN 0-226-01439-8 (pbk.)
     1. Feminist theory. I. Allen, Carolyn. II. Howard, Judith A.

HQ1190 .P78 2000
305.42′01 — dc21

                                                    00-033774

The paper used in this publication meets the minimum requirements of American
National Standard for Information Sciences — Permanence of Paper for Printed
Library Materials, ANSI Z39.48-1984.

Contents

Carolyn Allen
Judith A. Howard

Feminisms as Provocation

When scholars writing about ongoing debates and issues involving gender, race, class, culture, sexuality, and nation and their intersections — that is to say, feminist scholars — consider such scholarship at the beginning of the twenty-first century, what kinds of debates emerge as most pressing, what critical conversations are going on and ongoing, what methodologies are employed, what disciplinary boundaries are being crossed in interdisciplinary thinking? What questions are asked? Which questions recur? Do the forms of the questions indicate the disciplines of the askers, even in interdisciplinary contexts? How do feminist voices in an increasingly global world speak to and across one another? What lines of thought have been productive and which ones dead ends? Are there political concerns frequently voiced but not yet theorized? What is the relation of feminist thinking in the academy to the lives of women (and men?) outside the academy? This collection of recent essays in feminist thinking, published in *Signs: Journal of Women in Culture and Society* in the final four years of the twentieth century, raises these and other questions of crucial interest to feminist scholars at the beginning of the twenty-first century. Together these essays provide readers with a sense of what debates are most critical at the present moment of feminist scholarship.

When *Signs* came to the University of Washington in 1995, we as editors wanted to complement its long-standing reputation as the leading scholarly journal in women and gender studies by taking it in new directions and encouraging scholarly exchanges, perhaps even provoking some controversy, given the by now many and complicated versions of feminism alive in the United States and elsewhere. To that end, we began to invite responses to pieces of wide interdisciplinary interest. We looked especially to scholars whose work had been discussed in the germinating essay, but occasionally also to others with well-known interests in the topics of the essays. This volume collects some of those essays and responses published in *Signs* in recent years. It takes as its organizing principle *provocation,* in that it is designed both to provoke further response and to indicate the lively differences of opinion that characterize the most pressing debates in academic feminist work.

The first set of exchanges comes in response to Susan Hekman's essay,

"Truth and Method: Feminist Standpoint Theory Revisited." With responses by several of the best-known thinkers in feminist theory whose work collectively in large measure constitutes standpoint theory itself—Nancy Hartsock, Patricia Hill Collins, Sandra Harding, and Dorothy Smith—the exchange gives readers a sense of both the development of such thinking and the debates that are currently salient. The stakes include such questions as whether standpoint theory, centered as it is in the lives and experiences of women, has remained sufficiently labile to include the theorization of differences among women and the turn to postmodernism so characteristic of U.S. feminist thought in the eighties and nineties. At the same time, it raises, as its title indicates, questions of feminist standpoint theory as "truth," that is, as a privileged epistemology for thinking about issues of justice for women, and as "method," with its emphasis on the lived lives of women as grounds for understanding women's oppression. Hekman reads standpoint theories as more postmodern, more attentive to discourse than is ordinarily assumed and proposes an alternative epistemology, focused on Max Weber's "ideal types."

She works with an assumption that politics and epistemology are inseparable and argues that the central question of feminist standpoint theory has been how feminists justify the truth of the claim that women have been and are oppressed. She argues that women cannot resist oppression and gain political power unless they can legitimate this claim. The shift in standpoint theory during the 1980s originated in the demand for recognition of differences among women. She draws on Weber's work as an approach that explains and justifies the necessarily engaged, political role of the social analyst. She also attempts to explain and justify the conceptual status of the appeal to "women's experience" so that it does not fall prey to the epistemological confusions that the appeal has, in Hekman's view, generated. Throughout the essay, her purpose is to trace how standpoint theory, with its connections to the Enlightenment tradition, also deconstructs that tradition.

Her respondents speak back to her, pointing out ways in which differences among women are accounted for in their work and stressing, among other things, the importance not so much of individual experiences but of what Hill Collins calls, "the social conditions that construct" groups. Hartsock, Collins, Smith, and Harding are all concerned that in her emphasis on method, Hekman is in danger of undercutting the political efficacy of standpoint theorizing. As a group they also stress the importance, both theoretically and politically, of collective rather than individual standpoints.

The second exchange, like the first, also focuses on a well-known version of recent feminist thought—theories of sexual difference. Again, like the first exchange, its reach is global in that it centers differences among women at the heart of its provocation. Just as the first exchange refers to current debates over epistemological formations in feminist thought, so this second one focuses in part on the role of psychoanalytic discourses and sources in recent scholarship. The initiating essay, Rita Felski's "The Doxa of Difference," suggests that emphasis on sexual difference has led feminist scholars to exclude too readily other kinds of differences. In an argument that is both philosophical and political, she points to current gender work in postcolonial theory as a set of discourses that recognizes the difficulties of "diversity" when hierarchical differences are not also taken into account. She argues that "difference" has become "doxa," a "magical word of theory and politics radiant with redemptive meanings," and offers a systematic explanation of what she sees as theoretical inconsistencies as well as political problems evident in appeals to difference within feminist thought. Her aim is not so much to polemicize against difference but, instead, to deontologize it by offering a redescription of the status of equality and difference framed in pragmatic, rather than metaphysical, terms. She emphasizes that these terms exist in a condition of necessary philosophical and political interdependence, such that the very pursuit of difference returns always to the seemingly obsolete issues of equality. In the course of the essay she discusses sexual difference as doxa but argues for the productive dissension available in postcolonial feminisms.

Her respondents, whose work Felski critiques, are Rosi Braidotti, Drucilla Cornell, and Ien Ang. Each of them comments on Felski's critique but also goes beyond defending her earlier articulated positions to point to new insights in recently published or about-to-be published work. Thus, readers have a sense not only of how the respondents' differing global positions matter in their responses but also of how work such as Braidotti's on nomadism, and on the declining influence of French culture in Europe, Cornell's on a theory of equality based on the self-representation of what she calls our "sexuate being," and Ang's on the irreducible incommensurabilities among women of different cultural locations is moving feminist thinking forward in new and continuing attentions to "difference," to "equality," and to non-U.S. sites of provocation.

The next two exchanges may be read as taking up more specialized debates that situate themselves on the wider ground provided by the first two. Mary Hawkesworth's essay, "Confounding Gender," and the responses to it by Wendy McKenna and Suzanne Kessler, Steven G. Smith, Joan Wallach Scott, R. W. Connell, and Oyeronke Oyewumi, center on gender as a "useful category of analysis," as Joan Scott put it in a highly influential essay of the 1980s. The topic is especially crucial in this moment of focus on gender in realms as divergent as the renaming of some women('s) studies programs to gender studies, the attention to gender as performance, and the discussion of gender mobility in queer/transgender studies. Hawkesworth reads in detail four book-length studies of gender over the past twenty years, arguing that when they move from gender as analytic category to gender as explanation for social phenomena they unwittingly make presuppositions that may not be useful for feminist change and may be unrecognized by the writer. She argues that there are good reasons, both intellectual and political, for questioning gender, since it is a defining category of feminism. Her analysis focuses on buried assumptions that she sees constraining understandings of social and political problems and impairing the formation of political coalitions required to attain democratic solutions to those problems. Hawkesworth emphasizes a distinction between gender as analytic category and gender as explanation, cautioning against tautological, circular reasoning. She provides examples of ways in which different definitions of gender point toward different explanatory processes and argues that it is imperative to examine the adequacy of stipulative definitions of gender. She investigates the presuppositions of a number of accounts of gender and reads these as suggesting that an ideology of procreation surfaces frequently in them. She seeks to question the substantive claims about gender's work that she finds often implicit in feminist scholarship.

Her respondents, primarily authors of the studies she critiques, argue that they have not attempted to pose gender differences as causal and have not, as Hawkesworth proposes, given currency to procreationist ideologies by arguing for gender complementarity. Respondents also stress the ongoing usefulness, even essential recognition of paradoxes as crucial to feminist thinking (Scott), and point out the Western bias involved in taking gender itself to be an analytic category when other categories in non-Western cultures may be more salient (Oyewumi). In these ways this exchange, while centered on studies of gender, widens its scope to broader questions of feminist theory.

The final exchange begins with Debra Morris's "Privacy, Privation, Perversity: Toward New Representations of the Personal," and includes responses by Patricia Boling and Jean Bethke Elshtain. Morris argues for privacy as a reprieve from the workings of power, in a move to remove privacy from its dichotomized relation to "the public." Beginning her argument in a reading of Hanna Pitkin, and ending with attention to the relation of privacy and taboo in Patricia Williams's work, Morris argues for retaining what she calls the intractability of privacy as a hedge against the pressures of social control. She wishes for a critical reclamation of privacy and positions herself against those theorists who dismiss privacy as an ideological tool that works against examinations of oppression. Morris seeks a broadly interdisciplinary critical social theory of privacy, a theory sensitive to privacy's consequences for identity formation. Drawing on feminist, postmodernist, and radical-democratic critiques of liberal individualism, Morris establishes the utility of an emphasis on the singular, intractable dimensions of privacy for projects concerned with the political significance of identity. She turns away from the older public/private divide and argues for privacy as "transitional space," a place for navigating between the public and the personal, the systematic and the singular. She sees privacy as a reprieve from power, rather than an opposite of power.

For Boling, such an argument is "disquietingly unpolitical." For Elshtain, Morris does not sufficiently stress the social dimensions of both the public and the private. In taking on a debate central especially to feminist political theory, these writers revisit feminist interventions in a well-established territory of liberal democratic thought in order to shift terms and rethink the constructions of both the public and the private.

Points repeated in the exchanges indicate continuing issues for feminist thought, despite the differing disciplinary locations of the scholars included. Taken together the most obvious of these repetitions summarize both pressing concerns and continuing and future directions for feminist work.

1. Gender is culturally and historically located; in fact, feminist debates, whether they are about gender, sexual difference, or epistemology, are culturally located. See especially, for examples, Braidotti's comments on European and American feminisms and Felski's objection to her characterization of them and Oyewumi's discussion of seniority, rather than gender, as the primary organizing social category for the Yoruba.

2. Categories most often considered to be feminist purview (gender, race, sexuality, class, nation) are intersectional, but how those intersections work is not yet fully theorized. It is clear, however, that different primacies emerge for differently located individuals and groups.

3. Controversy continues to surround questions of method, critical discourse, citational politics, and the usefulness of established paradigms. The debates over the roles of psychoanalysis and of poststructuralist discourses more generally are most obvious, but all four exchanges contribute to these ongoing questions about what might be called critical framing.

4. Difference cannot be considered without its accompanying dynamic of dominance/hierarchy — without, that is, relations of power.

In fact, this last might be read as the most frequent touchstone for the essays collected here. Though not all the exchanges in the book focus exclusively on difference and dominance, most touch on it in some way. In one way or another, of course, "difference" has always been central to second-wave feminism. From its beginning in debates over women's difference from men, formulated in the "equality versus difference" discussions and the emphasis on "identity politics," in which communities defined themselves through difference from others, through analyses of differences among and within women, to current attempts to understand how such differences might intersect, difference has mattered. Scholarly work in each of these areas continues; there is no narrative of progress that accurately captures attention to difference in feminist thinking. But difference, as the feminisms represented here formulate it, also stresses crucial considerations of dominance, social hierarchies and their privileges, centers and margins, systematic structural inequalities, and their relation to each other and their effects on individual subjects. Especially in the first three exchanges, when difference appears, it is not to acknowledge pluralism or simple diversity but to recognize that differences among women signal simultaneously differing positions of access to social and economic privilege.

From the beginning, the difference that defines "debate" marks these feminist exchanges as provocative, calling forth arguments sometimes with politeness, sometimes with irritation. After all, to differ from others is how arguments—feminist or otherwise—move forward. The essays in this collection most often summarize these important and well-established fields of feminist thought, outline several of the debates within them, critique positions set forth previously, and conclude by suggesting new directions and new arguments that will extend the critical conversations they have already presented. At the same time, the essays also wrestle with questions of difference and debate questions of dominance in the very critical discourses within which they are framed. Marked often by differences in discourse as a consequence of their authors' institutional disciplinary "homes," the essays frequently engage difference by explicitly or implicitly arguing about feminisms' engagement with poststructural thinking, to which versions of difference are philosophically central.

These essays indicate that there is no longer a simple opposition between feminist thinkers who might identify their work with poststructuralism, postmodernism, or the "linguistic turn" in contemporary formulations and those who find these discourses to be detrimental to progressive social movements. Feminists with a strong ongoing commitment to the daily inequalities of everyday life (Dorothy Smith, e.g.) are also attuned, as her response to Hekman suggests, to the force of discourse in what she calls "brute reality." Similarly, theorists whose work calls on the various languages of poststructuralism are well aware of the material hierarchies that operate across individuals, cultures, and nations. In a parallel fashion, debates about whether gender inequities are best addressed at the macro level of societal structures and institutions or the micro level of individual consciousness and interaction have been replaced by calls for multilevel analyses. Given that gender tends to be analyzed more frequently in terms of private spheres and individual psychology, where race and class tend to be analyzed in terms of public spheres and social structures, multilevel analyses will also likely contribute to theorizing these intersections. The essays capture the productive complications of these debates over "difference" and "differences," and "micro" and "macro," as well as over their discursive formations and efficacies.

Sounding a note that reverberates in several of the provocations collected here, Ien Ang suggests that the complex political predicament of our time has a "deceptively simple" central inquiry: How are we to live together as the twenty-first century begins? "'We' and 'together' continue as the key sites of contestation," Ang writes. The exchanges in this volume, with their emphases on difference and dominance, point the way for future feminist work. For if the seventies saw the study of women become a serious scholarly endeavor, and the eighties complicated ideas of what constitutes "women," "race," and "gender," academic work in the nineties, captured at least in part by the essays in this collection, has tried to understand more completely those complications in specifying Ang's "we."

Still, much work remains to be done. Historically and culturally specific studies are increasingly crucial both for the still far-from-finished task of theorizing hierarchies and interactions of difference and dominance and for providing more information about, and interpretation of, lives that these differences in power continue to affect. These essays frequently point to work in postcolonial feminist theory and to sites outside the United States as crucial to future work in feminist studies. The currency in recent scholarship of such terms as *hybridity, border crossing,* and *intersectionality* speaks not only to the increasing attention to global contexts, complex racial ethnicities, transgendered possibilities, and nonnormative sexualities but also to the real difficulties in understanding exactly how these terms and the fields of power that produce and are produced by them work. Scholarship in the coming years needs to move beyond merely recognizing the absolute interrelatedness of various differences to more clearly understanding and detailing their formations, interactions, and effects in individuals and in groups.

Such understandings are necessary, but they are also daunting. The study of women and gender to date, incomplete as it is, has given scholars so much to do, so many directions to follow that actually deciding what to do has sometimes resulted in a kind of paralyzing "too-muchness" especially for younger scholars or for graduate students considering where to put their energies. Our varying feminist endeavors are grounded in "interdisciplinarity," yet most scholars are still trained in a particular discipline; learning the discourses and conventions of other knowledges is often not possible, for reasons of academic institutional structures. Cultural and economic networks are transnational, but scholarly training in multiple cultures, histories, and languages is rare—hence the focus on smaller sites of study informed by the larger networks of thought. Continually, however, feminist scholars need to stop and take account of these more local studies in order to see what new, more general theoretical gains might be made by working across them. The movement between the necessarily local and the theoretically general might be especially facilitated by an increased emphasis on collaboration in feminist work. Working groups of scholars, however traditionally trained, will benefit from mutual discussion of individually conceived studies. While such collaboration in the sciences and social sciences is a continuing practice, humanities scholars still labor largely alone. Interdisciplinary advances in feminist work will come from crossing these humanities/social science/natural science boundaries in collaborative projects.

It also remains true that scholars often follow their own emotional and identificatory interests so that who gets trained, who advances, who publishes, who is cited, and where those citations appear all influence the goal of making the study of women and gender fully inclusive and international. Journal and book publishing remains largely bound by national and linguistic borders and conference travel and Internet access are constrained by economic inequalities, so the sharing of work across borders is still limited in the face of the many possibilities. These barriers to increased global knowledges are beginning to fall, but future research accomplishments depend on ongoing efforts to cross these barriers, if the study of women and gender, with all their intersectional complexities, is to contribute to a more just world. This collection, with its provocative exchanges, references some of these challenges at the same time that it testifies to the ongoing power of feminist thinking.

Carolyn Allen
Department of English
University of Washington

                                                    Judith A. Howard
                                                    Department of Sociology
                                                    University of Washington

Truth and Method:
Feminist Standpoint Theory Revisited

I n 1983, the publication of Nancy Hartsock's *Money, Sex, and Power* changed the landscape of feminist theory. The scope of the book alone ensures it a prominent place in feminist thought. It includes a comprehensive critique of positivism, an indictment of masculinist theories of power, and even a textual analysis of Greek mythology. The central concern of the book, however, and the source of its lasting influence, is Hartsock's epistemological and methodological argument. Her goal is to define the nature of the truth claims that feminists advance and to provide a methodological grounding that will validate those claims. The method she defines is the feminist standpoint. Borrowing heavily from Marx, yet adapting her insights to her specifically feminist ends, Hartsock claims that it is women's unique standpoint in society that provides the justification for the truth claims of feminism while also providing it with a method with which to analyze reality.

In the succeeding decade, feminist standpoint theory has become a staple of feminist theory. Nancy Hartsock's essay in Sandra Harding and Merrill Hintikka's pathbreaking book *Discovering Reality* (1983) brought the concept to a philosophical audience. In a number of influential publications, Dorothy Smith developed a sociological method from the "standpoint of women." Harding featured feminist standpoint theory in her two important books on science and feminism. Patricia Hill Collins articulated a specifically black feminist standpoint. But in the late 1980s and early 1990s criticisms of the position mounted, and fewer discussions of it were published. Today the concept occupies a much less prominent position. Particularly among younger feminist theorists, feminist standpoint theory is frequently regarded as a quaint relic of feminism's less sophisticated past. Several developments in the late 1980s have led to this declining influence. First, the inspiration for feminist standpoint theory, Marxism, has been discredited in both theory and practice. Second, feminist standpoint theory appears to be at odds with the issue that has dominated feminist debate in the past decade: difference. Third, feminist standpoint theory appears to be opposed to two of the most significant influences in recent feminist

[*Signs: Journal of Women in Culture and Society* 1997, vol. 22, no. 2]

theory: postmodernism and poststructuralism. The Marxist roots of the theory seem to contradict what many define as the antimaterialism of postmodernism. For all of these reasons, the conclusion that feminist standpoint theory should be discarded seems obvious.

I think this conclusion is premature, that it is a mistake to write off feminist standpoint theory too quickly. Feminist standpoint theory raises a central and unavoidable question for feminist theory: How do we justify the truth of the feminist claim that women have been and are oppressed? Feminist standpoint theory was initially formulated in the context of Marxist politics. But from the outset, feminist standpoint theorists have recognized that feminist politics demand a justification for the truth claims of feminist theory, that is, that feminist politics are necessarily epistemological. Throughout the theory's development, feminist standpoint theorists' quest for truth and politics has been shaped by two central understandings: that knowledge is situated and perspectival and that there are multiple standpoints from which knowledge is produced. As the theory has developed, feminist standpoint theorists have explored, first, how knowledge can be situated yet "true," and, second, how we can acknowledge difference without obviating the possibility of critique and thus a viable feminist politics. Feminist standpoint theorists have answered these questions in a variety of ways; many of these answers have been unsatisfactory; the theory has been frequently reformulated. In the course of their arguments, however, these theorists have made an indispensable contribution to feminist theory.

It is my contention that feminist standpoint theory represents the beginning of a paradigm shift in the concept of knowledge, a shift that is transforming not only feminist theory but also epistemology itself. What Lorraine Code (1991) calls a "new mapping of the epistemic domain" that characterizes feminist theory owes much to the articulation and development of feminist standpoint theory. Finally, I assert that this theory remains central to contemporary feminism because the questions it raises are crucial to the future development of feminist theory and politics. Recently there has been much discussion among feminists of the parameters of a "politics of difference." I believe that feminist standpoint theory has laid the groundwork for such a politics by initiating the discussion of situated knowledges.

I. Defining the feminist standpoint

In an article originally published in *Quest* in 1975, Nancy Hartsock wrote: "At bottom feminism is a mode of analysis, a method of approaching life and politics, rather than a set of political conclusions about the oppression of women" (1981, 35). The power of feminist method, she asserts, grows out of the fact that it enables us to connect everyday life with the analysis of the social institutions that shape that life (36). This early article reveals the presupposition that defines her later formulation of the feminist stand-point: the belief that feminism, while necessarily political, at the same time must be centrally concerned with method, truth, and epistemology. Femi-nism, for Hartsock, is about truth claims and how we justify them. But at the very outset she refers to the issue that will complicate her search for truth in a feminist mode. She notes that the reality perceived by different segments of society is varied. Thus, she concludes, "Feminism as a mode of analysis leads us to respect experience and differences, to respect people enough to believe that they are in the best possible position to make their own revolution" (40).

For Hartsock, activity is epistemology: women and men create their own realities through their different activities and experiences. If this were the whole story, however, then both truth and reality would be multiple, even "relative," and Hartsock is very concerned to avoid this conclusion. When she presents her theory of the feminist standpoint in *Money, Sex, and Power* (1983c), this is the focus of her attention. She insists that "the con-cept of a standpoint rests on the fact that there are some perspectives on society from which, however well intentioned one may be, the real rela-tions of humans with each other and with the natural world are not visible" (117). Hartsock's goal in the book is to define the concept of a standpoint and apply it to the case of women. She outlines five criteria of a standpoint that she adapts from Marx's theory (118). Two potentially contradictory definitions of reality structure this discussion. First, in what today would be called a social constructionist argument, Hartsock asserts that material life structures and sets limits to an understanding of social relations. It follows that reality will be perceived differently as material situations differ. It also follows that the dominant (ruling) group in society will label its perspective as "real" and reject other definitions. Second, Hartsock insists that while the ruling group's perception of reality is "partial and perverse," that of the oppressed is not, that it exposes "real" relations among humans and is hence liberatory. Throughout her work Hartsock struggles with the relationship between these two definitions of reality. It constitutes a kind of fault line that runs through her articulation of the feminist standpoint. Although her formulation changes over the years, she continues to main-tain both that reality is socially and materially constructed and that some perceptions of reality are partial, others true and liberatory.

Further aspects of feminist standpoint theory emerge in Hartsock's well-known article "The Feminist Standpoint" (1983b). In this article Hartsock states that a specifically feminist historical materialism "might enable us to lay bare the laws of tendency which constitute the structure of patriarchy over time" (283). Her dualistic concept of reality structures this discussion as well. On the one hand, social constructionist themes recur throughout the argument: "I will sketch out a kind of ideal type of the social relations and world view characteristic of male and female activity in order to explore the epistemology contained in the institutionalized sexual division of labor" (289). The feminist standpoint "expresses female experience at a particular time and place, located within a particular set of social relations" (303). Quickly following this, however, is the statement that the feminist standpoint allows us to "go beneath the surface of appearances to reveal the real but concealed social relations" (304). Her thesis is that "women's lives make available a particular and privileged vantage point on male supremacy" (284).

In this article Hartsock introduces an approach that will become closely identified with standpoint theory: object-relations theory. The introduction of this theory highlights the tension inherent in her concept of reality—in a sense widening the fault line in that concept. In her discussion Hartsock appeals to object-relations theory to explain the difference between the male and female experiences of the world (1983b, 296). Bringing object-relations theory to bear on her Marxist assumptions, Hartsock argues that if material life structures consciousness, then women's relationally defined existence structures a life in which dichotomies are foreign and abstract masculinity is exposed as partial and perverse (298–99). Implicit in Hartsock's discussion is the assumption that object-relations theory is an appropriate and useful addition to feminist standpoint theory, not a major departure. In the context of her theory it seems to fit nicely with the Marxist thesis that reality is socially constructed and supplies a needed gendered component to that theory.

The incorporation of object-relations theory, however, represents a major theoretical departure in the development of standpoint theory. Feminist standpoint theory's identification with object-relations theory has changed the focus of the approach in two respects. First, object-relations theory, unlike Marxist theory, lacks a distinction between socially constructed and "true" reality. As feminist theorists in the 1980s discovered, object-relations theory effectively jettisons the concept of objective reality. Some advocates of feminist standpoint theory see this as an advantage, others as a disadvantage. But it becomes a problem that must be continually negotiated. Second, the incorporation of object-relations theory further problematizes the issue of difference. What was merely a troubling issue in feminist standpoint theory is a major stumbling block in object-relations theory. In object-relations theory the opposition between *the* experience of men and *the* experience of women is the centerpiece of the theory. The difficulty of theorizing differences among women and the variety of women's experiences that characterizes object-relations theory now becomes a major problem in feminist standpoint theory as well.[1]

In their perceptive discussion of the evolution of poststructuralist and postmodern thought, Rosalind Coward and John Ellis (1977) argue that the groundwork for the discursive concept of the subject that has become the new paradigm of subjectivity is already present in Marx's historically constituted subject. I would like to argue a similar thesis for the early definitions of feminist standpoint theory, particularly that of Hartsock. To establish this thesis I interpret Hartsock's criteria for a standpoint from the perspective of the work of one of the most prominent representatives of what I call the new paradigm of knowledge — Michel Foucault. Hartsock (1983c, 118) argues, first, that material life structures and sets limits to the understanding of social relations; second, that the ruling class structures the material relations of a society and hence its definition of the "real"; and, third, that the vision available to oppressed groups must be achieved through struggle. All of this translates nicely into Foucault's theory. First, his theories of sexuality, bio-power, the carceral society, and the evolution of the Western subject provide detailed analyses of how material/social life structures consciousness. Second, one of Foucault's central aims is to define how and to what extent hegemonic discourses (what Hartsock calls the ideology of the ruling class) define "reality" in any given society. Third, he is centrally concerned with defining how subjugated knowledges (the vision of the oppressed) can be articulated (Foucault 1980, 82).

But here the similarity ends. Hartsock further claims that the ruling group's vision is partial and perverse and that the vision of the oppressed exposes the "real" relations among humans. Foucault would counter that all visions are "partial and perverse" in the sense that all knowledge is necessarily from some perspective; we must speak from somewhere and that somewhere is constitutive of our knowledge. Most important, he would insist that the vision of the oppressed is itself another discourse, not the apprehension of "true" reality. It is undoubtedly a counterdiscourse, a dis-

---

[1] For an early discussion of the problem of difference, see Hartsock 1983a. She argues that in our society some empirical differences are reified into an ontologically significant "Difference" by the ruling class. She asserts that feminists should reject this construction of "Difference" and, rather, use empirical differences as sources of creativity and power. I find this to be an insightful and useful discussion of difference that has been unfortunately neglected in current discussions.

course that seeks to break the hold of the hegemonic discourse, but it is no closer to "reality" than the discourse it exposes. What it may be closer to, however, is a definition of a less repressive society.

It is my contention that the deconstruction of the concept of "true" reality is already implicit in Hartsock's definition of the feminist standpoint, just as the deconstruction of the transcendent subject was implicit in Marx's theory of the social construction of consciousness. If material life structures consciousness, if the different experiences of different groups create different realities, then this must hold for the oppressed as well as the oppressor. Hartsock might reply that the oppressed's conception of reality is true because it is based on a correct perception of material reality while that of the oppressor is false because it does not. But such an argument begs the question of how a correct perception of material reality is achieved. Ultimately, it must presuppose this reality as a given, as the standard by which truth and falsity are defined. Even in her early formulations of feminist standpoint theory Hartsock is defensive about the accuracy of the oppressed/women's conception of reality. The incorporation of object-relations theory makes her defense of this position even more difficult. If, as object-relations theory claims, our relations with others define our perceptions, then selecting one of these perceptions as "real" is instantly suspect. But Hartsock also realizes the centrality of this point. Unless women's standpoint can be shown to be truer, a reflection of reality itself, why bother with feminist analysis at all?

One of Hartsock's major claims is that while the discourse of the ruling class is ideological, that of the oppressed is not: it reflects the concrete reality of their lives. An important aspect of this claim is her assertion that the feminist standpoint is achieved, not given. The nature of their oppression is not obvious to all women; it is only through feminist analysis that the feminist standpoint can be articulated. What this comes down to is that although the feminist standpoint is discursively constituted, the material reality of women's lives on which it is based is not. This important distinction is lost in much subsequent feminist standpoint theory. The belief that the standpoint(s) of women resists the discursive constitution that defines all "partial and perverse" perceptions of reality is a major theme of feminist standpoint theorists in the 1980s; it structures these theorists' efforts to define a distinctive method for feminist analysis.

The clearest example of this belief is the work of Dorothy Smith. In her influential essay "Women's Perspective as a Radical Critique of Sociology" (1987b), Smith posits a contrast between the categories of sociology and the everyday life (what phenomenologists call the lifeworld) of women. She argues that the categories of sociology and sociological method embody what Hartsock calls "abstract masculinity." For the sociologist, objectivity is defined as the separation between knower and known, removal from the situatedness of knowledge. This method and these categories, she argues, obviate the experience of women, an experience that is always situated, relational, and engaged. Two conclusions follow from this. First, the lived reality of women's lives is absent from the domain of sociology; it is quite literally invisible to the sociologist. Second, the woman sociologist experiences a bifurcated consciousness: the abstract, conceptual world she encounters as a sociologist versus her lived reality as a woman (1987b, 90). The goal of Smith's work is to define a "reorganized sociology" that would solve both of these problems by foregrounding actual lived experiences.

Smith outlines this reorganized sociology, what she calls a sociology for women, in *The Everyday World as Problematic* (1987a). She defines the world of sociology as a *conceptual* world divorced from the lived, actual world of everyday experience. The world of women, in contrast, is "material and local," the world as we actually experience it. These definitions lead Smith to her definition of "women's standpoint" as the point outside textually mediated discourses in the actuality of everyday lives (1987a, 107). The standpoint of women, she claims, is related to Marx's method but constitutes an improvement on it because it is "anchored" in the everyday world (142). This method constitutes the "Copernican shift in sociology" that Smith is seeking (1979, 183).

Smith is quite clear about what she is attempting to do in her work; whether she is successful is another matter. She posits an absolute dichotomy between abstract concepts on the one hand and lived reality on the other, indicts sociology for inhabiting the conceptual world of abstractions, and advocates a move to the other side of the dichotomy. One of the curious aspects of Smith's account is that, although it is inspired by phenomenological method, it nevertheless departs from the phenomenologist's understanding of the nature of concept formation and the role of concepts in sociological analysis. Alfred Schutz (1967), whose theory of the lifeworld is the origin of Smith's approach, claims, like Smith, that sociological method must be rooted in the lived actuality of the social actors' reality (the lifeworld) and that the lived experiences of social actors must form the basis of sociological method and concepts. But, unlike Smith, Schutz argues, first, that the social actors' world is constituted by their concepts and, second, that the sociologist also employs concepts in order to study that lifeworld. Schutz claims that the sociology of the lifeworld that he advocates is more "adequate" than positivist sociology because, unlike that sociology, it is rooted in the concepts of social actors.

But he also makes it clear that his method is itself a complex conceptual apparatus with standards of truth and accuracy, that is, a discursive formation.

At times Smith seems to acknowledge that she is, in fact, advocating a conceptual shift and not a shift from concepts to reality. She asserts: "I am not suggesting, of course, that sociology can be done without knowing how to do it and that we approach our work with a naive consciousness" (1979, 174). In an explicit reference to Schutz, she claims that "as we evolve a discourse among women, it crystallizes the issues and concerns of those of us who got there first and have defined the types of statements, the relevances, the phenomenal universe, and the conventions that give it a social form independent of the particular individuals who are active in it" (1987a, 221). But these are isolated references. The overall theme of her work is to deny that she is either studying a conceptual reality (the world of the social actors) or fashioning a discourse and advocating a method. Her constantly reiterated thesis is that her approach is superior to "abstract sociology" because it is rooted in "an actual material setting, an actual local and particular place in the world" (1979, 181). What she refuses to acknowledge is that that "reality" is also discursively constituted. To do so would be to abandon the neat dichotomy between abstract concepts and lived reality on which her approach rests.

Other early formulations of feminist standpoint theory reflect this dichotomy between concepts and reality, specifically, the abstract world of men and the concrete world of women. Hilary Rose conceptualizes the dichotomy in terms of the material reality of women's labor and abstract masculinist science (1983, 1986); Iris Young calls for a "feminist historical materialism" rooted in "real social relations" (1980, 184–85); Mary O'Brien looks to the reproductive process to provide the material basis for her social theory (1981); and Alison Jaggar appeals to an explicitly Marxist understanding of the epistemological advantages of the oppressed view of reality (1983). Even Jane Flax, who later repudiates any naive conception of reality, argues that we need ways of thinking that can do justice to our experience (1983).

Despite their significant differences, all of these accounts share the conviction that the feminist standpoint is rooted in a "reality" that is the opposite of the abstract conceptual world inhabited by men, particularly the men of the ruling class, and that in this reality lies the truth of the human condition. There are three problems with this formulation. First, it assumes that the dichotomy between concepts and reality can be resolved by embracing reality and rejecting concepts. This strategy is self-defeating. The two elements of the dichotomy are interdependent; to embrace one is to acknowledge the epistemological validity of both sides of the dichotomy, not to solve the problem it poses. Second, it denies that the lifeworld is, like every other human activity, discursively constituted. It is a discourse distinct from that of abstract science, but a discourse nonetheless.[2] Third, as both Schutz and Max Weber clearly realized, one can argue that sociological analysis *should* begin with the actors' concepts and that any other approach will miss the object of its study—the lifeworld—but that this requires a specific *argument*. Opposing concepts to reality is not an argument and, furthermore, entails an epistemological fallacy.

II. The challenge of difference: Redefining the feminist standpoint

The original formulations of feminist standpoint theory rest on two assumptions: that all knowledge is located and situated, and that one location, that of the standpoint of women, is privileged because it provides a vantage point that reveals the truth of social reality. It is my thesis that the deconstruction of this second assumption is implicit in the first and that as the theory developed the problematic nature of the second assumption came to the forefront. Another way of putting this is that a new paradigm of knowledge was implicit in the first formulations of feminist standpoint theory, a definition of knowledge as situated and perspectival, but that these first formulations retained elements of the paradigm it was replacing.

Epistemologists have devoted much attention to the concept of "reality" in the past decade, offering powerful arguments against the notion of a given, preconceptual reality that grounds knowledge. The "linguistic turn" of twentieth-century philosophy and the influence of hermeneutics, postmodernism, and poststructuralism have all contributed to the present skepticism about "reality." These speculations are directly relevant to the evolution of feminist standpoint theory, an approach initially grounded in just such a concept of reality. But it was another discussion, the discussion of difference within the feminist community, that stimulated a reassessment of feminist standpoint theory in the late 1980s and early 1990s. Originally, feminist standpoint theorists claimed that the standpoint of women offers a privileged vantage point for knowledge. But if the differences among women are taken seriously and we accept the conclusion that women occupy many different standpoints and thus inhabit many realities, this thesis must be reexamined. The current reevaluation of feminist standpoint theory is an attempt to reconstitute the theory from the perspective of difference. These discussions focus on two questions that are central not

[2] See Grant 1993 for a similar critique.

only to this approach but also to feminist theory itself. First, if, as we must, we acknowledge that there are many realities that women inhabit, how does this affect the status of the truth claims that feminists advance? Second, if we abandon a single axis of analysis, *the* standpoint of women, and instead try to accommodate the multiple, potentially infinite standpoints of diverse women, do we not also lose the analytic force of our argument? Or, in other words, how many axes can our arguments encompass before they slip into hopeless confusion?[3] The political implications of these questions, furthermore, inform both of these arguments. If we abandon the monolithic concept of "woman," what are the possibilities of a cohesive feminist politics?

The concern both to accommodate difference and preserve the analytic and political force of feminist theory, specifically feminist standpoint theory, is prominent in the recent work of Nancy Hartsock. It is obvious that Hartsock cares very deeply about these issues. She is painfully aware of the evils of racism, particularly within the women's movement. She is also passionately committed to feminist social criticism as a force for social change and is determined not to let forces such as postmodernism erode that potential. These concerns emerge forcefully in a 1987 article, "Rethinking Modernism." The point of departure for Hartsock's argument is the differences among women. She asserts that we need to develop an understanding of difference by creating a politics in which previously marginalized groups can name themselves and participate in defining the terms that structure their world (1987, 189). Central to Hartsock's argument is the claim that unless we provide a systematic understanding of the world, we will be unable to change it. The object of her polemic in this and several other recent articles is postmodernism. In the past decade the issues of difference and multiplicity have come to be closely identified with postmodernism. Hartsock wants to reject this identification. She wants to valorize difference, to claim that the differences among women are significant both theoretically and practically, while at the same time rejecting postmodernism on the grounds that it obviates the possibility of the systemic knowledge that is necessary for social change.

Hartsock's efforts both to valorize difference and to retain at least some notion of reality and truth, of the "way the world is," produce some odd results. In "Rethinking Modernism," she significantly alters the basic thesis of feminist standpoint theory by asserting that although women are not a unitary group, white, ruling-class, Eurocentric men are (1987, 192). The ruling class, now referred to as the "center," is defined as unitary, while

---

[3] See Bordo 1990 for a cogent statement of this problem.

those on the periphery, the "others," are defined as heterogeneous. Hartsock's argument is that we must create a politics that lets the "others" into the center, a center that, she claims, will "obviously" look different when occupied by women and men of color (201). Hartsock's solution raises some troubling questions. It posits a center that is heterogeneous rather than homogeneous, but this suggests that it may not be a "center" at all. We might also ask whether, if the "others" have moved into the center, this move effectively eliminates the periphery. We can, I think, assume that Hartsock would not endorse a politics in which any group was marginalized. But it is difficult to retain the concept of "center," as she does, without a corresponding concept of periphery.[4]

All of these questions could be quite easily eliminated by abandoning the center/periphery dichotomy. But Hartsock is adamantly opposed to this move. Those of us who have been constituted as "other," she states, must insist on a world in which we are at the center rather than the periphery. The postmoderns, she claims, who want to eliminate the center, thereby deny us our right of self-definition. She also claims that they deny us the right to speak the truth about our subjugation, obviating the very possibility of knowledge and truth. Informing all of Hartsock's recent work is a fundamental dichotomy: either we have systemic knowledge of the way the world is or we have no knowledge, no truth, and no politics. For Hartsock, postmodernism represents the second term of this dichotomy (1990). I could argue, against Hartsock, that truth, knowledge, and politics are possible without an absolute grounding and that some postmodern writers make this argument quite persuasively. But I would like to examine Hartsock's position from a different angle. Her fears for the future of feminist analysis are not unfounded. If, as she realizes we must, feminism abandons *the* feminist standpoint and, with it, *the* correct view of reality, then we are in danger of abandoning the whole point of feminist analysis and politics: revealing the oppression of "women" and arguing for a less repressive society. If there are multiple feminist standpoints, then there must be multiple truths and multiple realities. This is a difficult position for those who want to change the world according to a new image.

I would argue that Hartsock has defined the problem correctly but is pursuing a solution in the wrong direction. She wants to embrace the "situated knowledges" that Haraway and others have theorized, but she cannot accept the logical consequence of this position: that no perspective/standpoint is epistemologically privileged. She wants to retain a notion

---

[4] Bar On 1993 offers an excellent account of the epistemological problems entailed by the claim to epistemic privilege and that of the center/margin dichotomy.

of privileged knowledge that can accommodate both diversity and locatedness. But her attempts to achieve this goal are not successful. "Situated knowledges," she claims, are "located in a particular time and place. They are therefore partial. They do not see everything from nowhere but they do see some things from somewhere." Borrowing postmodern terminology, she refers to the knowledges produced from the various subject positions of different women as "the epistemologies of these marked subjectivities." She then goes on to argue: "The struggles they represent and express, if made self-conscious, can go beyond efforts at survival to recognize the centrality of systemic power relations" (1989–90, 28–30). What this formulation requires is a sustained argument for how such systemic knowledge is possible. But such an argument is not forthcoming.

Other feminist standpoint theorists have also attempted to deal with the challenge of difference and its implications for the truth claims of the feminist standpoint. Dorothy Smith (1990a, 1990b) gets around the problem of difference by definitional fiat: she defines "women's actually lived experience" as a category that encompasses the diversity of women's lives and activities. She then opposes this category to the abstract concepts of sociological analysis, contrasting the "ideological" categories of the sociologist to "what actually happened" — the "primary narrative" (1990a, 157). But the method that she derives from this dichotomy is flawed and incomplete. First, despite the unmistakable influence of Schutz's work, Smith does not offer any argument for why the located knowledge of women is superior to the abstract knowledge of the sociologist; this is assumed to be obvious. Second, despite frequent references to Foucault and his theory of discourse, Smith refuses to identify the women's standpoint as a knowledge-producing discursive formation. She offers a detailed discussion of how the sociologist's discursive formations constitute the instruments of state power. At times she comes close to admitting that the discourse that women have developed about their lived reality, a discourse that includes concepts such as rape, sexual harassment, and battery, is also constituted. But ultimately she shies away from this conclusion. Like Hartsock, she continues to privilege the standpoint of women because she assumes that without such privileging the knowledge women claim loses its necessary grounding.

Patricia Hill Collins has a particular stake in theorizing difference: she wants to account for the unique standpoint of black women. She defines her problem in the context of the issue of difference: her goal, she states, is to articulate the unique aspects of black women's standpoint without denying the differences among black women. She tackles this problem by claiming, following Hartsock, that the black feminist standpoint she articulates, although rooted in everyday experiences, is constructed by the theorists who reflect on that experience. One of the goals of her own theory is to define the common experiences of black women that constitute their unique standpoint (1989; 1990, 208–21). Collins deals with the difficult issue of the truth status of the black feminist standpoint in an ambiguous way. In an early article she claims "objectivity" for the "outsider within" status of black women (1986, 15). In her more recent work, however, Collins retreats from this claim. In *Black Feminist Thought* she appeals to Donna Haraway's concept of standpoint as the most valid and concludes that "a Black women's standpoint is only one angle of vision," a "partial perspective" (1990, 234). But despite her endorsement of Haraway's position, Collins is unwilling to embrace the full implications of situated knowledge. She rejects the claim that the perspective of the oppressed yields "absolute truth," but she also rejects "relativism," which she defines as the claim that all visions are equal (1990, 235). Her final position holds out some hope for a redefined concept of objectivity. She asserts that black feminists who develop knowledge claims that can accommodate both black feminist epistemology and white masculinist epistemology "may have found a route to the elusive goal of generating so-called objective generalizations that can stand as universal truth." The ideas that are validated by different standpoints, she concludes, produce "the most objective truths" (1989, 773).

Other than Haraway herself, the only prominent feminist standpoint theorist to embrace fully what Collins labels the "relativist" position is Sara Ruddick. Citing Wittgenstein as her intellectual influence, Ruddick claims that feminism challenges the universality imperative of masculine thinking (1989, 128). In her discussion of "Maternal Thinking as a Feminist Standpoint," Ruddick appeals to both Hartsock and Foucault, apparently seeing no contradiction between Hartsock's definition of the feminist standpoint and Foucault's theory of subjugated knowledges (130). She concludes, "Although I count myself among standpoint theorists, I do not take the final step that some appear to take of claiming for one standpoint a truth that is exhaustive and absolute. . . . Although I envision a world organized by the values of caring labor, I cannot identify the grounds, reason, or god that would legitimate that vision" (135).[5]

Ruddick's solution to the problem of difference and privilege would not satisfy many feminist theorists. Like Collins and Hartsock, few feminist theorists are content to define the feminist standpoint as simply a "different

[5] For other recent accounts of standpoint theory, see Winant 1987; Aptheker 1989; Stanley and Wise 1990; and Campbell 1994.

voice" (or voices), one perspective among many. The difficulties of re-defining feminist standpoint theory in light of the epistemological issues raised by difference and the challenges to "reality" are most fully explored in the work of Sandra Harding. In her influential *The Science Question in Feminism* (1986) Harding defines three feminist epistemologies: feminist empiricism, feminist standpoint theory, and feminist postmodernism. Al-though sympathetic to standpoint epistemologies, Harding is persuaded that there cannot be *one* feminist standpoint; the situations of women are too diverse. Yet she also sees problems with the postmodern alternative. On her reading, postmodernism posits fractured identities, an apolitical approach, and the rejection of any kind of knowledge that results in an absolute relativism. In this book, Harding avoids choosing one epistemol-ogy over another by arguing for the necessary instability of feminist theo-ries. Coherent theories in an incoherent world, she concludes, are either silly, uninteresting, or oppressive (1986, 164).

In *Whose Science? Whose Knowledge?* (1991), Harding appears to reverse her position by fashioning a coherent theory for feminist science. The the-ory she offers, however, is a blend of diverse elements and thus continues the eclectic spirit of her earlier book. The aim of the book, she states, is not to resolve all tensions and contradictions between feminism and Western science but to "advance more useful ways for us to think about and plan their future encounters" (xi). Harding defines her position as "a postmod-ernist standpoint approach that is nevertheless committed to rethinking and revising some important notions from conventional metatheories of science" (49). In the course of developing her approach, Harding offers both a critique and a redefinition of standpoint theory, developing "the logic of the standpoint theory in ways that more vigorously pull it away from its modernist origins and more clearly enable it to advance some post-modernist goals" (106). For Harding, standpoint theory is attractive be-cause it offers an alternative to a crucial and seemingly irresolvable dichot-omy facing feminist theory: essentialism versus relativism. Her rejection of *one* feminist standpoint avoids the danger of essentialism; relativism is defeated by her claim that we must insist on an objective location — wom-en's lives — for the place where research should begin (134–42). But as her theory unfolds it becomes clear that Harding does not so much decon-struct this dichotomy as locate her position along the continuum it creates.

The ubiquitous issue of relativism leads Harding to her most signi-ficant contribution to standpoint theory: "strong objectivity." She be-gins by noting that "although diversity, pluralism, relativism, and differ-ence have their valuable and political uses, embracing them resolves the political-scientific-epistemological conflict to almost no one's satisfaction"

(140). Standpoint epistemologists, she argues, embrace historical-cultural-sociological relativism while rejecting judgmental or epistemological relativism (142). The "strong objectivity" she advocates recognizes the social situatedness of all knowledge but also requires "a critical evaluation to determine which social situations tend to generate the most objective knowledge claims" (142). It is significant that Harding follows traditional standpoint epistemology in assuming that the higher the level of oppression, the more objective the account: "It should be clear that if it is beneficial to start research, scholarship and theory in white women's situations, then we should be able to learn even more about the social and natural orders if we start from the situations of women in devalued and oppressed races, classes and cultures" (179–80).

Harding argues for keeping the concept of objectivity despite its historical associations with masculinist science because of its "glorious intellectual history" (160). The concept of objectivity she advocates departs from the masculinist definition in that it does not lay claim to "true beliefs" or "transhistorical privilege." But it also retains one important aspect of that definition: "Starting research in women's lives leads to socially constructed claims that are less false — less partial and distorted — than are the (also socially constructed) claims that result if one starts from the lives of men in the dominant groups" (185). The "less false stories" Harding advocates mediate between transhistorical universals on the one hand and absolute relativism on the other, forming a kind of middle ground between the polarities of this dichotomy. Harding intends this middle ground to be a critique of postmodern and poststructuralist positions. The postmodernists, Harding declares, assume that giving up on the goal of telling one true story about reality entails giving up on telling less false stories (187), a position that is unlikely to satisfy feminists' desire to know "how the world is" (304).

Once more, I could argue that Harding, like Hartsock, misinterprets the postmodern definition of knowledge and that at least one "postmodern" writer, Foucault, is very interested in telling stories that will result in a less oppressive social order. But, again, I will take a different tack in my criticism. Harding's reassessment of standpoint theory contains two serious oversights. First, she argues that starting research from the reality of women's lives, preferably those of women who are also oppressed by race and class, will lead to a more objective account of social reality. Like Hartsock, Harding offers no argument as to why this is the case. Particularly from the vantage point of the 1990s, it is not enough simply to assume that Marx got it right on such a crucial point. And, like Smith, Harding does not acknowledge that "the reality of women's lives" is itself a socially constructed discursive formation. It is a discourse that has been constructed, at least in part, by feminist standpoint theorists who define it as the ground of their method. The fact that it is closely tied to the social actors' own concepts and provides a counter to the hegemonic discourse of masculinist science makes it no less a discourse. Feminist standpoint theory can and, I argue, should be defined as a counterhegemonic discourse that works to destabilize hegemonic discourse. But this can be achieved without denying that it is a discourse or according it epistemological privilege.

Second, all of Harding's talk of "less false stories," "less partial and perverse accounts," and more "objective" research necessarily presupposes a shared discourse—a metanarrative, even—that establishes standards by which these judgments can be validated. Yet the centerpiece of Harding's critique of masculinist science is the denial of the possibility of such a metanarrative. She seems to assume that when feminist scholars offer their "less false stories" they will be universally acknowledged as such. This assumption fails both practically and theoretically. It seems abundantly obvious that within the masculinist discourse of science the accounts of feminist standpoint theorists have not been judged "better" than conventional scientific accounts. On the contrary, the scientific establishment has devoted much effort to discrediting feminist claims. Comparative statements such as those Harding advances require shared standards of judgment; no such standards bridge the gap between feminist and masculinist science. It is ironic that Harding's polemic against the metanarrative of masculinist science ultimately relies on the reconstruction of a similar standard for its validity.

III. Truths and methods: Toward a new paradigm

When feminist standpoint theory emerged in the early 1980s, it appeared to be exactly what the feminist movement needed: a method for naming the oppression of women grounded in the truth of women's lives. Standpoint theory constituted a challenge to the masculinist definition of truth and method embodied in modern Western science and epistemology. It established an alternative vision of truth and, with it, hope for a less repressive society. But the theoretical tensions implicit in the theory soon came to the forefront. The contradiction between social constructionist and absolutist conceptions of truth that characterizes Marx's theory were translated into feminist standpoint theory. As the theory developed in the late 1980s and early 1990s questions of how feminists should theorize differences among women and the status of feminism's truth claims became impossible to ignore—and equally impossible to answer within the confines of the original theory.

I argue that although it was conceived as an alternative vision of truth and reality, this vision does not constitute the theoretical legacy of feminist standpoint theory. Throughout the second half of the twentieth century a paradigm shift has been under way in epistemology, a movement from an absolutist, subject-centered conception of truth to a conception of truth as situated, perspectival, and discursive. It is my contention, first, that feminism was and continues to be at the forefront of this paradigm shift and, second, that feminist standpoint theory has contributed an important dimension to that shift within feminist theory. Because of the dualistic conception of truth and reality that characterized its original formulation, feminist standpoint theory has had the effect of problematizing absolutes and universals, focusing attention instead on the situated, local, and communal constitution of knowledge.

Another way of putting this is that in attempting to interpret feminist standpoint theory, we should look to Kuhn, not Marx. Feminist standpoint theory is part of an emerging paradigm of knowledge and knowledge production that constitutes an epistemological break with modernism. Feminist standpoint theory defines knowledge as particular rather than universal; it jettisons the neutral observer of modernist epistemology; it defines subjects as constructed by relational forces rather than as transcendent. As feminist standpoint theory has developed, the original tension between social construction and universal truth has dissolved. But it is significant that this has been accomplished, not by privileging one side of the dichotomy, but by deconstructing the dichotomy itself. The new paradigm of knowledge of which feminist standpoint theory is a part involves rejecting the definition of knowledge and truth as either universal or relative in favor of a conception of all knowledge as situated and discursive.

This new paradigm of knowledge necessarily defines a new approach to politics. Modernist epistemology defines politics in terms of the dichotomies that inform it. Thus for the modernist, politics must be grounded in absolute, universal principles and enacted by political agents defined as universal subjects. Under the new paradigm, politics is defined as a local and situated activity undertaken by discursively constituted subjects. Political resistance, furthermore, is defined as challenging the hegemonic discourse that writes a particular script for a certain category of subjects. Resistance is effected by employing other discursive formations to oppose that script, not by appealing to universal subjectivity or absolute principles.

As a way of illustrating my thesis that a new paradigm is emerging, it is useful to look at the three epistemic positions that Harding defines in her 1986 book. In the course of a decade the distinctions between these categories have nearly collapsed. Feminist empiricism has been radically redefined by epistemologists such as Lynn Hankinson Nelson and Helen Longino. Nelson (1990) provides a redefinition of empiricism from a feminist perspective that conforms to what I call the new paradigm of knowledge. Relying on the work of W. V. Quine, Nelson defines an empiricism in which, as she puts it, the world matters, but scientific communities produce knowledge. Her principal thesis is that it is not individuals but communities who know. Nelson's empiricism involves evidence, but it is evidence defined and constrained by public standards, not data observed from an Archimedean point by a neutral observer.[6] Longino offers a similar argument in *Science as Social Knowledge* (1990). She defines her position as "contextual empiricism," a view of science in which scientific knowledge is socially created and objectivity is a function of community practices. It is significant that both Nelson and Longino reject what they call "relativism," but they do so by appealing to widely shared but communal — that is, constructed — standards of evidence.

Harding herself has been instrumental in blurring the distinction between feminist standpoint theory and feminist postmodernism with her advocacy of "a postmodernist standpoint approach." The principal theme of feminist standpoint theory, that knowledge is situated in the material lives of social actors, has become the definitive characteristic not only of feminists influenced by postmodernism but of feminist theory as a whole. The major distinction between postmodernism and standpoint theory, the claim of privileged knowledge and one true reality, has been almost entirely abandoned. Both Hartsock and Harding radically modify the claim to privileged knowledge. Ruddick abandons any claim to privileged knowledge at all. Flax, an early proponent of the feminist standpoint, has enthusiastically embraced postmodernism and the multiple truths it entails. The notion of a feminist standpoint that is truer than previous (male) ones, she now claims, rests on problematic and unexamined assumptions (1990, 56).[7] What these theorists are effecting is what Lorraine Code calls "remapping the epistemic terrain into numerous fluid conversations" (1991, 309). What is significant about this remapping, however, is that for all of these theorists, defining reality as socially constructed and multiple does not obviate but, rather, facilitates critical analysis.

[6] See Tuana 1991 for a compatible analysis of Nelson.
[7] See also Hirschmann 1992; and Bar On 1993.

The feminist theorist who has done the most to define what I am calling the new paradigm of truth and method is Donna Haraway. Her famous essay "A Manifesto for Cyborgs," even though it does not mention feminist standpoint theory, can be read as an attempt to refashion that theory in light of the challenge to privileged reality. Haraway asks, What would another political myth for socialist feminism look like? What kind of politics can embrace fractured selves and still be effective and socialist feminist? (1990, 199). Implicit in these questions is the assumption that the "myth" of socialist feminism—feminist standpoint theory—cannot be sustained and that feminists must look for another. What is also implicit is that, for Haraway, what we must look for is not "truth" and "reality" but, rather, another story. "Women's experience," she claims, "is a fiction and a fact of the most crucial, political kind. Liberation rests on the construction of consciousness, the imaginative apprehension, of oppression, and so of possibility" (191).

In an equally famous article, "Situated Knowledges," Haraway relates her position directly to feminist standpoint theory: "There is no single feminist standpoint because our maps require too many dimensions for that metaphor to ground our visions. But the feminist standpoint theorists' goal of an epistemology and politics of engaged, accountable positioning remains eminently potent. The goal is better accounts of the world, that is, 'science'" (1988, 590). In this passage Haraway defines what I see as the central problem facing feminist theory today: given multiple standpoints, the social construction of "reality," and the necessity of an engaged political position, how can we talk about "better accounts of the world," "less false stories"? And, indeed, how can we talk about accounts of the world at all if the multiplicity of standpoints is, quite literally, endless? In the past several years, a number of feminist theorists have tried to answer these questions by articulating what might be called "quasi-universals." Martha Nussbaum (1992) and Susan Moller Okin (1994) have argued for a revival of the notion of basic human needs and a common humanity on which to ground ethics and feminist theory. They argue, as another theorist puts it, that "successful coalitions and political action require a substantial concept of common humanity grounded in an explicit notion of human nature" (Kay 1994, 21). These authors argue for what they call a "rich" and historically situated concept of human nature. But implicit in these arguments is the assumption that we need a concept of how the world *really* is, a metanarrative that provides standards for cross-cultural judgments, if we are to fashion a feminist, or any kind of, politics.

In conclusion, I would like to suggest another answer to these questions. The problem of constructing a viable method for feminist analysis, a method that also provides the basis for a feminist politics, is twofold. First, if we take the multiplicity of feminist standpoints to its logical conclusion, coherent analysis becomes impossible because we have too many axes of analysis. Ultimately, every woman is unique; if we analyze each in her uniqueness, systemic analysis is obviated. So is feminist politics: we lose the ability even to speak for certain categories of women. Second, if we acknowledge multiple realities, multiple standpoints, how do we discriminate among them? How do we select the perspectives and standpoints that are useful to us, that will help us achieve our theoretical and practical goals, or are we necessarily condemned to the "absolute relativism" that some critics fear?

In discussing the problems of developing a method for feminist analysis, Jane Flax argues, "Any feminist standpoint will necessarily be partial. Thinking about women may illuminate some aspects of a society that have been previously suppressed by the dominant view. But none of us can speak for 'woman' because no such person exists" (1990, 56). The problem here, as Flax realizes, is not to replace the absolutism implicit in the claim to *the* feminist standpoint with a relativistic stance but to deconstruct the dichotomy, to articulate a method and, hence, a politics, grounded in a different epistemology. I suggest that the methodological tool that meets these requirements, a tool that fits the methodological and epistemological needs of feminism at this juncture, can be found in a source rarely employed in feminist discussions: Weber's methodology and, specifically, his concept of the ideal type. Weber's methodology has many advantages for the current debate over feminist methodology. Most fundamental is that his approach presupposes that social analysis is always undertaken by situated, engaged agents who live in a discursively constituted world. Although a range of contemporary theorists — most notably Foucault — share this presumption, Weber's position supplies three elements that these contemporary approaches lack. First, Weber provides a detailed analysis of the conceptual tool that can effect this analysis: the ideal type. Second, he provides extensive examples of how this concept operates in empirical analysis. Third, he develops an elaborate justification for the partial and circumscribed approach he advocates.

At the root of Weber's concept of the ideal type is his claim that no aspect of social reality can be apprehended without presuppositions: "As soon as we attempt to reflect about the way in which life confronts us in immediate concrete situations, it presents an infinite multiplicity of successively and coexistently emerging and disappearing events" (1949, 72). Weber argues that we bring order to this multiplicity by relying on values and, specifically, cultural values: "Order is brought into this chaos only on the condition that in every case only a *part* of concrete reality is interesting and *significant* to us, because only it is related to the *cultural values* with which we approach reality" (78; emphasis in original). The cultural values of a society, thus, impose an initial ordering of the multiplicity of possible meanings that confront social actors. But Weber argues that values also structure the meaning apprehension of the social scientist. It is the investigator's individual value choice that guides the selection of a subject of analysis: "Without the investigator's evaluative ideas, there would be no principle of selection of subject-matter and no meaningful knowledge of the concrete reality" (82). The result of the investigator's choice is the conceptual tool that Weber calls the "ideal type": "An ideal type is formed by the one-sided *accentuation* of one or more points of view and by the synthesis of a great many diffuse, discrete, more or less present and occasionally absent *concrete individual phenomena,* which are arranged according to one-sidedly emphasized viewpoints into a unified *analytic* construct" (90; emphasis in original).[8]

For Weber, ideal types are neither hypotheses nor descriptions of reality but "yardsticks" to which reality can be compared; they are neither historical reality nor "true reality" but are purely limiting concepts or "utopias"; the purpose of ideal types is to provide a means of comparison with concrete reality in order to reveal the significance of that reality (90–93). This aspect of Weber's concept is crucial. We cannot justify ideal types by claiming that they accurately reproduce social reality. No concept can do that—all positions are partial and perspectival. But neither can we justify ideal types on the grounds that they uncover the universal truth of social reality, that they have the status of the universal laws of the natural sciences. Universal laws, Weber claims, can reveal nothing about what social scientists want to explain: the meaning and significance of social reality. Unlike universal laws, ideal types cannot be refuted by contradictory cases; the discovery of contradictory cases reveals the irrelevance of the concept to the problem at hand, not its "error" (1975, 190). The only justification we can appeal to, Weber concludes, is significance: an ideal type is valid if it helps us understand social reality.

Weber's concept of the ideal type can be useful in explaining the epistemological status of feminist research. First, it makes explicit that no perspective is total, all are partial; ideal types are, in his words, one-sided. Knowledge is always situated in a particular locality, the particular standpoint of these particular women. Second, it specifies that the subject of any

---

[8] See Hekman 1983, 1995.

analysis is dictated by the interest of the investigator. It is the values of feminist researchers and their political goals that have motivated them to investigate issues like wife battery, rape, incest, and even the origins of patriarchy itself. In Weber's terminology, what feminist social science has accomplished is to create a set of ideal types that allow us to "see" a different social world. Carole Pateman's "sexual contract" (1988), Arlie Hochschild's "second shift" (1989), and Karen Sacks's "centerwoman" (1988) are but a few examples of this conceptual set. Third, the ideal type rests on the assumption that what the social researcher studies, the activities and concepts of social actors, is already constituted; it is, in postmodern jargon, a discursive formation that constitutes "reality" for those who participate in it. This is a crucial point for the critique of many versions of feminist standpoint theory. Hartsock, Smith, and even, occasionally, Harding make the mistake of assuming that women's daily lives constitute a given reality that provides the necessary grounding for feminist theory. Weber's concept emphasizes that, like all other aspects of social life, women's daily life is a reality constituted by shared concepts.

The epistemology of Weber's ideal type also provides an answer to the charge of "absolute relativism" that many feminist theorists have raised. The problem is this: How do we convince nonfeminists that the ideal types of feminist analysis, concepts informed by the values of feminist researchers, are useful and insightful? How do we construct an argument for *these* ideal types rather than for the infinite variety of concepts that is possible? Weber argues that there is no metanarrative to which we can appeal to justify our value choices. Thus he would argue that the values that lead feminists to investigate the workings of patriarchy cannot be shown to be "objectively" correct. But Weber does have an answer to this problem. Although he argues that values are necessarily irreconcilable, he maintains that the logic of analysis itself rests on universal grounds (1949, 58). His argument is that although we cannot agree that we should be studying a particular topic—this is a value choice—we can agree on whether the analysis is logical. I would not offer quite so optimistic an answer. Weber's neat separation between facts and values is unfeasible. But this need not be cause for despair. Wittgenstein (1958) offers an argument that can be useful here. He asserts that our society is held together by certain basic values and assumptions that constitute what he calls "a form of life"; one of these assumptions is a very broadly based and loosely defined concept of what constitutes a persuasive argument. Because of the long-standing domination of patriarchy, these assumptions are masculinist; rationality, as many feminists have argued, is gendered masculine. But it does not follow that feminists cannot use these masculinist assumptions for their own purposes and, in so doing, transform them. We may not be able to persuade nonfeminists that the institutions of patriarchy are evil and should be dismantled. But we may be, and indeed have been, able to persuade them, through the use of skillful arguments, that sexual harassment, marital rape, and wife battery should be defined as crimes.

I am not claiming that the ideal type solves all the epistemological and methodological problems of feminist theory. I am claiming that it is highly appropriate to some of the problems that feminist theory is currently confronting, problems raised in large part by the development and evolution of feminist standpoint theory. The ideal type emphasizes that there is no metanarrative, either normative or methodological, to which we can appeal. Nor is there a truth about social totality that is waiting to be discovered. But this does not mean that the systemic analysis of the institutions of patriarchy is necessarily precluded. Weber's ideal type makes it clear that social analysis is a necessarily political activity, undertaken by agents who live in a world constituted by language and, hence, values. We engage in specific analyses because we are committed to certain values. These values dictate that certain analyses are trivial and others are important; all are not equal.[9] It is our values, then, that save us from the "absolute relativism" that the defenders of modernism so feared. Feminists cannot prove their values to be the objectively correct ones. On this point the postmoderns are correct: we live in a world devoid of a normative metanarrative. But we can offer persuasive arguments in defense of our values and the politics they entail. Some of these arguments will be persuasive: in the past decades feminists have been successful in beginning to change the parameters of patriarchal economic and political institutions. Other arguments will not be persuasive.[10] But by advancing both persuasive and unpersuasive arguments, feminists are, in the process, changing the norms of what constitutes an argument.

I think that recasting feminist standpoint theory in terms of the epistemology of the ideal type can make a significant contribution to contemporary feminist theory. Such a recasting would involve defining the feminist standpoint as situated and engaged knowledge, as a place from which feminists can articulate a counterhegemonic discourse and argue for a less repressive society. Women speak from multiple standpoints, producing multiple knowledges. But this does not prevent women from coming

[9] Flax 1993 makes a similar argument.
[10] MacKinnon's antipornography argument (1987) is a notable example.

together to work for specific political goals.[11] Feminists in the twentieth century have done precisely this and have, as a consequence, changed the language game of politics. And, ultimately, this is the point of feminist theory.

Department of Political Science
University of Texas at Arlington

References

Aptheker, Bettina. 1989. *Tapestries of Life: Women's Work, Women's Consciousness and the Meaning of Daily Experience.* Amherst: University of Massachusetts Press.

Bar On, Bat-Ami. 1993. "Marginality and Epistemic Privilege." In *Feminist Epistemologies,* ed. Linda Alcoff and Elizabeth Potter, 83–100. New York: Routledge.

Bordo, Susan. 1990. "Feminism, Postmodernism, and Gender-Skepticism." In *Feminism/Postmodernism,* ed. Linda Nicholson, 133–76. New York: Routledge.

Campbell, Richmond. 1994. "The Virtues of Feminist Empiricism." *Hypatia* 9(1):90–115.

Code, Lorraine. 1991. *What Can She Know? Feminist Theory and the Construction of Knowledge.* Ithaca, N.Y.: Cornell University Press.

Collins, Patricia Hill. 1986. "Learning from the Outsider Within: The Sociological Significance of Black Feminist Thought." *Social Problems* 33(6):14–32.

———. 1989. "The Social Construction of Black Feminist Thought." *Signs: Journal of Women in Culture and Society* 14(4):745–73.

———. 1990. *Black Feminist Thought.* Boston: Unwin Hyman.

Coward, Rosalind, and John Ellis. 1977. *Language and Materialism: Developments in Semiology and the Theory of the Subject.* London: Routledge & Kegan Paul.

Flax, Jane. 1983. "Political Philosophy and the Patriarchal Unconscious: A Psychoanalytic Perspective on Epistemology and Metaphysics." In Harding and Hintikka 1983, 245–81.

———. 1990. "Postmodernism and Gender Relations in Feminist Theory." In *Feminism/Postmodernism,* ed. Linda Nicholson, 39–61. New York: Routledge.

———. 1993. *Disputed Subjects: Essays on Psychoanalysis, Politics and Philosophy.* New York: Routledge.

Foucault, Michel. 1980. *Power/Knowledge.* New York: Pantheon.

Grant, Judith. 1993. *Fundamental Feminism: Contesting the Core Concepts of Feminist Theory.* New York: Routledge.

Haraway, Donna. 1988. "Situated Knowledges: The Science Question in Feminism and the Priviledge of Partial Perspective." *Feminist Studies* 14:575–99.

———. 1990. "A Manifesto for Cyborgs: Science, Technology and Socialist Femi-

---

[11] In a similar argument, Judith Grant asserts that political similarities can be cultivated to help feminists speak across suppressed differences (1993, 123).

nism in the 1980s." In *Feminism/Postmodernism*, ed. Linda Nicholson, 190–233. New York: Routledge.

Harding, Sandra. 1986. *The Science Question in Feminism*. Ithaca, N.Y.: Cornell University Press.

———. 1991. *Whose Science? Whose Knowledge? Thinking from Women's Lives*. Ithaca, N.Y.: Cornell University Press.

Harding, Sandra, and Merrill Hintikka, eds. 1983. *Discovering Reality: Feminist Perspectives on Epistemology, Metaphysics, Methodology, and the Philosophy of Science*. Dordrecht: Reidel.

Hartsock, Nancy. 1981. "Fundamental Feminism: Prospect and Perspective." In *Building Feminist Theory*, ed. Charlotte Bunch, 32–43. New York: Longman.

———. 1983a. "Difference and Domination in the Women's Movement: The Dialectic of Theory and Practice." In *Class, Race and Sex*, ed. Amy Swerdlow and Hanna Lessinger, 157–72. Boston: Hall.

———. 1983b. "The Feminist Standpoint: Developing the Ground for a Specifically Feminist Historical Materialism." In Harding and Hintikka 1983, 283–310.

———. 1983c. *Money, Sex, and Power*. New York: Longman.

———. 1987. "Rethinking Modernism: Minority vs. Majority Theories." *Cultural Critique* 7:187–206.

———. 1989–90. "Postmodernism and Political Change: Issues for Feminist Theory." *Cultural Critique* 14:15–33.

———. 1990. "Foucault on Power: A Theory for Women?" In *Feminism/Postmodernism*, ed. Linda Nicholson, 157–75. New York: Routledge.

Hekman, Susan. 1983. *Weber, the Ideal Type and Contemporary Social Theory*. Notre Dame, Ind.: University of Notre Dame Press.

———. 1995. "A Method for Difference: Feminist Methodology and the Challenge of Difference." Paper presented at the annual meeting of the American Political Science Association, Chicago.

Hirschmann, Nancy. 1992. *Rethinking Obligation: A Feminist Method for Political Inquiry*. Ithaca, N.Y.: Cornell University Press.

Hochschild, Arlie, with Anne Machung. 1989. *The Second Shift*. New York: Viking.

Jaggar, Alison. 1983. *Feminist Politics and Human Nature*. Totowa, N.J.: Rowman & Allanheld.

Kay, Judith. 1994. "Politics without Human Nature? Reconstructing a Common Humanity." *Hypatia* 9(1):21–52.

Longino, Helen. 1990. *Science as Social Knowledge*. Princeton, N.J.: Princeton University Press.

MacKinnon, Catharine. 1987. *Feminism Unmodified: Discourses on Life and Law*. Cambridge, Mass: Harvard University Press.

Nelson, Lynn Hankinson. 1990. *Who Knows: From Quine to a Feminist Empiricism*. Philadelphia: Temple University Press.

Nussbaum, Martha. 1992. "Human Functioning and Social Justice: In Defense of Aristotelian Essentialism." *Political Theory* 20(2):202–46.

O'Brien, Mary. 1981. *The Politics of Reproduction*. New York: Routledge & Kegan Paul.

Okin, Susan Moller. 1994. "Gender Inequality and Cultural Differences." *Political Theory* 22(1):5–24.

Pateman, Carole. 1988. *The Sexual Contract*. Stanford, Calif.: Stanford University Press.

Rose, Hilary. 1983. "Hand, Brain and Heart: A Feminist Epistemology for the Natural Sciences." *Signs* 9:73–90.

———. 1986. "Women's Work: Women's Knowledge." In *What Is Feminism? A Re-examination*, ed. Juliet Mitchell and Ann Oakley, 616–83. New York: Pantheon.

Ruddick, Sara. 1989. *Maternal Thinking: Toward a Politics of Peace*. Boston: Beacon.

Sacks, Karen. 1988. *Caring by the Hour: Women, Work and Organizing at the Duke Medical Center*. Urbana and Chicago: University of Illinois Press.

Schutz, Alfred. 1967. *The Phenomenology of the Social World*, trans. George Walsch and Frederick Lehnert. Evanston, Ill.: Northwestern University Press.

Smith, Dorothy. 1979. "A Sociology of Women." In *The Prism of Sex*, ed. Julia Sherman and Evelyn Beck, 135–87. Madison: University of Wisconsin Press.

———. 1987a. *The Everyday World as Problematic: A Feminist Sociology*. Boston: Northeastern University Press.

———. 1987b. "Women's Perspective as a Radical Critique of Sociology." In *Feminism and Methodology*, ed. Sandra Harding, 84–96. Bloomington: Indiana University Press.

———. 1990a. *The Conceptual Practices of Power: A Feminist Sociology of Knowledge*. Boston: Northeastern University Press.

———. 1990b. *Texts, Facts, and Femininity: Exploring Relations of Ruling*. London: Routledge.

Stanley, Liz, and Sue Wise. 1990. "Method, Methodology and Epistemology in Feminist Research Processes." In *Feminist Praxis: Research, Theory and Epistemology*, ed. Liz Stanley, 20–60. London: Routledge.

Tuana, Nancy. 1991. "The Radical Future of Feminist Empiricism." *Hypatia* 7(1):100–114.

Weber, Max. 1949. *The Methodology of the Social Sciences*, trans. and ed. Edward Shils and Henry Finch. New York: Free Press.

———. 1975. *Roscher and Knies*, trans. Guy Oakes. New York: Free Press.

Winant, Terry. 1987. "The Feminist Standpoint: A Matter of Language." *Hypatia* 2(1):123–48.

Wittgenstein, Ludwig. 1958. *Philosophical Investigations*. New York: Macmillan.

Young, Iris. 1980. "Socialist Feminism and the Limits of Dual System Theory." *Socialist Review* 10(2/3):169–88.

Comments and Reply

Comment on Hekman's "Truth and Method: Feminist Standpoint Theory Revisited": Truth or Justice?

Nancy C. M. Hartsock, Department of Political Science, University of Washington

$\int$ usan Hekman's article (in this volume) begins with a good summary of the current situation of feminist standpoint theories. She makes several important points that are often unrecognized in discussions of standpoint theories. First, she notes that standpoint theories come in a variety of forms. Second, she argues that these theories must be understood as a counterhegemonic discourse, that is, as centrally concerned with politics. And third, she reminds us that at least my version of standpoint theory operates with a social constructivist theory of the subject. There is much that is useful in her article, but here I want to address three areas where I think she reads standpoint theories through a kind of American pluralism that prefers to speak not about power or justice but, rather, about knowledge and epistemology. She is not alone in this.[1]

First, there is the question of the nature of the subject — If not pregiven but, rather, socially constructed, how is the subject exactly constructed, and what is the nature of this subject (subjected/collective/historically specific, etc.)? Second, What is the nature of the knowledge produced by this subject? Here I want to take up the question of whether truth, as usually understood, is the relevant category for the knowledge that is a social production. What is meant by truth, and how can it be achieved or justified? And third, What kind of privilege can one claim (or is one justified in claiming) for knowledge that arises from any particular social location, with the

I would like to thank Judy Aks and Karen Stuhldreher for comments on an earlier draft of this comment. I also want to thank Nancy Hirschman for organizing a panel on standpoint theory at the 1994 American Political Science Association meetings, where a number of these ideas were discussed.

[1] See also Brown 1995 for an account that not only treats my work as putting forward a model of subjects as pregiven but also argues that my work should be put in the same category as that of Allan Bloom!

[*Signs: Journal of Women in Culture and Society* 1997, vol. 22, no. 2]

understanding that social locations are fundamentally structured by power relations?

As I read Hekman's article, and other critiques of standpoint theories as well, I am struck by the extent to which the Marxist roots of standpoint theories have gone unrecognized. This leads to the criticism that standpoint theories are by nature essentialist, that they assume a fixed human nature for individuals with pregiven selves and pregiven needs and wants. While many would argue against a "return to the fathers," I think there are a number of both helpful and harmful ideas to be taken, used, translated, and also discarded. In writing the article "The Feminist Standpoint: Developing the Ground for a Specifically Feminist Historical Materialism," I was attempting to translate the concept of the standpoint of the proletariat into feminist terms (Hartsock 1983). Marx, in *Capital* (1967, 1:19), adopted a simple two-class model in which everything exchanged at its value, and only a few pages before the end of volume 3, more than two thousand pages later, he returns to the problem of class, which will now be shown to be more complicated and demanding of subtle treatment. The manuscript, however, breaks off only a few pages later without presenting such an analysis. Given the fruitfulness of Marx's strategy, I adopted by analogy a simple two-party opposition between feminist and masculinist representatives of the patriarchy. Following Lukacs's (1971) essay, "Reification and the Standpoint of the Proletariat," I wanted in my article to translate the notion of the proletariat (including its privileged historical mission) into feminist terms. I was arguing that, like the lives of proletarians in Marxist theory, women's lives in Western capitalist societies also contained possibilities for developing a critique of domination. By examining the institutional sexual division of labor, I argued that a feminist standpoint could be developed that would deepen the critique available from the standpoint of the proletariat and that would allow for a critique of patriarchal ideology. In following this strategy I committed an error similar to that of Marx. While he made no theoretical space for any oppression other than class, by following his lead I failed to allow for the importance of differences among women and differences among other various groups—power differences all.

But given this, why should I raise, once again, the importance of a nineteenth-century European patriarch for late twentieth-century feminist theory? Why Marx? Why now? The fall of the Soviet state, along with the Berlin Wall, has occasioned a global celebration of the market and of capitalism's successes. Fredric Jameson notes that for those who do not distinguish clearly between "Marxism itself as a mode of thought and analysis, socialism as a political and societal aim and vision, and Communism as a historical movement," Marxism can appear to be an embarrassing remnant of the past.[2] And certainly Teresa Ebert is right when she suggests that, "under the pressure of the dominant discourses of Postmodernism, Marxism and historical materialism are becoming lost revolutionary knowledges for the current generation of feminists" (1996, x). Still, even figures such as Derrida, regarding *The Communist Manifesto,* argue, "I know of few texts in the philosophical tradition, perhaps none, whose lesson seemed more urgent today" (1994, 13, quoted in Ebert 1996, xx). I would add that in the context of capitalism, which has truly become global, and in which more and more of life is commodified, much of Marx's critique of capitalism remains very apt.[3]

Still, I see Marx as an anti-Enlightenment figure on balance, although it must be recognized that his relationship to the Enlightenment and whole tradition of Western political thought is that of both the inheriting son and the rebellious son (see, e.g., Benhabib 1990, 11). Thus, his account of the process of labor itself can be seen in sexual/gendered terms: Marx theorizes the relation of the worker to his own activity as an alien activity not belonging to him: "Activity as suffering, strength as weakness, *begetting as emasculating,* . . . self-estrangement" (Marx and Engels 1978, 76; emphasis mine). Marx's account of estranged labor thus uses some of the "second homosocial birth" images I have found in many works in the history of Western political thought.[4] As I read Marx, he argues that the worker encounters himself in a world he has himself created, albeit in a very negative form.

Feminism, too, exists in an ambivalent relation to the Enlightenment. On the one hand, feminist theorists sometimes argue for a "me too" position in order to work for women's inclusion in a number of societal institutions.[5] On the other hand, women as women have never been the "subjects" of Enlightenment/liberal theory, and so women's insistence on speaking at all troubles those theories (see, e.g., Eisenstein 1981; and Kipnis 1988). (It is certainly my suspicion that this, along with decolonization and struggles for recognition by racial and ethnic groups, is one reason why European and North American theorists have lost some of their certainties.)

But let me now turn to the several questions I want to address. First, the question of truth. In the modernist/Enlightenment version, truth has

[2] Jameson 1996, 14; see also Brown's statement (1995, 4).

[3] See Haraway's chapters (1996) on Oncomouse and vampire culture.

[4] Achilles was one of the first to want to be born again in legend and song. He prayed that he would do some great thing first before he died and so could live on in legend and song.

[5] See Ferguson 1993 for a discussion of this issue.

to do with discovering a preexisting external something that, if it meets some criteria, can be labeled as true. Moreover, it must be discovered from nowhere in particular so that Truth can retain its pristine qualities. The definition of truth that I relied on, and still do, is more complex than this and is heavily indebted to my own reading of Marx. I do not claim to give an accurate reading of Marx, nor do I think it is important to rehabilitate him for contemporary feminist theory; rather, I want to suggest in a shorthand way how standpoint theories approach the question of truth. In the "Theses on Feuerbach," Marx argues against an understanding of "things" as "objects," especially objects of contemplation: "Man must prove the truth, i.e., the reality and power, the this-worldliness of his thinking in practice" (Marx and Engels 1975, 6). Finally, there is Marx's famous conclusion: "The philosophers have only *interpreted* the world in various ways; the point is to *change* it" (8).

The Marxian project, then, changes the criteria for what counts as knowledge: to have knowledge, for Marx, includes seeing, tasting, feeling, and thinking. If truth is the reality and power of ideas in action, then knowledge and truth must be treated in a much more historically specific way and attention should be devoted to the social, historical, and ultimately conventional form of all definitions of truth. (And on this point, one can be reminded of Foucault's claim that truth is simply error codified.) One is reminded that the search for knowledge is a human activity, structured by human requirements.

But here I become uncomfortable with the language of truth. The search for truth is not at all the way to understand Marx's project. The point, most fundamentally, is to understand power relations — in this case, power relations centered on the development of capitalism and the commodification of increasingly greater areas of human existence. But the point of understanding power relations is to change them. And to this end, Marx's categories move and flow and enact the fluidity that many postmodernist theorists insist on. To give just a few examples, capital is described as raw materials, instruments of labor, and means of subsistence of all kinds that are utilized to produce new raw materials, new instruments of labor, and new means of subsistence, as "accumulated labours," as "living labour serving accumulated labour," as "a bourgeois production relation, a social relation of production," and as "an independent social power" (Marx and Engels 1978, 176, 207, 208).

The result is a very complex idea of what constitutes "truth," which now becomes a difficult term to retain if one is to avoid falling back into Enlightenment categories of analysis. Hekman is right to point to Marx's claims about truth and their congruence with a number of Foucault's positions. She states tellingly that, despite these similarities, Foucault would argue that the discourses of the oppressed are just that and are not closer to "reality." She recognizes that these discourses, however, may be closer to "a definition of a less repressive society" (345). Standpoint theories are technical theoretical devices that can allow for the creation of accounts of society that can be used to work for more satisfactory social relations.

Marxist theories (and feminist standpoint theories) also remind us that the categories and criteria that come most immediately to mind for judging truth are likely to be those of the dominant groups. Thus, Marx can argue that everything appears reversed in competition, that the accumulation of wealth in capitalism (currently being celebrated on a global scale) is at the same time the accumulation of misery. Yet these categories and criteria are made true for all members of society. One can think of many ideas such as this — for example, compulsory heterosexuality enforced as a "truth," not discovered but made real through a variety of practices. My arguments for adopting a feminist standpoint recognize the danger of the biblical promise, "Ye shall know the truth and the truth shall set you free." In the context of power relations extant across many parts of the globe, "knowing the truth" is much more likely to get one jailed or make one disappear.

To turn to the second issue — the nature of the subject — I found in Marx the kinds of social constructivist theories of the subject that others have encountered in poststructuralism. But in contrast to the American tendency (certainly with the help of some European poststructuralists themselves) to interpret these theories in liberal pluralist, and in some cases libertarian, terms, terms that rely on accounts of the microprocesses of power, I found in the Marxian tradition an insistence on what some have called a "global" as opposed to a "totalizing" theory (see Hennessy 1993). The focus is on the macroprocesses of power, those that, although they may be played out in individual lives, can be fully understood only at the level of society as a whole. To claim that we can understand the totality of social relations from a single perspective is as futile an effort as to claim that we can see everything from nowhere.

A focus on large-scale social forces highlights different aspects of the subject. Thus, Marx can be read as providing a theory of the subject as subjected, as does Foucault. That is, one can read the essay on estranged labor or the theory of surplus value in *Capital* (which I would argue are two versions of the same philosophical argument) as accounts of how men (and they are) constitute themselves as subjected, pouring their lives into the objects that belong to another. Yet Marx's theory of subjects/

subjection differs from Foucault's in its stress on potentials and possibilities for developing other forms of subjectivity.[6] In addition, the Marxian theory of subjectivity is rightly classified as a "theoretical anti-humanism," an idea developed under this heading by Althusser and passed on by him to his students, Foucault and Derrida (see Hartsock 1991). That is, the subjects who matter are not individual subjects but collective subjects, or groups.

These groups must not be seen as formed unproblematically by existing in a particular social location and therefore seeing the world in a particular way. My effort to develop the idea of a feminist standpoint, in contrast to "women's viewpoint," was an effort to move in this direction. Chela Sandoval's notion of the importance of strategic identity for women of color represents an important advance in understanding this process, as does her development of the notion of oppositional consciousness.[7]

Sandoval argues that U.S. Third World feminism can function as a model for oppositional political activity. She proposes that we view the world as a kind of "topography" that defines the points around which "individuals and groups seeking to transform oppressive powers *constitute themselves* as resistant and oppositional subjects" (1991, 11; emphasis mine). She holds that once the "subject positions" of the dominated are "self-consciously recognized by their inhabitants," they can be "transformed into more effective sites of resistance" (11). She discusses a "differential consciousness," which she states operates like the clutch of an automobile, allowing the driver to engage gears in a "system for the transmission of power" (14).

Here, Sandoval's views parallel those of Gramsci, who suggests that we rethink the nature of identity: "Our capacity to think and act on the world is dependent on other people who are themselves also both subjects and objects of history" (Gramsci 1971, 346). In addition, one must reform the concept of individual to see it as a "series of active relationships, a process in which individuality, though perhaps most important, is not the only element to be taken into account." Individuality, then, is to be understood as the "ensemble of these relations. . . . To create one's personality means

[6] As I would like to adapt Marx to the use of contemporary feminism, I would like to change the potential of the proletariat, its "historic mission," to what bell hooks has described as a yearning for a different (and I would argue, better) world. See hooks 1990, esp. the essay "Postmodern Blackness."

[7] Sandoval (1990) makes an excellent point in her article on the development of the category of "women of color" out of the consciousness-raising sessions at the 1981 National Women's Studies Association meeting. Much of what follows comes from Sandoval's (1991) article on U.S. Third World feminism.

to acquire consciousness of them and to modify one's own personality means to modify the ensemble of these relations" (352). Moreover, Gramsci holds that each individual is the synthesis of these relations and also of the history of these relations, a "précis of the past" (353). The constitution of the subject, then, is the result of a complex interplay of "individuals" and larger-scale social forces. Groups are not to be understood, as Hekman seems to do, as aggregates of individuals. Moreover, the constitution of the "collective subject" posited by standpoint theories requires an always contingent and fragile (re)construction/transformation of these complex subject positions. As Kathi Weeks has put it, "This project of transforming subject-positions into standpoints involves an active intervention, a conscious and concerted effort to reinterpret and restructure our lives. . . . A standpoint is a project, not an inheritance; it is achieved, not given" (1996, 101).

I turn now to my third point, the issue of privileged knowledge. Fundamentally, I argue that the criteria for privileging some knowledges over others are ethical and political rather than purely "epistemological." The quotation marks here are to indicate that I see ethical and political concepts such as power as involving epistemological claims on the one hand and ideas of what is to count as knowledge involving profoundly important political and ethical stakes on the other. Hekman is right that I want to privilege some knowledges over others because they seem to me to offer possibilities for envisioning more just social relations. I believe there is a second aspect to the idea that some knowledges are "better" than others, and here I think Sandoval has stated the most important point: the self-conscious transformation of individuals into resistant, oppositional, and collective subjects.

The most important issue for me is the question of how we can use theoretical tools and insights to create theories of justice and social change that address the concerns of the present. Marx, for all of the difficulties with both his theoretical work and the state of actually (non)existing socialism, calls our attention to certain macrolevel issues to be addressed. In addition, one can find in the work of theorists such as Gramsci a much more useful and complex theorization of relations between "individuals" and society as a whole, one that opens up possibilities for both new knowledges and new collectivities.

References

Benhabib, Seyla. 1990. "Epistemologies of Postmodernism." In *Feminism/Postmodernism*, ed. Linda Nicholson, 107–30. New York: Routledge.

Brown, Wendy. 1995. *States of Injury: Power and Freedom in Late Modernity.* Princeton, N.J.: Princeton University Press.

Derrida, Jacques. 1994. *Spectres of Marx,* trans. Peggy Kamuf. New York: Routledge.

Ebert, Teresa. 1996. *Ludic Feminism and After: Postmodernism, Desire and Labor in Late Capitalism.* Ann Arbor: University of Michigan Press.

Eisenstein, Zillah. 1981. *The Radical Future of Liberal Feminism.* New York: Longman.

Ferguson, Kathy. 1993. *The Man Question: Visions of Subjectivity in Feminist Theory.* Berkeley and Los Angeles: University of California Press.

Foucault, Michel. 1980. *Language, Counter-Memory, Practice: Selected Essays and Interviews.* Ithaca, N.Y.: Cornell University Press.

Gramsci, Antonio. 1971. *Selections from the Prison Notebooks,* ed. and trans. Quintin Hoare and Geoffrey Nowell Smith. New York: International.

Haraway, Donna. 1996. *Modest_Witness@Second_Millennium.FemaleMan© Meets _Oncomouse™: Feminism and Technoscience.* New York: Routledge.

Hartsock, Nancy. 1983. "The Feminist Standpoint: Developing the Ground for a Specifically Feminist Historical Materialism." In *Discovering Reality: Feminist Perspectives on Epistemology, Metaphysics, Methodology and Philosophy of Science,* ed. Sandra Harding and Merrill Hintikka, 283–310. Dordrecht: Reidel/Kluwer.

———. 1991. "Louis Althusser's Structural Marxism." *Rethinking Marxism* 4(4):10–40.

Hennessy, Rosemary. 1993. *Materialist Feminism and the Politics of Discourse.* New York: Routledge.

hooks, bell. 1990. *Yearning: Race, Gender, and Cultural Politics.* Toronto: Between-the-Lines.

Jameson, Fredric. 1996. "Actually Existing Marxism." In *Marxism beyond Marxism,* ed. Saree Makdisis, Cesare Casarino, and Rebecca E. Karl, 14–54. New York: Routledge.

Kipnis, Laura. 1988. "Feminism: The Political Conscience of Postmodernism." In *Universal Abandon? The Politics of Postmodernism,* ed. Andrew Ross, 149–66. Minneapolis: University of Minnesota Press.

Lukacs, George. 1971. "Reification and the Standpoint of the Proletariat." In his *History and Class Consciousness.* Boston: Beacon.

Marx, Karl. 1967. *Capital,* vol. 1. New York: International.

Marx, Karl, and Friedrich Engels. 1975. *Collected Works,* vol. 5, 3d ed. New York: International.

———. 1978. *The Marx-Engels Reader,* ed. Robert Tucker, 2d ed. New York: Norton.

Sandoval, Chela. 1990. "Feminism and Racism: A Report on the 1981 National Women's Studies Association Conference." In *Making Face, Making Soul/ Haciendo Caras,* ed. Gloria Anzaldúa, 55–71. San Francisco: Aunt Lute.

———. 1991. "U.S. Third World Feminism: The Theory and Method of Oppositional Consciousness in the Postmodern World." *Genders* 10 (Spring): 1–24.

Weeks, Kathi. 1996. "Subject for a Feminist Standpoint." In *Marxism beyond Marxism*, ed. Saree Makdisi, Cesare Casarino, and Rebecca E. Karl, 89–118. New York: Routledge. ∎

Comment on Hekman's "Truth and Method: Feminist Standpoint Theory Revisited": Where's the Power?

Patricia Hill Collins, Department of African-American Studies, University of Cincinnati

My reading of standpoint theory sees it as an interpretive framework dedicated to explicating how knowledge remains central to maintaining and changing unjust systems of power. While the main arguments in Susan Hekman's article (in this volume) contain surface validity, because standpoint theory never was designed to be argued as a theory of truth or method, Hekman's article simply misses the point of standpoint theory overall. By decontextualizing standpoint theory from its initial moorings in a knowledge/power framework while simultaneously recontextualizing it in an apolitical discussion of feminist truth and method, Hekman essentially depoliticizes the potentially radical content of standpoint theory.

First, the notion of a standpoint refers to historically shared, *group*-based experiences. Groups have a degree of permanence over time such that group realities transcend individual experiences. For example, African Americans as a stigmatized racial group existed long before I was born and will probably continue long after I die. While my individual experiences with institutionalized racism will be unique, the types of opportunities and constraints that I encounter on a daily basis will resemble those confronting African Americans as a group. Arguing that Blacks as a group come into being or disappear on the basis of my participation seems narcissistic, egocentric, and archetypally postmodern. In contrast, standpoint theory places less emphasis on individual experiences within socially constructed groups than on the social conditions that construct such groups.

I stress this difference between the individual and the group as units of analysis because using these two constructs as if they were interchangeable clouds understanding of a host of topics, in this case, the very notion of a group-based standpoint. Individualism continues as a taproot in Western theorizing, including feminist versions. Whether bourgeois liberalism positing notions of individual rights or postmodern social theory's celebration of human differences, market-based choice models grounded in individualism argue that freedom exists via the absence of constraints of all sorts, including those of mandatory group membership. Freedom occurs when individuals have rights of mobility in and out of groups, much as we join clubs and other voluntary associations.

But the individual as proxy for the group becomes particularly problematic because standpoint theory's treatment of the group is not synonymous with a "family resemblance" of individual choice expanded to the level of voluntary group association. The notion of standpoint refers to groups having shared histories based on their shared location in relations of power—standpoints arise neither from crowds of individuals nor from groups analytically created by scholars or bureaucrats. Take, for example, the commonality of experiences that emerges from long-standing patterns of racial segregation in the United States. The degree of racial segregation between Blacks and Whites as *groups* is routinely underestimated. Blacks and Whites live in racially segregated neighborhoods, and this basic feature generates distinctive experiences in schools, recreational facilities, shopping areas, health-care systems, and occupational opportunities. Moreover, middle-class Blacks have not been exempt from the effects of diminished opportunities that accompany racial segregation and group discrimination. It is common location within hierarchical power relations that creates groups, not the results of collective decision making of the individuals within the groups. Race, gender, social class, ethnicity, age, and sexuality are not descriptive categories of identity applied to individuals. Instead, these elements of social structure emerge as fundamental devices that foster inequality resulting in groups.

To ignore power relations is simply to misread standpoint theory—its raison d'être, its continuing salience, and its ability to explain social inequality. Hekman's treatment of groups as an accumulation of individuals and not as entities with their own reality allows her to do just this. Note the slippage between individual and group standpoint in the following passage: "If we take the multiplicity of feminist standpoints to its logical conclusion, coherent analysis becomes impossible because we have too many axes of analysis. Ultimately, every woman is unique; if we analyze each in her uniqueness, systemic analysis is obviated. So is feminist politics: we lose the ability even to speak for certain categories of women" (28). Hekman clearly identifies the very construct of standpoint with the idea of individual perspective or point of view. This assumption allows her to collapse the individual and group as units of analysis and proceed to reason that *individuals* and *collectivities* undergo similar processes. But because she remains focused on the individual as proxy for the group, it becomes difficult to construct the group from such "unique" individuals. Arriving at the dead end of the impossibility of systemic analysis that leads to systemic change appears as the result. By omitting a discussion of group-based realities grounded in an equally central notion of group-based oppression, we move into the sterile ground of a discussion of how effectively standpoint theory serves as an epistemology of truth.

In contrast to Hekman's view that attention to multiplicity fosters incoherence, current attention to the theme of intersectionality situated within assumptions of group-based power relations reveals a growing understanding of the complexity of the processes both of generating groups and accompanying standpoints. Initially examining only one dimension of power relations, namely, that of social class, Marx posited that, however unarticulated and inchoate, oppressed groups possessed a particular standpoint on inequality. In more contemporary versions, inequality has been revised to reflect a greater degree of complexity, especially that of race and gender. What we now have is increasing sophistication about how to discuss group location, not in the singular social class framework proposed by Marx, nor in the early feminist frameworks arguing the primacy of gender, but within constructs of multiplicity residing in social structures themselves and not in individual women. Fluidity does not mean that groups themselves disappear, to be replaced by an accumulation of decontextualized, unique women whose complexity erases politics. Instead, the fluidity of boundaries operates as a new lens that potentially deepens understanding of how the actual mechanisms of institutional power can change dramatically while continuing to reproduce long-standing inequalities of race, gender, and class that result in group stability. In this sense, group history and location can be seen as points of convergence within hierarchical, multiple, and changing structural power relations.

A second feature of standpoint theory concerns the commonality of experiences and perspectives that emerge for groups differentially arrayed within hierarchical power relations. Keep in mind that if the group has been theorized away, there can be no common experiences or perspectives. Standpoint theory argues that groups who share common placement in hierarchical power relations also share common experiences in such power relations. Such shared angles of vision lead those in similar social locations to be predisposed to interpret these experiences in a comparable fashion. The existence of the group as the unit of analysis neither means that all individuals within the group have the same experiences nor that they interpret them in the same way. Using the group as the focal point provides space for individual agency. While these themes remain meritorious, they simply do not lie at the center of standpoint theory as a theory of group power and the knowledges that group location and power generate.

Unfortunately, the much-deserved attention to issues of individual agency and diversity often overshadow investigating the continued salience of group-based experiences. But group-based experience, especially that of race and/or social class, continues to matter. For example, African-American male rates of incarceration in American jails and prisons remain the highest in the world, exceeding even those of South Africa. Transcending social class, region of residence, command of English, ethnic background, or other markers of difference, all Black men must in some way grapple with the actual or potential treatment by the criminal justice system. Moreover, as mothers, daughters, wives, and lovers of Black men, Black women also participate in this common experience. Similarly, children from poor communities and homeless families are unlikely to attend college, not because they lack talent, but because they lack opportunity. Whatever their racial/ethnic classification, poor people as a group confront similar barriers for issues of basic survival. In this sense, standpoint theory seems especially suited to explaining relations of race and/or social class because these systems of power share similar institutional structures. Given the high degree of residential and occupational segregation separating Black and/or working-class groups from White middle-class realities, it becomes plausible to generate arguments about working-class and/or Black culture that emerge from long-standing shared experiences. For both class and race, a much clearer case of a group standpoint can be constructed. Whether individuals from or associated with these groups accept or reject these histories, they recognize the saliency of the notion of group standpoint.

But gender raises different issues, for women are distributed across these other groups. In contrast to standpoints that must learn to accommodate differences within, feminist standpoints must be constructed across differences such as these. Thus, gender represents a distinctly different intellectual and political project within standpoint theory. How effectively can a standpoint theory that was originally developed to explicate the wage exploitation and subsequent impoverishment of European, working-class populations be applied to the extremely heterogeneous population of women in the contemporary United States, let alone globally? For example, Black women and White women do not live in racially integrated women's communities, separated from men and children by processes such as gender steering into such communities, experience bank redlining that results in refusal to lend money to women's communities, attend inferior schools as a result of men moving to all-male suburban areas, and the like.

Instead, Black and White women live in racially segregated communities, and the experiences they garner in such communities reflect the racial politics operating overall. Moreover, proximity in physical space is not necessarily the same as occupying a common location in the space of hierarchical power relations. For example, Black women and women of color routinely share academic office space with middle-class and/or White women academics. It is quite common for women of color to clean the office of the feminist academic writing the latest treatise on standpoint theory. While these women occupy the same physical space—this is why proximity should not be confused with group solidarity—they occupy fundamentally different locations in hierarchical power relations. These women did not just enter this space in a random fashion. An entire arsenal of social institutions collectively created paths in which the individuals assigned to one group received better housing, health care, education, and recreational facilities, while those relegated to the other group did with worse or did without. The accumulation of these different experiences led the two groups of women to that same academic space. The actual individuals matter less than the accumulation of social structures that lead to these outcomes. In this sense, developing a political theory for women involves confronting a different and more complex set of issues than that facing race theories or class-based theories because women's inequality is structured differently.

There is a third theme of standpoint theory in which power is erased, namely, the significance of group consciousness, group self-definition, and "voice" within this entire structure of power and experience. Collapsing individual and group identity emerges here as significant because applying standpoint theory to the individual as proxy for the group becomes particularly problematic in comparing individual voice with group voice or standpoint. Typically, this process operates via imagining how *individuals* negotiate self-definitions and then claiming a "family resemblance" positing that *collectivities* undergo a similar process. Because collectivities certainly do construct stories in framing their identity, this approach appears plausible. But can the individual stand as proxy for the group and the group for the individual? Moreover, can this particular version of the individual serve as the exemplar for collective group identity?

If an individual reasons from his or her own personal experiences by imagining that since "*we* are all the same under the skin, therefore, what *I* experience must be the same as what everybody else experiences," then a certain perception of group narrative structure emerges. If an individual believes that his or her personal experiences in coming to voice, especially the inner voices within his or her own individual consciousness hidden from hierarchal power relations, not only reflect a common human experience but, more to the point, also serve as an exemplar for how *group* consciousness and decision making operate, then individual experience becomes the model for comprehending group processes. This approach minimizes the significance of conflict within groups in generating group narratives. In the model in which an individual conducts inner dialogues among various parts of his or her "self," the process of mediating conflicting identities occurs within each individual. The individual always holds complete power or agency over the consciousness that he or she constructs in his or her own mind and the voice that she or he uses to express that consciousness.

Shifting this mode of coming to voice to the level of the small group provides space to think of groups as collections of individuals engaged in dialogue with one another. As equal and different, the concern lies in finding rules to decide whose voice has most validity. By asking, "If we acknowledge multiple realities, multiple standpoints, how do we discriminate among them?" (28), Hekman continues the search for rules that everyone can follow in order to come to a collective "voice." Within the scope of individuals engaged in face-to-face interaction, this seems reasonable. But does this work with the understanding of *group* that underlies standpoint theory?

Hekman quite rightly recognizes that multiple realities yield multiple perspectives on reality. But again, her concern with the question of who has the best, "truest," or privileged standpoint remains grounded in ambiguous notions of group that omit group-based conflicts and how hierarchical power relations generate differences in group voice or standpoint. Bracketing the question of power and restricting argument solely to the question of truth certainly reveals the limitations of using epistemological criteria in defense of privileged standpoints. But within the reality of hierarchical power relations, the standpoints of some groups are most certainly privileged over others. The amount of privilege granted to a particular standpoint lies less in its internal criteria in being truthful, the terrain in which Hekman situates her discussion, and more in the power of a group in making its standpoint prevail over other equally plausible perspectives. Within hierarchical power relations, it seems reasonable that groups disadvantaged by systems of power might see their strength in solidarity and collective responses to their common location and subjugation. In contrast, it seems equally plausible that those privileged by these types of group placements might want to do away with notions of the group altogether, in effect obscuring the privileges they gain from group membership.

Again, gender raises some particular challenges in using standpoint theory to represent the standpoint of women. One fundamental contribution of feminist movement grounded in standpoint theory was that it aimed to bring women's group consciousness into being. Early emphasis on women's coming to voice via the process of consciousness-raising and claiming individual "voice" inadvertently laid the foundation for the type of conceptual ambiguity between individual and group as categories of analysis. Contemporary feminist theorizing, especially the emergence of postmodern social theory's theme of deconstructing the subject, aggravates this long-standing commitment to bringing individual women to voice as emblematic of the collective struggle of women for "voice." Collapsing the processes of individual and group voice and using the process of individual women coming to voice as emblematic of women's collective coming to voice reinforces this notion that individual and collective voice or standpoint are the same. For many contemporary feminists, voicing their discontent with oppression is sufficient—actually changing institutional power relations seems less important. Gaining voice only to lose it again to a standpoint theory that replaces the freedom of individually negotiated friendships or sisterhood with the obligations of race, class, and gender "families" seems unacceptable to those with the means to escape.

Standpoint theory argues that ideas matter in systems of power. In this sense, standpoints may be judged not only by their epistemological contributions but also by the terms of their participation in hierarchical power relations. Do they inherently explain and condone injustice, or do they challenge it? Do they participate in relations of rule via creating knowledge, or do they reject such rule by generating cultures of resistance? Extracting any claims about knowledge from the power relations in which they are embedded violates the basic premise of standpoint theory because such theory exists primarily to explicate these power relations. Thus, attempts to take the knowledge while leaving the power behind inadvertently operate within the terrain of privileged knowledge. While I respect postmodern contributions in deconstructing languages of power, standpoint theory encompasses much more than changing the "language game of politics" (32). Oppression is not a game, nor is it solely about language—for many of us, it still remains profoundly real. ∎

Comment on Hekman's "Truth and Method: Feminist Standpoint Theory Revisited": Whose Standpoint Needs the Regimes of Truth and Reality?

Sandra Harding, Departments of Women's Studies, Education, and Philosophy, University of California, Los Angeles

I agree with several of Susan Hekman's central arguments (in this volume). Feminist standpoint theory has indeed made a major contribution to feminist theory and, as she indicates at the end, to late twentieth-century efforts to develop more useful ways of thinking about the production of knowledge in local and global political economies. We can note that feminists are not the only contemporary social theorists to struggle with projects of extricating ourselves from some of the constraints of those philosophies of modernity that began to emerge in Europe three or more centuries ago. Moreover, Hekman is certainly right that current reevaluations of marxian projects, of the "difference" issues, and of poststructuralism are three sites of both resources and challenges to the further development of standpoint theories, as they must be also for other contemporary social theorizing.

These last three sets of issues are intimately related. The modern understanding of how to go about knowledge seeking, retained in the marxian epistemology, assumed that one should imagine a kind of single, ideal knower, "homogeneously" constituted since he purportedly represented no particular cultural identity, interests, or discourses. The proletarian standpoint, once it was generalized as the truly human standpoint, provided just such an ideal unitary knower no less than did social contract theory's "rational man." Issues neither of differences between knowers nor of the cultural constitution of knowledge — the multicultural and poststructuralist issue about discourses — could arise as long as knowledge acquisition was figured as performing the "God-trick," as Donna Haraway famously put the point (1988). Thus, early articulations of feminist standpoint theory retained some of these problematic modernist assumptions about truth and reality.

However, it seems to me that Hekman distorts the central project of standpoint theorists when she characterizes it as one of figuring out how to justify the truth of feminist claims to more accurate accounts of reality. Rather, it is relations between power and knowledge that concern these thinkers. They have wanted to identify ways that male supremacy and the production of knowledge have coconstituted each other in the past and to explore what heretofore unrecognized powers might be found in women's lives that could lead to knowledge that is more useful for enabling women to improve the conditions of our lives. This language about truth and reality certainly is one that can be found in early and some continuing standpoint accounts—including the title of the very book in which Nancy Hartsock's essay first appeared (1983), for which I am half responsible! Marxian and other older modernist discourses provided the framework for the feminist standpoint project initially, including the language about truth and reality. However, at least this standpoint theorist thinks that feminist standpoint projects and the modernist discourses they used turned out to be on a collision course. We can talk usefully about "less false beliefs"—ones apparently, as far as we can tell, less false than all *and only those* against which they have so far been tested—without invoking the notion of truth or reality in the conventional senses of these terms. That way we can avoid the truth claimant's position that "the one true story" has, now and forever, already been identified and that as far as the truth claimant is concerned, the matter is closed, *fini*, ended. And we can talk about such less false accounts of "nature and social relations," or however we want to refer to the object of our thoughts and research, without invoking the idea of a static, eternally fixed state of affairs "out there" that our representations have managed uniquely to capture. As N. Katharine Hayles puts the point, many highly useful but conflicting representations can be consistent with "how the world is," although none can be uniquely congruent with it (Hayles 1993; see also Dupre 1993; Van Fraassen and Sigman 1993).

Relatedly, Hekman's account loses the point that standpoint epistemologies and methodologies were constructed in opposition to the all-powerful dictates of rationalist/empiricist epistemologies and methodologies ("positivism") in the natural and social sciences and in public institutions such as the law, medicine, state economic policy, and so forth. They were also constructed in opposition to the "interpretationist" oppositions to them imagined by most philosophers and social theorists to be the only possible such alternatives. Moreover, for such positivist and antipositivist theorists in philosophy and the social sciences, at least in the United States, marxian approaches lay beyond the pale of reasonable discussion.

For the standpoint theorists, however, the marxian epistemology/ sociology of knowledge provided the only resources powerful enough to counter the prevailing conceptual frameworks for the kinds of natural and social science projects of feminism in the 1970s and early 1980s. At that time, poststructuralism did not yet seem to offer the resources for feminist science and social science studies that, at least for me, have now been identified in it. Discussions of ideology appeared to be able to handle the cultural configurations that are more richly and accurately, in my view, understood through poststructuralist analyses of socially constituted discourses.[1]

In the brief space remaining to me, I want to try to make vivid the (or, rather, a) "logic" of standpoint theory as it emerged in such a context. I shall try to show how the issues about truth and reality on which Hekman and others have focused need not arise if we reflect on this logic through the resources provided by the past three decades of work in the social studies of science and technology, on the one hand, and multicultural and global science studies and feminisms, on the other hand. This account will also help to clarify some aspects of my work that Hekman finds puzzling.

"Natural experiments" as a clue to standpoint logic. Standpoint theories argue that the social world in effect provides a kind of laboratory for "experiments" that can enable one to observe and explain patterns in the relations between social power and the production of knowledge claims. Recollect that ancient lesson from elementary school science classes: "Is that stick in the pond that appears to be bent really bent? Walk around to a different location and see that now it appears straight—as it really is." Then, theories of optics were invoked to explain the causes of the initially distorted appearances. In an analogous way, standpoint theorists use the "naturally occurring" relations of class, gender, race, or imperialism in the world around us to observe how different "locations" in such relations tend to generate distinctive accounts of nature and social relations. (They do not *determine* them, but only "tend to generate" accounts different from the dominant ones in distinctive ways.) Thus, the kinds of daily life activities socially assigned to different genders or classes or races within local social systems can provide illuminating possibilities for observing and explaining systemic relations between "what one does" and "what one can know." Observing these differing relations is like walking around the pond. Distinctive gender, class, race, or cultural positions in social orders provide different opportunities and limitations for "seeing" how the social order works. Societies provide a kind of "natural experiment" enabling accounts of how knowledge claims are always "socially situated."

Like the stick-bent-in-water example, although all knowledge claims are determinately situated, not all such social situations are equally good ones from which to be able to see how the social order works. Dominant groups have more interests than do those they dominate in not formulating and

---

[1] It should also be noted that while for Europeans, poststructuralism is a kind of postmarxism, for many U.S. poststructuralists, it is a *premarxism*. Like Hekman, they attach it to diverse liberal social science discourses—in her case, those of Thomas Kuhn and Max Weber.

in excluding questions about how social relations and nature "really work." From the perspective of women's lives (as articulated by different and sometimes conflicting feminist accounts), such questions emerge as these: Are women "really" capable of only a lesser rationality than men's? Is the double day of work "really" a matter of nature's, not culture's, design? In social relations organized by domination, exploitation, and oppression, the "conceptual practices of power" (Smith's phrase [1990]) will construct institutions that make seem natural and normal those relations of domination, exploitation, and oppression.

This kind of structural political "difference" was exactly the point of standpoint theory projects, although which "system of domination" was centered depended on whether marxist men or northern feminists or male antiracists and postcolonialists were doing the thinking. However, it took feminists of color, multicultural and global feminisms, to develop the powerful resources of "intersectionality" necessary to analyze social relations from the standpoint of their daily lives, which were shaped by the mutually supportive or sometimes competitive relations between androcentrism, Eurocentrism, and bourgeois projects (e.g., hooks 1981; Anzaldúa 1987; Collins 1991). Moreover, also not initially centered in standpoint logics and epistemologies was "mere difference"—the cultural differences that would shape different knowledge projects even where there were no oppressive social relations between different cultures (although the persistent attention to women's daily lives clearly required accounting for cultural differences in "what women do").

The "intersectionality" approaches use resources provided by thinking from both of these kinds of differences among women to shape what is often referred to as multicultural and global feminisms. If one starts asking questions about standard accounts of the growth of modern science, for example, from the lives of peoples who suffered from that growth and from the associated European expansion that made it possible and benefited from it (lives articulated through diverse "constructed" discourses), one—anyone—learns more than if such questions were not asked. Postcolonial science studies and the critiques of development, including feminist work in these fields, have asked such questions. They provide resources that northern and northern feminist science studies cannot provide. The reason for this is not because poor, Third World women are "more oppressed," as Hekman misstates my point, but, rather, because thought that begins from conceptual frameworks developed to answer questions arising in *their* lives starts from outside the Eurocentric conceptual frameworks within which northern and northern feminist science studies have been largely organized. Hekman's comment about more oppressed women (23), contrary to what I am sure were her intentions, functions to

reinstate the Eurocentrism of dominant conceptual frameworks of northern discourses, including feminist ones, by encouraging hostile competitive relations between northern and southern women ("Who's most
oppressed?").

One way to characterize what it is about different cultural locations (including those in relations of domination) that invariably will generate both
enabling and limiting knowledge claims is the following. Cultures have
different locations in the heterogeneous natural world (exposure to the
demands of babies or factories, cancer-producing sunlight or too little sun,
deserts or rain forests). They bring different interests even to the "same"
natural or social environment (e.g., interests to fish, travel, mine, harvest
seaweed from, desalinize, etc., the Atlantic Ocean). They draw on, and are
positioned in different ways with respect to, culturally distinctive discursive
resources — metaphors, models, narratives, conceptual frameworks — with
which to think about themselves and the worlds around them. Moreover,
they have culturally distinctive ways of organizing the production of
knowledge, usually highly related to how they produce everything else —
to work (see Harding 1997, and in press).

This kind of framework can be used to explain differences in knowledge
possibilities of the kinds of cultures conventionally of interest to anthropologists and historians. In fact, I draw it from the post-Kuhnian social
studies of science and technology and the postcolonial cross-cultural studies of modern sciences as much like other local knowledge systems (see,
e.g., Watson-Verran and Turnbull 1995). It could have been drawn as easily from analyses of northern American societies, as were most of the original standpoint writings.

Hekman's administrator perspective.   From this perspective, Hekman's
questions about truth and reality can be avoided. Other questions that do
much of the same work do arise — for example, about evidence, Eurocentric conceptual frameworks in every discipline, the culturally diverse purposes of science, and the relations between the expansion of European
power and hegemonic conceptual apparatuses. But Hekman's preoccupa-
tions with truth and reality arise, I suggest, only from the standpoint of a
Eurocentric reaction to these postcolonial accounts. Let us ask what social
location one could infer for the author of the following (purportedly value
neutral?) passage in which Hekman reacts to a statement by Haraway with
what Hekman sees as "the central problem facing feminist theory today."[2]
My question is: Who is the "we" in these passages? "Given multiple stand-

[2] Hekman says here that it is Haraway who defines the problem Hekman formulates below; however, this is not Haraway's formulation of it — it is Hekman's.

points, the social construction of 'reality,' and the necessity of an engaged political position, how can we talk about 'better accounts of the world,' 'less false stories'? And, indeed, how can we talk about accounts of the world at all if the multiplicity of standpoints is, quite literally, endless?" (27). In the next paragraph she repeats her statement of this problem:

> First, if we take the multiplicity of feminist standpoints to its logical conclusion, coherent analysis becomes impossible because we have too many axes of analysis. Ultimately, every woman is unique; if we analyze each in her uniqueness, systemic analysis is obviated. So is feminist politics: we lose the ability even to speak for certain categories of women. Second, if we acknowledge multiple realities, multiple standpoints, how do we discriminate among them? How do we select the perspectives and standpoints that are useful to us, that will help us achieve our theoretical and practical goals, or are we necessarily condemned to the "absolute relativism" that some critics fear? (28)

Who is the repeated "we" of these paragraphs, with "too many axes of analysis," trying to "speak for certain [other?] categories of women," forced to acknowledge multiple realities with no guides to discriminating among them, no justifiable guides for selecting "the perspectives and standpoints that are useful to us," and so forth? Not women in their everyday lives, who must and do make reasoned, evidence-dependent judgments about such matters. In centering these questions, Hekman's standpoint remains that of the administrator faced with managing all those culturally local people, with their conflicting perspectives, claims, and demands. If "our" one true story of a world that is out there and available for the telling is not *the* true story, then the modernist paranoia begins: "We" are going to have to admit the legitimacy of everyone's story and world—some of which will probably conflict with our favored ones. Lost is the analysis of how knowledge projects are designed for local situations, including diverse interests in gaining and exercising power. This is not, of course, where Hekman wants to be positioned, but it seems to me that it is where the conceptual framework of her article is positioned.

Clarifications. This brings me to some clarifications. "Less false accounts." Science never gets us truth; it always promised something much better than truth claims. Truth claims were supposed to be thought of as expressing a relation to the world claimed only by religious or other dogmatic beliefs. Scientific procedures are supposed to get us claims that are less false than those—and only those—against which they have been tested. Further evidence can be collected, and conceptual shifts cast old claims into new frameworks. Thus, scientific claims are supposed to be held not as true but, only provisionally, as "least false" until counter-evidence or a new conceptual framework no longer provides them with the status of "less false" than those against which they have been tested. Thus, my discussions of "strong objectivity" and of "less false" claims were intended to distance standpoint thinking from remnants of popular modernist ideology that did not even match modernist science theory. Another way to put this point is that claims to truth are harmless as long as they promise no more than the evidence that can be produced in support of such a claim. Of course the standards for what counts as "less false" can be at issue or change over time. The standards for knowledge claims, too, are provisional and tend to change over time. We need not avoid the useful notion of "less false" claims just because we turn away from the absolutist standards of modernism.

Hekman says I "offer no argument" as to why it is that "starting research from the reality of women's lives . . . will lead to a more objective account of social reality" (23). Yet chapter 5 of *Whose Science? Whose Knowledge?* did precisely that, pointing to diverse such arguments already "out there" in older history and social science research (Harding 1991). I had already pointed to some of these in my earlier analysis of the differences between several feminist standpoint theory arguments (Harding 1986). Hekman is right, in my view, about the necessity to understand "women's lives" or, in her terms, "the reality of women's lives," as socially constructed discursive formations. But, that some such discursive accounts provide richer resources than others for understanding natural and social worlds — that they are epistemically privileged in this sense — I did argue for, as has every other standpoint theorist. It is odd that nowhere in her article does she take up just what it is that Hartsock, Smith, Collins, myself, and others have identified in the women's lives that seemed to us to justify claims of epistemic preference. She seems to be interested not in the substantive claims of standpoint theories but only in their troubled participation in a truth/reality discourse.

Finally, something must be said about the misleading chronology for the development of feminist standpoint theory that Hekman gives in the first few paragraphs. Smith's first standpoint essay, the one Hekman references to my 1987 anthology, originally appeared in 1974 (Smith 1974). Three more essays were published by 1981 (Smith 1977, 1979, 1981). By 1979, four years before Hartsock's publications, Marcia Westkott could already include a review of the wide influence on sociologists of several of Smith's standpoint essays in her *Harvard Educational Review* essay (1979).

It was Smith, not Hartsock, to whom Collins stated her indebtedness — which makes sense since Smith and Collins are both sociologists. Hartsock's two versions of her important essay appeared in the same year, 1983, as did published standpoint essays by Alison Jaggar, Hilary Rose (as Hekman indicates later on p. 16) and Harding. Moreover, there were a number of colloquia on Smith's and Harding's work in the late 1980s and early 1990s and discussions of feminist standpoint epistemologies in diverse journal articles, feminist philosophy collections, and disciplinary association meetings (evidently excluding political science discourses) during this period.

More than factual errors are at issue here. Hartsock's essay has indeed been immensely and justifiably influential. It does not devalue the brilliance of her work to recognize, however, that in retrospect one can see that feminist standpoint epistemology was evidently an idea whose time had come, since most of these authors worked independently and unaware of each other's work. (Standpoint theory would itself call for such a social history of ideas, would it not?) It was a project "straining at the bit" to emerge from feminist social theorists who were familiar with the marxian epistemology. If one was familiar with Marx's, Engles's, and Lukacs's writings on epistemology, the potential parallels Hartsock so incisively delineates between the situations of "proletarians" and of "women" in thinking about relations between power and knowledge began to leap off the page. Moreover, standpoint theory's subsequent development tended to be constrained by the familiar disciplinary borders that evidently still limit Hekman's grasp of this history. These disciplinary development routes also created distinctively different standpoint theor*ies,* in the plural, each drawing on different disciplinary and other research interests, resources, and methodologies. Different political projects have also shaped how standpoint epistemologies have been developed.

My point is that the ways we think about these different versions of standpoint theory — these multiple standpoints on standpoint theory that are located in different disciplines and other cultures, with different interests, discursive resources, and typical ways of organizing the production of epistemologies/methodologies — replicate the situations that are Hekman's overt topic. Our analyses, too, are socially situated and constituted by the often hard-to-detect politics of the conceptual frameworks we adopt, intentionally or not.

Whose locations, interests, discourses, and ways of organizing the production of knowledge are silenced and suppressed by taking the administrative standpoint on standpoint theory that Hekman centers?

References

Anzaldúa, Gloria. 1987. *Borderlands/La Frontera*. San Francisco: Spinsters/Aunt Lute.

Collins, Patricia Hill. 1991. *Black Feminist Thought: Knowledge, Consciousness, and the Politics of Empowerment*. New York: Routledge.

Dupre, John. 1993. *The Disorder of Things: Metaphysical Foundations for the Disunity of Science*. Cambridge, Mass.: Harvard University Press.

Haraway, Donna. 1988. "Situated Knowledges: *The Science Question in Feminism* and the Privilege of Partial Perspective." *Feminist Studies* 14(3):575–99. Reprinted in her *Simians, Cyborgs and Women: The Reinvention of Nature*. New York: Routledge, 1991.

Harding, Sandra. 1983. "Why Has the Sex-Gender System Become Visible Only Now?" In *Discovering Reality: Feminist Perspectives on Epistemology, Metaphysics, Methodology, and Philosophy of Science*, ed. Sandra Harding and Merrill Hintikka, 311–24. Dordrecht: Reidel/Kluwer.

———. 1986. *The Science Question in Feminism*. Ithaca, N.Y.: Cornell University Press.

———. 1991. *Whose Science? Whose Knowledge? Thinking from Women's Lives*. Ithaca, N.Y.: Cornell University Press.

———. 1997. "Women's Standpoints on Nature: What Makes Them Possible?" *Osiris* 12:186–200.

———. In press. "Multicultural and Global Feminist Philosophies of Science: Resources and Challenges." In *Feminism, Philosophy and the Philosophy of Science*, ed. Lynn Hankinson Nelson and Jack Nelson. Dordrecht: Reidel.

Hartsock, Nancy. 1983a. "The Feminist Standpoint: Developing the Ground for a Specifically Feminist Historical Materialism." In *Discovering Reality: Feminist Perspectives on Epistemology, Metaphysics, Methodology, and Philosophy of Science*, ed. Sandra Harding and Merrill Hintikka, 283–310. Dordrecht: Reidel/Kluwer.

———. 1983b. "The Feminist Standpoint: Toward a Specifically Feminist Historical Materialism." In her *Money, Sex, and Power*, 231–51. New York: Longman.

Hayles, N. Katherine. 1993. "Constrained Constructivism: Locating Scientific Inquiry in the Theater of Representation." In *Realism and Representation*, ed. George Levine, 27–43. Madison: University of Wisconsin Press.

hooks, bell. 1981. *Ain't I a Woman? Black Women and Feminism*. Boston: South End.

Jaggar, Alison. 1983. "Feminist Politics and Epistemology: Justifying Feminist Theory." In her *Feminist Politics and Human Nature*, 353–89. Totowa, N.J.: Rowman & Allenheld.

Rose, Hilary. 1983. "Hand, Brain and Heart: A Feminist Epistemology for the Natural Sciences," *Signs: Journal of Women in Culture and Society* 9(1):73–90. Reprinted in Sandra Harding and Jean O'Barr, eds., *Sex and Scientific Inquiry*, (Chicago: University of Chicago Press, 1987).

Smith, Dorothy. 1974. "Women's Perspective as a Radical Critique of Sociology."

Sociological Inquiry 44:7–14. Reprinted in Sandra Harding, ed., *Feminism and Methodology: Social Science Issues* (Bloomington: Indiana University Press, 1987).

———. 1977. "Some Implications of a Sociology for Women." In *Woman in a Man-Made World: A Socioeconomic Handbook,* ed. Nona Y. Glazer and Helen Waehrer, 15–29. Chicago: Rand-McNally.

———. 1979. "A Sociology for Women." In *The Prism of Sex: Essays in the Sociology of Knowledge,* ed. Julia Sherman and Evelyn T. Beck, 135–87. Madison: University of Wisconsin Press.

———. 1981. "The Experienced World as Problematic: A Feminist Method." Sorokin Lecture no. 12, University of Saskatchewan, Saskatoon.

———. 1990. *The Conceptual Practices of Power: A Feminist Sociology of Knowledge.* Boston: Northeastern University Press.

Van Fraassen, Bas, and Jill Sigman. 1993. "Interpretation in Science and in the Arts." In *Realism and Representation,* ed. George Levine, 77–99. Madison: University of Wisconsin Press.

Watson-Verran, Helen, and David Turnbull. 1995. "Science and Other Indigenous Knowledge Systems." In *Handbook of Science and Technology Studies,* ed. Sheila Jasanoff et al., 115–39. Thousand Oaks, Calif.: Sage.

Westkott, Marcia. 1979. "Feminist Criticism of the Social Sciences." *Harvard Educational Review* 49:422–30. I

Comment on Hekman's "Truth and Method: Feminist Standpoint Theory Revisited"

Dorothy E. Smith, Department of Sociology, Ontario Institute for Studies in Education

I have written this grudgingly. Susan Hekman's (in this volume) interpretation of my work is so systematically out to lunch that it is difficult to write a response that does not involve a replication of what I have already said, at length and in various versions, elsewhere. But that would interest neither me nor readers. So I have asked myself: Apart from lack of care and thought, what is she doing that leads to her systematic misreading? And what might be systematic about other mistakes such as the chronology of "standpoint theory"'s development (a work published in 1979 is attributed to the decade following, 1983), or that its roots were in Marxism (Where's the women's movement?), or that it is less used and interesting currently (speak for your own discipline, Susan; in sociology it flourishes), or that feminist standpoint theory has become identified with "object-relations" theory (news to me).

A major problem is the reification of "feminist standpoint theory." Feminist standpoint theory, as a general class of theory in feminism, was brought into being by Sandra Harding (1986), not to create a new theoretical enclave but to analyze the merits and problems of feminist theoretical work that sought a radical break with existing disciplines through locating knowledge or inquiry in women's standpoint or in women's experience. Those she identified had been working independently of one another and have continued to do so. In a sense, Harding created us. I do not think there was much interchange among us. As standpoint theorists, we became identifiable as a group through Harding's study. And as a construct of Harding's text, we appeared as isolated from the intellectual and political discourses with which our work was in active dialogue. I cannot speak here for Nancy Hartsock, Patricia Hill Collins, or others mentioned in Hekman's article, but, for myself, I am very much aware of being engaged with the debates and innovations of the many feminist experiments in sociology that, like mine, were exploring experience as a method of discovering the social from the standpoint of women's experience.

But Hekman goes beyond Harding to constitute us as a common theoretical position, indeed as a foundationalist theory justifying feminist theory as knowledge. A coherence is invented for us: "Despite their significant differences, all of these accounts share the conviction that the feminist standpoint is rooted in a 'reality' that is the opposite of the abstract conceptual world inhabited by men, particularly the men of the ruling class, and that in this reality lies the truth of the human condition" (Hekman, 16). Given the realities of our nonexistence as a group except on paper, she *must* distort in order to bring off this representation. The quotation comes on page 16, after Hartsock and Smith have been thoroughly worked over, and Smith at least (Hartsock is speaking for herself) has been tortured into the shape that fits this conclusion. What's wrong with this account so far as I am concerned?

First, I am not proposing a *feminist standpoint* at all; taking up women's standpoint as I have developed it is not at all the same thing and has nothing to do with justifying feminist knowledge. Second, I am not arguing that women's standpoint is rooted in a reality of any kind. Rather, I am arguing that women's standpoint returns us to the actualities of our lives as we live them in the local particularities of the everyday/everynight worlds in which our bodily being anchors us. As I use the term, *actuality* is not defined. The notion of "actual" in my writing is like the arrow on the map of the mall saying "You are here," that points in the text to a beyond-the-text in which the text, its reading, its reader, and its concepts also *are*. It is, so to speak, where we live and where discourse happens and does its constituting of "reality." Third, I do not embrace reality and reject concepts (Hekman, 16). It is precisely the force of women's standpoint (at least as I have developed it) that it folds concepts, theory, discourse, *into actuality* as people's actual practices or activities (a fully reflexive notion applying to the concepts of such a sociology). The contrast I draw between the abstract conceptual modes of ruling and a location of consciousness in the particularizing work that women do in relation to children does not constitute two equivalent regions, and the move I propose is not from concepts to reality. Rather, it is to recognize that concepts are also in actuality and that the objectifications of what I early on described as the relations of ruling are themselves people's socially organized practices in the actual locations of their lives. I and others working with this approach have developed a body of systematic study in which concepts and theories are examined for how they are activated in organizing social relations (Smith 1987; Walker 1990; Campbell and Manicom 1995). I realize that this is a bit tricky to grasp, but Hekman's (prince-pleasing) glass slipper will not fit the feet of this ugly sister.

In the end, the oddest thing is to find Hekman restoring us to the law of the father: Alfred Schutz, Michel Foucault, and, finally, Max Weber. Sandra Harding remarks, in her comments on Hekman, that she (Hekman) "loses the point that standpoint epistemologies and methodologies were constructed" oppositionally (51). Somehow Hekman misses altogether that such epistemologies and methods came out of and were dialogically implicated in a women's movement that offered a profound challenge to established discourses in almost every region of the political, artistic, and intellectual discourses. In various ways, those who have been identified with "feminist" standpoint theory became active in working with other women in our fields to undermine social science's embedding of the standpoint of white men as hidden agent and subject. Its distinctively experiential methodology was only a systematization of a political methodology that had been foundational to the women's movement.

Beginning in women's experiences told in women's words was and is a vital political moment in the women's movement. Experience is a method of speaking that is not preappropriated by the discourses of the relations of ruling. This is where women began to speak from as the women's movement of our time came into being. When we assembled *as* "women" and spoke together *as* "women," constituting "women" as a category of political mobilization, we discovered dimensions of "our" experience that had no prior discursive definition. In this political context, the category "women" is peculiarly nonexclusive since it was then and has remained open-ended, such that boundaries established at any one point are subject to the disruption of women who enter speaking from a different experience as well as an experience of difference. It is this commitment to the privileges of women to speak *from* experience that opens the women's movement to the critique of white and/or heterosexist hegemony from those it marginalizes and silences. The authority of experience is foundational to the women's movement (which is not to say that experience is foundational to knowledge) and has been and is at once explosive and fruitful.

Experience is a method of talk, a language game, in which what is not yet spoken struggles dialogically to appropriate language sedimented with meaning before the moment in which she speaks. It is through and through saturated with the social relations, including the social relations of discourse, in which what is being spoken of is embedded as well as those of which the moment of speaking is part. Experience gives direct access to the necessarily social character of people's worlds; it is in *how* people talk, the categories they use, the relations implicitly posited among them, and so forth, and in what is taken for granted in their talk, as well as in what they can talk about. It is the saturation of experience as a language game with social relations that makes nonsense of Hekman's notion that standpoint ultimately dissolves into the endless idiosyncratic consciousnesses of unique individuals.

The knowledge people have by virtue of their experience is a knowledge of the local practices of our everyday/everynight worlds. It is for the most part what Michael Polanyi (1967) called "tacit knowledge"—a knowing that is the very texture of our daily/nightly living in what we know how to do, how we go about things, and what we can get done. We know how and where to go shopping; we know how to read a book in the less-than-aware dimensions of turning pages from left to right; we know washing dishes, sweeping floors, cleaning; we know putting on makeup and washing our hair; we know how to recognize the boundary between street and sidewalk; we may not know what it is to be battered by a man, but we would know if we had been; some of us know what it is to suckle children; some of us know menstruation; some of us know getting on a bus and going to work; we know how to do our work and who works with us; we know . . . ; we know . . . ; we know as a matter of doing. This is a knowing that is of the socially organized ground of our participation in living with others, some of it, indeed, altogether beyond consciousness, but no less what we know how to do.[1]

Such tacit knowing, of course, becomes a knowledge only at that point when it is entered into the language game of experience, that is, in the

---

[1] Ethnomethodology is that sociology that seeks to uncover the taken-for-granted that is prenormative and prior to discursive positing (Garfinkel 1967).

course of telling. For the most part, it remains the secret underpinning of everything we do. We discover it vividly as we learn from small children that they truly do not know the same world that we do or when we travel among a people whose everyday/everynight living is radically different from ours. A sociology built on such a social ontology differs from Hekman's interpretation of Weber (and I have some reservations about the accuracy of her interpretation) as resting "on the assumption that what the social researcher studies, the activities and concepts of social actors, is already constituted" (30). Rather, I take the view that the social is always *being brought into being* in the concerting of people's local activities. It is never already there.

The women's movement and its methodology of working from experience began to unearth the tacit underpinnings of gender. But at the very moment when experience is summoned by what women can find they have in common, it is being translated into the universalizing discourse of a movement making political claims across a variety of fronts. It has seemed to me that in the women's movement, some women have wanted to be able to go directly from what we know by virtue of how we participate in social relations to claims to knowledge at the level of a universalizing discourse. The critique of "essentialism" aims at this move. Standpoint theory is often understood, as I think Hekman understands it, as foundational to knowledge claims of this kind according to which women's experience is privileged. I do not make this claim. Rather, taking women's standpoint and beginning in experience gives access to a knowledge of what is tacit, known in the doing, and often not yet discursively appropriated (and often seen as uninteresting, unimportant, and routine). Here is where I have held we might begin, as sociologists committed to discovering society from where people are as participants in it.

I do not, therefore, argue, as Hekman says I do, that the "knowledge of women is superior to the abstract knowledge of the sociologist" (20), in part, of course, because my interest is in a sociology that does not displace what people know as the local practices of our everyday/everynight living but, rather, seeks to build on and enlarge it beyond the horizon of any one person's daily experience. I call this taking for sociology the problematic of the everyday/everynight world (Smith 1987). To take up Sandra Harding's metaphor in her comment in this exchange, I want a sociology that would seek to discover the shape of the pond that positions the people and their perspectives vis-à-vis one another.

People's tacit knowledge of what they know as a matter of daily/nightly practices surfaces as people speak and as what they speak of is taken seriously, undistilled, untranslated. Speaking for themselves and from their experience has been a fundamental commitment of the women's movement, and it remains foundational to the method of inquiry I have been trying to develop for sociology. I stress "method of inquiry" since what I do as theory is not really an epistemology, although it must wrestle with epistemological problems; it is surely not a theory foundational to feminist theory, nor yet a theory of history, society, the laws of social systems, or anything of that kind. As a theory it is a systematic formulation of a method of developing investigations of the social that are anchored in, although not confined by, people's everyday working knowledge of the doing of their lives.

Since I want to take people's experience as a place to start, Weber's notions of "ideal types" leaves me cold. What could this be but an assertion of the right of the social scientist to impose her framework on the world and to resume the effectivity of the relations of ruling in subordinating voices speaking from people's experience in and of their lived actualities. "Ideal type" methodology brokers differences among intellectual colleagues but is wholly unreflexive with respect to observer-observed relations. Different idealizations could be constructed of the same historical events. They could coexist without being either exhaustive with respect to those events or necessarily in contradiction with one another.[2] But ideal type methodology creates no commitments to how things are experienced by those who live them. It creates no openness toward those it studies. The sociologist working with this method is not committed to hearing and honoring what the other has to say. Despite Weber's commitment to an interpretive sociology, his specification of *Verstehen* as a method in social science clearly privileges the standpoint of the external observer. For example, in his specification of "direct observational understanding" he discusses in terms of alternative motivational accounts the problem of explaining why a woodcutter is cutting wood in the forest:[3] Is he cutting wood to sell it? for his own use? because he is angry? But shift the standpoint to that of people's actual experience. The question of why he is cut-

---

[2] Note that much more needs to be done to show that Carole Pateman, Arlie Hochschild, or Karen Sacks makes use of ideal-type analyses. Hekman seems to conflate ideal types with concepts and typifications; the latter is in general use in the analysis of ethnographic types of materials in social science, and neither is the same as Weber's systematic exploration of the logic, say, of rational legal forms of authority.

[3] This instance is extensively analyzed and discussed along with others in a chapter of my *The Everyday World as Problematic: A Feminist Sociology* (Smith 1987, n. 1). In that chapter, I examine how the relations between observer and observed enter into (and can be found in) the accounts that are produced from the encounter.

ting wood does not arise for the woodcutter who is *in the course of* cutting wood to sell, because he is angry, for his own use. From the Archimedean perch of social scientific discourse, the reality that comes into being only in relation to it (constituted by it, if you will) appears puzzling and confusing.[4] So it was for Weber, who struggled to comprehend the complexities of historical change and found in his "ideal type" a method of wresting order from what he conceded was beyond ordering. But from the standpoint of experience in and of the everyday/everynight actualities of our lives, it is the oppressively routine organization, the persistence, the repetition, of capitalist forms of exploitation, of patriarchy, of racial subordination, of the forms of dominance Foucault (1980) has characterized as "power/knowledge," as the local contouring of people's lives that constitute a sociological problematic. The system of sociological principles that Weber developed and on which his "ideal type" methodology is based is incompatible with a sociology *for* women, or *for* people.

References
Campbell, Marie, and Ann Manicom, eds. 1995. *Experience, Knowledge, and Ruling Relations.* Toronto: University of Toronto Press.
Foucault, Michel. 1980. *Power/Knowledge: Selected Interviews and Other Writings, 1972–1977.* New York: Pantheon.
Garfinkel, Harold. 1967. *Studies in Ethnomethodology.* Englewood Cliffs, N.J.: Prentice Hall.
Harding, Sandra. 1986. *The Science Question in Feminism.* Ithaca, N.Y.: Cornell University Press.
Polanyi, Michael. 1967. *The Tacit Dimension.* Garden City, N.Y.: Doubleday.
Smith, Dorothy E. 1987. *The Everyday World as Problematic: A Feminist Sociology.* Boston: Northeastern University Press.
Stinchcombe, Arthur. 1983. "Origins of Sociology as a Discipline." *Ars Sociologica* 27(1):11.
Walker, Gillian. 1990. *Family Violence: The Politics of Conceptualization in the Women's Movement.* Toronto: University of Toronto Press. **I**

[4] The problem is endemic to a sociology that begins from a standpoint in its own self-sustaining theoretically constructed world and constitutes an Archimedean point for its discursive subject. "The disorganized flow of empirical social reality is the only thing that creates problems difficult enough to make it worthwhile to have a discipline trying to tame the flow into theoretically and methodologically unimpeachable sociology," writes Arthur Stinchcombe (1983, 10).

Reply to Hartsock, Collins, Harding, and Smith

Susan Hekman, Department of Political Science, University of Texas at Arlington

My purpose in writing "Truth and Method: Feminist Standpoint Theory Revisited" (in this volume) was to reopen the debate over feminist standpoint theory and to refocus the discussion of the central issues raised by the theory. The comments in this issue by Patricia Hill Collins, Sandra Harding, Dorothy Smith, and Nancy Hartsock on my article indicate that I have been at least partially successful in that purpose. I welcome the opportunity to further extend this discussion.

Patricia Hill Collins, Sandra Harding, and Nancy Hartsock all raise an objection that goes to the heart of the approach that I develop in the article. They argue, although in different ways, that I, as Collins puts it, "depoliticize" feminist standpoint theory. Claiming that standpoint theory was not designed to be argued as a theory of truth and method, Collins asserts that my "apolitical discussion of feminist truth and method" (43) denies the potentially radical content of standpoint theory. Similarly, Harding argues that I "distort" the central project of standpoint theorists by characterizing the approach as an attempt to justify the truth of feminist claims to more accurate accounts of reality. Against this she claims that it is "relations between power and knowledge that concern these thinkers" (50). Finally, Hartsock argues that I read feminist standpoint theory through "a kind of American pluralism that prefers to speak not about power or justice but, rather, about knowledge and epistemology" (35).

It is precisely the relation between power and knowledge that concerns me in the article. I begin my analysis of feminist standpoint theory with an assumption that is also the centerpiece of Hartsock's approach: politics and epistemology are inseparable. I argue that the central question of feminist standpoint theory has been how we justify the truth of the feminist claim that women have been and are oppressed. My claim is that women cannot resist oppression and gain political power unless they can legitimate this claim. I further argue that the shift in the theory that occurred in the 1980s had a political origin: the demand for recognition of differences among women. Finally, I turn to Weber's ideal type because it is an approach that explains and justifies the necessarily engaged (political) role of the social analyst. I do not think that this approach either distorts or depoliticizes feminist standpoint theory. On the contrary, I think it continues the tradition established by that theory: the necessary connection between knowledge and power.

Collins continues her criticism of the alleged depoliticization of my approach in her discussion of group-based experience. She claims that because I "remain focused on the individual as proxy for the group, it becomes difficult to construct the group from such 'unique' individuals" (45). Hartsock advances a similar criticism with her claim that I erroneously define groups as aggregates of individuals. Although I do argue that multiplicity fosters incoherence, the intent of this argument is to criticize an approach that denies the use of any general concepts. Far from advocating a feminism based in individual experiences, I see the move toward a highly individualistic feminist social theory as a danger to be avoided, a move that would paralyze feminist social analysis. The intent of my exploration of feminist ideal types is to explain and justify the use of general concepts, including those describing group experience, that can foster useful feminist social analysis and provide for the possibility of collective political action.

Sandra Harding approaches the relationship between knowledge and power in feminist standpoint theory from a different perspective than the one that I present in my article. In her discussion of what she calls "the logic of standpoint theory" Harding appeals to work in the social studies of science and technology, multicultural global science studies, and feminism to make her argument for "less false accounts" of the social and natural worlds. She uses these resources to argue that some social situations are good ones from which to see how the social order works and that some discursive accounts provide richer resources for understanding the natural and social world. Despite my criticism of aspects of her work, I agree with these claims. Our difference lies in the means by which we justify them. Relying on the perspectives provided by Weber and Wittgenstein, I argue that, ultimately, all we can do is to present what we hope will be persuasive arguments for the analytic/political perspective we adopt. In the absence of a universal metanarrative we can only argue that the feminist position we advocate will alleviate the oppression of women and that this is a good worth striving for. And, finally, as Wittgenstein wrote, at the end of reasons comes persuasion.

Harding's reference to my alleged "administrative standpoint" is a more disturbing criticism. Who, Harding asks, is the "we" that I refer to in my article? Not, she claims, women in their everyday lives, but an "administrator" faced with managing "all those culturally local people" (55). I would like to offer a different answer: the "we" is feminist social analysts who want to understand the world with the aim of changing it. No, this "we" is not "everyday women." It is women who are engaged in an activity that is worthwhile and has the potential for radically changing social reality: feminist social analysis. The perspective of the feminist social analyst is partial because all perspectives are partial. But it is a perspective that, I would argue, has the potential to change the world for the better. Part of my purpose in appealing to Weber's ideal type was to make explicit the necessarily partial nature of all analytic concepts while at the same time justifying their use.

My differences with Dorothy Smith are the most fundamental. Our disagreement hinges on my claim that she roots women's standpoint in the reality of women's experience and that this results in the (in my view, futile) attempt to replace concepts with brute reality/experience. Smith denies this charge. In her refutation she claims, rather, that "women's standpoint returns us to the actualities of our lives as we live them in the local particularities of the everyday/everynight worlds in which our bodily being anchors us." She concedes that this distinction is "a bit tricky to grasp" (61). I agree. I still don't grasp it.

Far from denying the validity of women's experience, I am trying to explain and justify the conceptual status of the appeal to "women's experience" so that it does not fall prey to the epistemological confusions that this appeal has generated. I turn to Weber's theory because he makes it explicit that, as social analysts, we are using concepts that are different from, although related to, those of social actors. This is the case because our goal is different. Unlike actors operating in the social world, our goal is to understand and clarify that world. To deny this seems to me to lead to yet more epistemological confusion. Ideal-type methodology, contrary to Smith's claim, is useful precisely because it *is* reflexive about the epistemological complexities of the observer/observed relationship.

In her comments on my article, Nancy Hartsock raises the vexed issue of the relationship of both feminism and Marxism to Enlightenment thinking. Her argument that Marx is an anti-Enlightenment thinker is a controversial one, but one that I will not take issue with here. Her claim that feminism has an "ambiguous" relationship to the Enlightenment, however, is germane to my central thesis regarding feminist standpoint theory. Hartsock claims that "women's insistence on speaking at all troubles those theories" (37). Although the context of this remark is different than that of my article, our arguments have important parallels. My purpose in writing the article was to trace the way in which feminist standpoint theory, a theory that emerged out of the Enlightenment tradition, deconstructed (if you will) that tradition. Women speaking their truth had the effect of transforming truth, knowledge, and power as the Enlightenment defined them. I identify this transformation as the emergence of a new paradigm. Although Hartsock and I differ in the ways we define this transformation, we are in agreement that the Enlightenment certainties have been exploded and that it is the speech of women that has accomplished this. And, ultimately, this is what the feminist standpoint is all about.

The Doxa of Difference

It is tempting, writes Derrida scholar Rodolphe Gasché, to read the philosophical history of difference as exemplifying the progressive emancipation of difference from identity (1994, 82). Our own time is uniquely prone to such a reading. As Gasché notes, difference reigns supreme in critical thought, whereas identity barely dares to show its face. Emblazoned on book covers, routinely invoked in intellectual debates, "difference" functions as an unassailable value in itself, seemingly irrespective of its referent or context. Difference has become doxa, a magic word of theory and politics radiant with redemptive meanings.

Feminism has its own distinctive version of this story of the triumph of difference over identity. The origins of feminist thought are usually attributed to such figures as Mary Wollstonecraft, who drew on Enlightenment ideals to protest against the subordination of women. Yet such ideals, it soon transpired, were not congenial friends of feminism but merely masks for a phallocentric logic based on the tyranny of identity. Second-wave feminists sought instead to reclaim the feminine; women's liberation lay in the affirmation of their irreducible difference rather than in the pursuit of an illusory goal of equality. This gynocentric ideal in turn has lost much of its power, thanks to the ascent of poststructuralism as well as to extensive criticisms of its political exclusions and biases. As a result, we are now in a postmodern condition, where female difference has fragmented into multiple differences and any appeal to general ideals or norms can only be considered politically questionable and theoretically naive.

This story has been told on numerous occasions and in various registers. For some it is a narrative of progress, as feminism sheds its essentialisms and universalisms to achieve a more sophisticated stage of theoretical consciousness. For others it is a narrative of the fall, as feminism is lured from its true goals by internecine squabbles and the spurious prestige of French avant-garde thought. Many feminist scholars are familiar with this story;

The writing of this article was aided by a University of Virginia summer grant. I would like to thank my *Signs* readers and Farzaneh Milani for their help in drafting the final version.

[*Signs: Journal of Women in Culture and Society* 1997, vol. 23, no. 1]

we may encounter it in scholarly articles, reproduce it in our classes, repeat it in our own academic writing. Indeed, it undoubtedly contains a grain of truth, at least as a description of the recent trajectory of mainstream feminist theory in the humanities. I want, however, to dislodge at least partially this narrative of feminism's evolution from identity to difference. Its unidirectional structure obscures the actual simultaneity and interdependence of different feminist positions. Like all metanarratives, furthermore, it confuses the internal logic of a particular set of theoretical debates with the condition of the world as a whole. In other words, the political interests and needs of the world's women do not necessarily move in step with the various phases of academic feminist theory.

Of course, no doxa ever gains universal acceptance, and there have been various challenges to the preeminence of difference within contemporary feminism. Already in 1986, in an article ably summarized by its title, "The Instability of the Analytical Categories of Feminist Theory," Sandra Harding warned against grounding feminism in a single political-philosophical idea, arguing that Enlightenment ideas, gynocentric politics, and postmodern critiques of identity are all woven into the complex fabric of contemporary feminism. "We should learn how," writes Harding, "to regard the instabilities themselves as valuable resources" (664). Chela Sandoval has also criticized conventional taxonomies of feminism as a historical series of developmental phases, making an argument for a "tactical subjectivity" that can deploy different forms of feminist politics according to context (1991). In addition, as I show below, some postcolonial theorists have challenged the current vogue of difference within Western feminism for glossing over fundamental hierarchies and conflicts between women.

Relatively little attention has been paid, however, to a systematic examination of the theoretical inconsistencies as well as political problems evident in appeals to difference within feminist thought. Indeed, for the most part, the conceptual primacy of difference remains uncontested. While particular notions of difference may be subject to criticism for reproducing an androcentric or imperialist conception of the Other, this critique assumes, if only tacitly, the existence of a "real," more authentic difference existing beyond the deceptive snares of the oppressor's language. One of the aims of this article is to question such visions of alterity as the ultimate truth of feminist theory and politics. My aim is not to polemicize against difference but, rather, to deontologize it by offering a redescription of the status of equality and difference that is framed in pragmatic rather than metaphysical terms. However, I am less interested in arguing that these terms constitute distinct if equally valid choices for feminists (Snitow 1990) than in showing that they exist in a condition of necessary philosophical and political interdependence, such that the very pursuit of difference returns one, inexorably, to the seemingly obsolete issue of equality.[1]

Sexual difference: The supreme difference?

As Michèle Barrett (1987) points out, the concept of difference is used in various, not always compatible, ways within feminist theory. Most commonly, it is used to denote the difference between women and men, whether this difference is attributed to biological, psychological, or social causes. Second, it is used to denote the difference between women as shaped by hierarchies of class, race, sexual preference, age, and so on. This second definition is often used to challenge the claims of the first: the experiential diversity of real women mitigates against any general claims about the nature of female difference. Third, difference in its Derridean inflection as *différance* has been used by feminist theorists to address the relational and unstable nature of linguistic meaning and the positioning of the feminine as a key site of such instability. Finally, the concept of sexual difference is deployed by Lacanian feminists to highlight the "great divide" of masculine/feminine as an inescapable if unstable psycholinguistic relation structuring the symbolic order.

In this article I consider two influential currents within contemporary feminist thought: psychoanalytical theories of sexual difference as developed within feminist philosophy and analyses of cultural and material differences between women within postcolonial theory. These two approaches exemplify some of the most sophisticated current writing on difference within feminism. They both proceed from a recognition of the limitations of essentialist notions of female experience and seek, although in dissimilar ways, to redeem the notion of difference by radicalizing and extending its claims. They thus provide an ideal starting point from which to explore the ramifications of concepts of alterity, heterogeneity, and difference within feminist thought.

Sexual difference theory first came to the fore in the United States in the late 1970s as a result of the dissemination of the writings of the so-called French feminists (Hélène Cixous, Luce Irigaray, and Julia Kristeva). While this work undoubtedly generated new insights and perspectives in feminist thought, it was also extensively criticized for its essentialist, idealist, and Eurocentric tendencies (Jones 1981; Spivak 1987). At the present

---

[1] Some useful general critiques of the idealization of difference include McGowan 1991; Gasché 1994; Taylor et al. 1994. Helpful feminist discussions include Sypnowich 1993; Collin 1994; Young 1995.

time, we are witnessing the emergence of what might be called a "second generation" of sexual difference theorists writing in Europe, Australia, and the United States, exemplified by such figures as Rosi Braidotti, Drucilla Cornell, and Elizabeth Grosz. For the most part, these writers are more conscious than their predecessors of the pitfalls involved in theorizing the category of woman. As a result, they seek to legitimate sexual difference as a foundational category of feminist thought while simultaneously emptying it of any normative or essentialist content. I will consider the feasibility of such a goal by addressing the philosophical as well as political aspects of recent formulations of sexual difference. Given that the current visibility and prestige of this writing derives from its perceived affiliations with "high theory," it is important to address its arguments in these terms and to consider whether its deployment of poststructuralist ideas is in fact a theoretically cogent one.

Rosi Braidotti, for example, defines the guiding questions of feminist philosophy in the following manner: "Can we formulate otherness, difference without devaluing it? Can we think of the other not as other-than, but as a positively other entity?" (1991, 177). Braidotti, like her colleagues, prefers *sexual difference* to *gender* because of the latter's overly sociological connotation that masculine and feminine are externally imposed roles to be eventually discarded in a putative androgynous future. Sexual difference feminists, by contrast, stress the structural centrality of sexual division to the formation of human culture, arguing that the symbolic order is predicated on the sovereignty of the phallus and the erasure of the feminine except as a phantasmic object of male desire. The goal of feminism is thus not to deny difference—which would merely endorse the logic of phallocentrism as male-defined sameness—but to recover the feminine within sexual difference, to generate an autonomous female imaginary beyond existing stereotypes of woman (Braidotti 1994).

The recent work of Drucilla Cornell offers a detailed elucidation of sexual difference theory. Cornell, like Braidotti, acknowledges her affiliation to the work of Lacan and Derrida, whom she regards as potential allies of feminism in their diagnosis and critique of phallocentrism. This affiliation renders Cornell suspicious of any reference to female essences or universals. She devotes considerable effort to refuting the arguments of feminist legal theorists Robin West and Catharine MacKinnon, whose vision of a universal female destiny she explicitly rejects. Yet Cornell, like other feminist philosophers, is also wary of a perceived slippage between women and the feminine in the writings of Derrida and other male theorists, whereby the feminine becomes a position in language available to either sex. If the feminine is always already a metaphor, it is one with which actual women have a particularly urgent connection and affiliation.

How, then, can we avoid either essentializing women or dematerializing them? The solution proposed by Cornell can best be described as a formal theory of sexual difference; it affirms the importance of the feminine while refusing to give it any substantive content. Such a strategy seeks to avoid a will to definition and closure deemed to be quintessentially phallocentric. Rather, the feminine is that which resists definition, which embodies multiplicity and otherness. It is not to be equated with the false femininity of existing gender stereotypes but embodies a utopian gesturing toward an alternative imaginary beyond the constraints of patriarchal thought. "Feminism," writes Cornell, "demands nothing less than the unleashing of the feminine imaginary—an imaginary made possible, paradoxically, by the lack of grounding of the feminine in any of the identifications we know and imagine as Woman" (1995, 147).

The value of such a position, according to Cornell, is that it allows for an affirmation of the feminine without the need for essentialist or naturalist descriptions of woman (1993, 57). A psycholinguistic model of sexual difference, in its emphasis on relation rather than essence, can accommodate rather than exclude the complex variables of race, class, and culture. Thus, by refusing to give any determinate or normative content to the feminine, the feminist philosopher hopes to avoid the charge of ethnocentrism, arguing that such a framework can include all rather than only some women. Feminine difference exists outside the binary structures of patriarchal thought, including, paradoxically, the very distinction between masculine and feminine. It is not part of the already thought, but a principle of opposition to it; the feminine simply *is* the sign of a radical heterogeneity, the privileged marker of difference.

I remain troubled, however, by certain contradictions within this seemingly nonprogrammatic feminist program. Its vision of autonomous femininity seems incompatible with the poststructuralist paradigm on which theorists of sexual difference simultaneously rely. Within such a paradigm, there can be no rupture between an existing male symbolic and a future female imaginary, simply because any recognition of irreducible otherness necessarily presupposes an existing set of conventions, assumptions, and traditions against which this singularity can be recognized *as* other (Gasché 1994, 2). Thus Braidotti's wish to conceptualize difference not as "other-than" but as "positively other" collides with the most basic premise of structuralist and poststructuralist thought, the recognition that the sign has no inherent, positive meaning but exists only through its differential relationship to other signs. In other words, it is hard to see how a quasi-utopian vision of authentic, self-defined femininity can be reconciled with a semiotic model that defines meaning as fundamentally relational, unstable, and impure (were such alterity to exist, it would, of course, constitute pure identity, the ultimate metaphysics of presence).

Thus Cornell's view of feminism is framed for the most part in absolutist terms; either women seek to articulate a radical otherness beyond the already thought or we remain forever imprisoned within the iron cage of phallocentrism. This dichotomy follows inevitably from the Lacanian premises on which she relies (although orthodox Lacanians would undoubtedly regard such a vision of woman-as-alterity as reconfirming rather than transcending phallocentrism). Yet the Lacanian view of history and culture as fundamentally phallocentric homogenizes important differences within that history, including the diverse positions and social practices of women.[2] Were all the multitudes of women in history who engaged in cultural activities — the artists, the revolutionaries, the mothers, the teachers — really nothing more than the passive vehicles of phallocentrism? If not, then feminism needs a more supple framework for analyzing women's complex and varied relations to particular axes of power. And if this is indeed the case, as Cornell frequently implies in her presentation of culture as an exclusively male creation, why should contemporary feminists be able to free ourselves from the ubiquitous grip of phallocentric thought when all previous women in history have failed? What epistemological break renders our position more authentic than theirs?

Cornell's championing of feminine difference is passionately and avowedly utopian, yet there are important reasons utopianism has lost much of its luster in recent years. The founding premise of utopian thought is a quintessentially modernist ideal of self-invention, of the absolutely new that will follow the moment of rupture from the alienated and inauthentic past. It thus tends to devalue existing political struggles as superficial with a concomitant preference for the gesture of grand refusal (Fraser 1995, 165). An opposition between (feminine) revolution and (male-defined) reformism often appears in the work of sexual difference theorists, yet the framing of political struggles in such starkly antithetical terms has lost much of its persuasive force in recent times (McGowan 1991, 154). This modernist ideal of self-creation ex nihilo is another instance of a political

---

[2] As Nancy Fraser notes, such a position "misleadingly posits unity and coherence among what are actually a diverse plurality of discursive regimes, subject positions, signifying practices, public spheres, and significations — including divergent and conflicting significations of femininity, which are surely not all reducible to 'lack'" (1995, 165).

topos strangely at odds with the poststructuralist assumptions on which it ostensibly draws, most obviously the deconstructive critique of any notion of authentic origin. Any oppositional politics, surely, operates by means of a complex array of identifications, partial self-recognitions, and critical refusals, whereby subordinate social groups negotiate their ambivalent relationships to the representations that define them. Women both are and are not "women." A vision of femininity as pure otherness cannot speak to this messy blend of tradition and innovation, of recuperation and re-creation, of borrowing from the past and imagining the future, that shapes feminist practice.

Furthermore, the annexation of difference as the authentic feminine principle frequently engenders the reverse claim: that the feminine is in turn to be understood as the exemplary symbol of alterity. Cornell, for example, claims that "the 'feminine' is not celebrated just because it is the feminine, but because it stands in for the heterogeneity that undermines the logic of identity purportedly established by phallologocentrism" (1991, 34). In this regard, theories of sexual difference, even as they seek to empty femininity of any substantive content and thereby rid it of essentialist biases, continue to assume the overarching priority of the male/female divide. The feminine serves as the privileged marker of difference, standing in for all the forms of diversity that are repressed in contemporary societies. Braidotti, for example, refers to the difference between men and women as the prototype of all differences (1991, 210), describing feminism as *the* discourse of modernity (10).[3]

To equate "difference" and "the feminine" in this way, however, is patently questionable; it subsumes and incorporates manifold forms of diversity within the framework of sexual difference at the very moment that it claims to acknowledge their independent existence. As has often been pointed out (e.g., Spelman 1988), it is only certain women who have the luxury of perceiving the male/female divide as the foundational division, simply because their own (privileged) class or race position remains unmarked and hence invisible. An exclusive focus on the category of sexual difference must inevitably gloss over these fundamental hierarchies between women, irrespective of whether it draws on the discourse of identity politics or of poststructuralist theory. Some sexual difference theorists have not been unaware of such criticisms and have sought to incorporate

---

[3] Compare Irigaray's claim that "sexual difference is one of the major philosophical issues, if not the issue, of our age. According to Heidegger, each age has one issue to think through, and one only. Sexual difference is probably the issue in our time which could be our 'salvation' if we thought it through" (1993, 5).

discussions of race into their work. Cornell, for example, reads Toni Morrison's *Beloved* as a distinctive retelling of the Medea myth, arguing that the novel dramatizes the very difference of African-American motherhood (1991, 195). Yet the continuing reliance on the master grid of Lacanian theory begs numerous questions in subsuming the multicausal politics of race within a psychoanalytic framework. Retaining an equation of power with the phallus and of subversion with the feminine, such a model upholds the convenient fiction that power is an exclusively male phenomenon and fails to consider the agency and complicity of women *as women* in the exercise of class and race hierarchies.

Furthermore, while theorists of sexual difference insist on the fissures and contradictions within femininity, they frequently retain a monochromatic view of phallic power and privilege, thereby obscuring the diverse and conflictual relationship of men of different classes, races, and sexualities to signifiers of maleness. Masculinity is represented in many, contradictory ways in our culture. While the transcendental signifier—God and his various religious, political, and juridical stand-ins—is gendered male, this does not mean that all males are therefore suffused with transcendental authority. While women of color, for example, have challenged the sexism within their own communities, they are less likely to see masculinity per se as the enemy or to assume a self-evident connection between men and cultural power. Similarly, some lesbian activists, particularly since the AIDS crisis and the advent of queer theory, perceive their affiliation with gay men as equal to or more important than their kinship with heterosexual feminists. Women may have perfectly cogent reasons for choosing to identify or ally with men rather than other women around specific political issues. Insofar as ontologies of sexual difference presume the overarching significance of the male-female distinction, which is only subsequently "filled in" by the particulars of class, race, sexuality, and so on, they cannot account for such a refusal to prioritize gender except in terms of some notion of false consciousness or its equivalent.

Difference as dissension: Postcolonial feminism

Sexual difference feminism thus results in an impasse. Either feminine difference is given a substantive definition and is thereby subject to charges of essentialism, or it is feted as an asocial principle of alterity and is thereby robbed of any meaningful political content, resulting in the creation of what Laura Donaldson dubs "The Woman without Qualities" (1992, 126). At this point I would like to turn to a discussion of feminist perspectives within postcolonial theory in order to consider some alternative imaginings of difference.

Postcolonial feminism is a contested term that would not be unequivocally endorsed by all the writers I discuss.[4] I understand *postcolonial* as designating the historical condition of countries recently liberated from colonial rule, and *postcolonial theory* as addressing the complex dynamics of cultural formation and interchange in such geopolitical contexts. Even within these parameters, however, the term has been criticized for homogenizing fundamental differences between national cultures (e.g., India and Australia), for glossing over racial differences and hierarchies within these cultures (Australia may be postcolonial to white settlers, but not to indigenous peoples), and for implying a clear-cut historical transition to a postcolonial condition that ignores ongoing Western influences in the cultural and economic, if not political, realms (Frankenberg and Mani 1993; McClintock 1994). Furthermore, the increasing visibility of postcolonial studies as an academic field has engendered suspicion about the ease with which displays of alterity can be commodified and neutralized with Western institutions (Spivak 1989; Chow 1993). Clearly, *postcolonial* does not function as a neutral label for an already existing field but actively demarcates particular processes of inclusion and exclusion.

Like any contested term, then, it can only serve as a starting point, rather than an end point, for inquiry and needs to be combined with conjunctural analyses of specific historical and geopolitical contexts (Frankenberg and Mani 1993). My concern in this article, however, is less with the ultimate value of *postcolonial* as a description of empirical historical realities than with elucidating the ways in which debates within postcolonial feminism help to crystallize the conceptual and political ambiguities of difference. While these discourses are necessarily heterogeneous, they are nevertheless characterized by certain family resemblances and recurring argumentative moves.

One of these moves involves an intensification and further fragmentation of the concept of difference. Criticizing the homogeneous view of the third world woman propagated by Western feminism, postcolonial feminists affirm the irreducible particularity and complex diversities characterizing the lives of non-Western women. For example, Chandra Mohanty's

[4] Perhaps the most detailed case against the value of postcolonial theory for feminism has been made recently by Carole Boyce Davies (1994, chap. 4). In my view, however, Davies overstates her case; there is a much more substantial feminist presence in postcolonial studies than she acknowledges.

influential article "Under Western Eyes" (1984) critically examines the intersection of feminist theories of women's oppression with a Euro-American conception of the third world to produce the composite image of the "Third World Woman." This woman is depicted as sexually repressed, tradition bound, and uneducated, in explicit contrast to the educated, modern, autonomous, first world feminist. The third world woman is thus appropriated by Western feminism as ultimate proof of the universality of patriarchy and female bondage. She is depicted as both same, part of a putative global sisterhood, and yet mysteriously other, an allegory of enigmatic yet undifferentiated cultural alterity.

Against such an ethnocentric perspective, Mohanty argues for context-specific, differentiated analyses of the ways in which women are produced as a sociopolitical group within particular historical and cultural locations. Such analyses of the complicated intersections of gender with ethnicity, class, religion, and numerous other determinants inevitably undermine an established Western feminist narrative of male power and female power-lessness. In this sense, postcolonial feminist theory articulates a difference from dominant Western feminist conceptions of difference by complicating and further fragmenting the notion of alterity.

Mohanty's emphasis on the specific and the local, as opposed to the homogeneous and the systematizing, seems to indicate skepticism regarding the claims of large-scale social theory. In another context, however, Mohanty insists on the need for a broader perspective on the international-ization of economies and labor forces, emphasizing the value of cross-national and cross-cultural analyses as a way of conceptualizing the system-atic socioeconomic and ideological processes within which women of the third world are enmeshed (1991, 2). Here she seeks to retain the category of the "Third World Woman" as a way of demarcating possibilities of polit-ical coalition among diversely positioned women through the creation of "imagined communities." Thus the emphasis on particularity is modified by a recognition of the value of systematic analyses of global disparities. In a similar vein, Gayatri Spivak warns of the limitations of microanalyses that remain oblivious to "the broader narratives of imperialism" (1988, 291), and Rey Chow questions the current fetish for cultural/local/ethnic differ-ence as a preordained fact, given that difference cannot be separated from, but is fundamentally related to, the broader structures of communication and domination within which it occurs (1993, 47; see also Trinh 1989).

This suspicion of the Western feminist politics of difference is expressed with particular force and clarity in a recent article by Ien Ang. "As a woman of Chinese descent," Ang writes, "I suddenly find myself in a position in which I can turn my 'difference' into intellectual and political capital, where 'white' feminists invite me to raise my 'voice,' *qua* a nonwhite woman, and make myself heard" (1995, 57). The politics of assimilation, Ang notes, has given way to that of multiculturalism. Yet this seemingly benevolent attentiveness to multiple voices reinforces fundamental hierarchies between women, as feminist discourse reproduces the logic of Western imperialism in its unthinking appropriation of the difference of the other. "Difference is 'dealt with' by absorbing it into an already existing feminist community without challenging the naturalised legitimacy and status of that community *as* a community" (60).

Ang thus complicates an idealized vision of multiple differences by drawing attention to the real, often profound gulf that separates women. This is, in her phrase, "the tension between difference as benign diversity and difference as conflict, disruption, dissension" (68). While the appeal to a common female identity is increasingly untenable within feminism, the turn toward a politics of diversity is an inadequate alternative if it ignores systematic inequalities among women in access to power, knowledge, and material resources. For Ang, such inequalities are fundamentally connected to the structural insurmountability of white, Western hegemony, which she defines as "the systemic consequence of a global historical development over the last 500 years — the expansion of European capitalist modernity throughout the world, resulting in the subsumption of all 'other' peoples to its economic, political and ideological logic and mode of operation" (65).

These and similar arguments within postcolonial feminism undercut any vision of alterity as positive or subversive by reaffirming the inextricable connections between difference and hierarchy. Against Braidotti's attempt to recast difference as "positively other," they insist on the continuing relevance of difference as "other than," on the need for comparative analysis across social groups as a means of elucidating pervasive inequities of power, materials, and resources. At an epistemological level, furthermore, such analysis implies the possibility of a systematic and normative critique that transcends a mere perspectivalism of multiple viewpoints. The diagnosis of inequality assumes a norm of equality that is found to be lacking. In this sense, equality functions not simply as a "phallocentric" or "imperialist" concept but, rather, as an indispensable term for uncovering and criticizing the pathologies of patriarchy and imperialism.

In this respect, the field of postcolonial feminism is marked by an ongoing tension between the particular and the universal, between the "thick description" of specific cultural practices and the macrosystemic analysis of transnational structures of inequality. While "local" and "global" may in fact constitute permeable and unstable markers for cultural modalities that thoroughly infiltrate each other (Grewal and Kaplan 1994, 11), there are nevertheless significant differences of emphasis in the work of individual writers. In general, however, postcolonial feminist work is characterized by a refusal to isolate gender from multiple other determinants, including those of race and class, and by a typical (although by no means universal) emphasis on material and institutional, rather than purely linguistic, structures of power (Mohanty 1991).

At the same time, this commitment to the analysis of material inequalities is often combined with a deconstructive critique of identity. Against nativist visions of autonomous racial or cultural difference, postcolonial theorists are likely to note that such distinctions are no longer feasible in an era of pervasive migration, media globalization, and transnational information flow. The colonized's fashioning of an insurgent counteridentity is inevitably shaped by the experience of colonization; the colonizer's culture is irrevocably altered by contact with the native. As a result, a conception of distinct, singular, internally homogeneous groupings gives way to a model of *métissage,* of borrowing and lending across porous cultural boundaries.

Such concepts as hybridity, creolization, and *métissage,* while not uncontested within postcolonial studies, strike me as offering the most viable alternative to the current doxa of difference. I have no particular investment in the word *hybrid* as such. As Robert Young (1995) notes, the term may indeed be compromised by its connections to the discourses of nineteenth-century racist genetics and the assumptions of compulsory heterosexuality. Yet, as Young also acknowledges, the power and value of the term lies in its encapsulation of the logic of both/and. "Hybridity thus makes difference into sameness, and sameness into difference, but in a way that makes the same no longer the same, the different no longer simply different," thereby engendering "difference and sameness in an apparently impossible simultaneity" (26).

Such a reformulation strikes me as a crucial paradigm shift. Metaphors of hybridity and the like not only recognize differences within the subject, fracturing and complicating holistic notions of identity, but also address connections between subjects by recognizing affiliations, cross-pollinations, echoes, and repetitions, thereby unseating difference from a position of absolute privilege. Instead of endorsing a drift toward an ever greater atomization of identity, such metaphors allow us to conceive of multiple, interconnecting axes of affiliation and differentiation. Affiliation, I would stress, does not preclude disagreement but, rather, provides its necessary precondition; it is only in the context of shared premises, beliefs, and vocabularies that dissent becomes possible.

For this reason, while I am sympathetic to much of Ang's argument, I am not fully persuaded by her recourse to the idea of incommensurability to describe the relations between women of different races. This claim arises out of Ang's discussion of competing readings of Madonna as symptomatic of the racial gulf within feminism. While most white feminists, according to Ang, have celebrated Madonna as a symbol of resistive postmodern femininity, black critics such as bell hooks are critical of the racist subtext underpinning such media images of idealized whiteness. Ang comments: "What we see exemplified here is a fundamental *incommensurability* between two competing feminist knowledges, dramatically exposing an irreparable chasm between a white and a black feminist truth. No harmonious compromise or negotiated consensus is possible here" (1995, 64).

Ang's own example, however, surely does not warrant such a strong conclusion. Thus, both black and white feminist readings of Madonna are shaped by overlapping conceptual frameworks and discursive regimes (within which terms such as *identity, the self,* and *oppression* become meaningful and usable), even as they both partake of the distinctive, historically specific "language game" of cultural studies in interpreting a media phenomenon such as Madonna as emblematic of broader social structures and processes. At the same time, their differing political locations result in conflicting interpretations of the resistive potential of this particular cultural icon.[5] The relationship here is surely one of complicated entanglement, overlapping, and disagreement, not a clash of incommensurable discursive universes.

Furthermore, it is precisely this entanglement that makes criticism possible, that allows hooks to point out the contradictions between feminism's claim to represent all women and its actual race blindness, and that enables some white as well as black feminists to explore the racial politics of Madonna (Bordo 1993). Incommensurability, by contrast, does not allow for disagreement, critique, or persuasion because there are no common terms that would allow one argument to latch onto and address another. Furthermore, it is important to realize that the recourse to incommensurability necessarily *works both ways.* It does not simply address the refusal of women of color to have their political concerns subsumed within inappropriate

---

[5] I remain unconvinced, furthermore, that race is necessarily the primary or most salient issue in disagreements over Madonna, which are also heavily shaped by generational and disciplinary divisions. While cultural studies has enabled numerous feminist readings of Madonna as sublime parodist, white feminists in other disciplines, and particularly those still affiliated with the movement feminism of the 1970s, are often very critical of Madonna, whom they perceive as buying into, rather than subverting, patriarchal notions of feminine beauty.

categories but simultaneously legitimates—indeed posits as inevitable—
the inaccessibility of such concerns to white women, who are thereby relieved of any need to engage with them. Thus, an actual incommensurability between the positions of white women and women of color would in
fact undermine Ang's own argument, making it incomprehensible to those
very readers to whom it is ostensibly addressed.

I read Ang's argument as a strategic intervention into a specific debate,
a provocation intended to startle white Western feminists out of arrogant
assumptions about female commonality beyond racial and cultural difference. While I sympathize with the need for such a provocation, and while
I agree that "idealized unity" cannot provide a basis for feminism, the turn
toward a model of incommensurability strikes me as counterproductive, as
theoretically tenuous and politically defeatist. It is theoretically tenuous
because it does not acknowledge actual overlappings of vocabularies,
frameworks, and assumptions; it is politically defeatist because it rules out,
in advance, the possibility of one discourse acting on and influencing another. Yet how else, one wonders, is politics possible? Of course Ang is
right to point out that the vast material and cultural divisions between
women cannot be overcome by mere fiat or good intention. Yet her statement, "We might do better to start from point zero and realise that there
are moments at which no common ground exists whatsoever, and when
any communicative event would be nothing more than a speaking past
one another" (1995, 60) seems to offer only the alternative of silence and
separatism. It is hard to see how such an a priori conviction of the impossibility of communication can be squared with Ang's own carefully enunci-
ated critique of Western feminism (why bother with such a critique if your
audience is incapable of understanding you?) or with the ongoing imperative for political coalitions and alliances among different (unequally) subordinate groups.

At the same time, Ang rightly insists that cultural interchange does not
occur on an equal footing, that instances of borrowing and citation are
framed by asymmetrical grids of power. In this context, the trope of hybridity has been subject to criticism for effacing material conflicts between
the colonizer and the colonized and denying the agency of the oppressed
(e.g., Parry 1987). While this criticism may apply to the work of specific
writers, it does not, in my view, follow inevitably from its use. To acknowledge the cultural leakages and interconnections between cultures is not
necessarily to deny their asymmetrical placement. Neither is it to affirm
uncritically a condition of cultural fragmentation and geographical displacement that is often experienced as painful rather than liberating, as has
occurred in contemporary celebrations of the nomadic subject. The point

is not to idealize and essentialize hybridity as a new source of political value, as a code word for the radically authentic or subversive. It is simply to acknowledge cultural impurity as the inescapable historical backdrop of all contemporary struggles — including those that may invoke politically necessary slogans of tribalism and nativism — in a global culture marked by pervasive and ongoing processes of both voluntary and involuntary cultural interchange.

In other words, the motif of hybridity disrupts the frequent association of political struggle with an assumed need for cultural authenticity free of any taint of the oppressor's culture. Thus, recent postcolonial theory has often stressed the politics of translation, as exemplified in the cultural and temporal specificity of enunciative acts.[6] Rather than demarcate certain concepts (e.g., modernity, equality, technology, the human) as intrinsically "Western" and thus forever tied to the enforcement of an imperialist agenda, recent postcolonial theory has been attentive to the diverse appropriations and rearticulations of such vocabularies across various global sites. The complex interminglings of indigenous traditions and external influences are such that discourses once linked to the colonizer may acquire very different meanings when adopted by the colonized to challenge their own condition. Such a pragmatic concern with the utility of discourse rather than its ontological purity strikes me as a more viable — and more hopeful — basis for politics.

Rethinking difference

In the final section of my article I elaborate the contradictory and impure status of difference as a philosophical category, its necessary imbrication with the very norms and ideals it seeks to negate. I will begin by noting that the common opposition between equality and difference within feminist thought is in fact a false antithesis (Scott 1988). The opposite of equality is not difference but, rather, inequality, a principle to which presumably no feminist would subscribe. Similarly, the antonym of difference is not equality but identity. Thus a difference-based feminism refuses a logic of identity that would subsume women within male-defined norms. It does not, however, reject equality but, rather, argues for an expanded understanding of equality that can simultaneously respect difference. Cornell helpfully refers us to Amartya Sen's notion of equivalence as a way of conceptualizing this vision of "equal differences": "'Equivalence' means of equal value, but not of equal value *because of likeness*" (Cornell 1993, 141).

[6] Appadurai 1993; Gilroy 1993; Bhabha 1994; Grewal and Kaplan 1994; Loomba 1994.

As such a formulation implies, the affirmation of difference presumes a tacit appeal to an ideal of equality, if it is not to result in a mere endorsement of existing hierarchies. "Equivalence" includes both an attention to the irreducible particularity of certain forms of experience and a normative argument for treating that experience justly. Enlightenment ideals of equality thus cannot simply be counterposed against an incommensurable principle of "difference." Rather, the very critique of such ideals as lacking presumes, if only implicitly, an expanded, more adequate notion of equality that is genuinely open to diversity. Similarly, any defense of difference and specificity necessarily relies on a universal maxim that transcends particulars, for example, the claim that "all differences should be treated with respect." As soon becomes evident, however, this minimalist norm is not very helpful. What differences are being talked about here—those of gender, race, class, sexuality, age, intelligence, opinion, politics, lifestyle? Are all these differences equal? Can they all be given equal respect simultaneously? For example, can the Ku Klux Klan's desire to express their political difference from the values of mainstream U.S. culture be reconciled with the wishes of specific racial groups to have their own cultural differences respected? The appeal to difference does not transcend but embroils the individual more deeply within the problematic but inevitable condition of normative judgment.

Two distinct issues come to the fore here: a claim for the *significance* of a particular form of difference and a claim for its *value*. As Charles Taylor notes, the defense of difference does not preclude but, rather, presumes a shared horizon of meaning against which this defense is articulated. At any given moment, there is an infinite array of differences in the world. The very identification of certain traits—gender, class, age, sexual preference, ethnic background—as more important than others—shoe size, ability to sing in tune—necessarily involves an appeal to intersubjective norms. "Defining myself means finding what is significant in my difference from others" (Taylor 1991, 35–36). Of course, one cannot predict in advance which differences will matter; the social movements of the past twenty years have been precisely about expanding the criteria for what constitutes "significant difference." In the future, no doubt, these criteria will shift again. However, they are never simply private or autonomous but always already formed in relation to broader discursive and social structures.

The second question relates to the value of particular forms of difference. Thus certain axes of differentiation may be significant without being worthy of preservation. One example might be the "difference" generated by the experience of severe poverty or starvation. Alternatively, someone who is sympathetic in principle to ideological diversity may nevertheless balk at celebrating the "difference" of the racist or misogynist. Contemporary affirmations of difference often assume, in an oddly naive way, that all differences are necessarily benevolent and hence deserve recognition. Yet this is clearly not the case; difference cannot form a value in itself, not only because some differences may be simply inconsequential and uninteresting, as Taylor notes, but also because they may actually be harmful to the survival of other life forms or cultural practices. To argue for openness to diversity thus does not do away with but, rather, exacerbates the problem of formulating values and norms that can mediate between the claims of competing forms of difference. Such "contingent foundations" (Butler 1995) are inescapable yet subject to ongoing revision; their status is rhetorical rather than ontological.

In a similar vein, Steven Connor (1992) has argued persuasively that appeals to difference and incommensurability within poststructuralist theory are themselves paradoxically beholden to norms, values, and universalizable assumptions. The recourse to absolute alterity is thus conceptually incoherent, if only because equality and difference, identity and otherness, and universality and particularity constantly infiltrate and implicate each other philosophically and politically. Much poststructuralist thought still remains caught within a surface/depth opposition, whereby the discourse of equality is seen as an illusory veil concealing the hidden "truth" of difference. Yet difference is not a foundation but a relation, not an inherent property but a distinction engendered within a given semiotic framework. Depending on the criteria used, it is clearly possible in principle to demonstrate that any two randomly chosen objects in the world are either similar to or different from each other. In other words, there is no reality-in-itself that can provide ultimate proof of the significance or value of either difference or similarity. Both the construction of commonality among subjects and the assertion of difference between subjects are rhetorical and political acts, gestures of affiliation and disaffiliation that emphasize some properties and obscure others. It is only in such contingent terms that their value can be assessed.

It might be objected at this point that my argument continues to reproduce rather than to overturn traditional philosophical oppositions such as difference/identity and universality/particularity. While this reproach is routinely deployed in contemporary theory as a way of disarming one's opponents, its logic is often specious. Specifically, it is frequently based on a misunderstanding of deconstruction (which recognizes by contrast that dualisms cannot be overcome, but at best displaced),[7] as well as on a

---

[7] One might express this recognition by noting that any argument that claims to overcome binary oppositions inevitably sets up a new opposition between binary and nonbinary thought.

received reading (or as Gasché would say, misreading) of Hegel, whereby dialectical opposition is seen as a tyrannical logic leading to an inevitable subsumption of difference by identity.

Yet feminist attempts to overcome philosophical dualism, most evident in the work of sexual difference theory, have been spectacularly unsuccessful. They result either in a regression to a reductive monism (the isolation of difference as a foundational category) or to a reproduction of the same dualism at a more abstract level (the male/female opposition is negated only to be reinstated as a division between phallocentrism and feminine difference). The problem for feminism, I suggest, is less that of dualism per se than of the ways in which particular oppositions have been reified as invariably and ontologically gendered. This problem can be addressed not by reiterating the same oppositions at a more abstract level but, rather, by questioning such a gendering of conceptual oppositions and simultaneously destabilizing them to show their necessary interdependence (recall Young's reference to making difference into sameness and sameness into difference, thereby engendering "difference and sameness in an apparently impossible simultaneity").

In other words, it is surely possible to conceptualize dualistic distinctions in terms of an ongoing oscillation and productive conflict between distinct terms that is not resolved through a Hegelian synthesis. I have sought to discuss the equality/difference distinction in such a light, as a way of demonstrating the necessary interdependence and complex slippage between these terms. Furthermore, I have questioned the assumption that the subject of feminism can be tied to either side of this dialectic by suggesting that particular groups within feminism may ally themselves contingently, variously, and indeed simultaneously to different sides of the equality/difference divide.

Thus, a double strategy comes into play: a *deconstructive* reading of the equality/difference distinction as philosophically unstable and internally independent needs to be combined with a *pragmatic* analysis of the contingent political utility adhering to either side of this dialectic for specific groups of women. For example, some reasons for the current feminist focus on difference might include the unprecedented move of women into traditionally male institutional structures, with a consequent collision of vocabularies, experiences, and forms of life; the impact of poststructuralism on intellectual work in the humanities; and the sustained critique of the exclusionary biases of Western feminism. At the same time, the status of difference as a grounding category for feminism remains radically contested. Many women are unlikely to dismiss equality—whether legal, educational, or economic—as passé, as mere male-defined reformism, given the continuing and vast disparities in the global distribution of power and resources. As Chow notes, the recent feminist affirmation of female autonomy and its subversive power derives from the specific material and ideological conditions linked to both the achievements and privileges of Western feminism and cannot be carelessly generalized (1993, 66). The status of difference is differentially articulated, just as the political meanings accruing to the struggle for equality are not always equal.

In this context, I conclude by noting that the categories often invoked disparagingly by feminist theorists — equality, reason, history, modernity — are not stable, uniform entities but are reproduced and changed by the specific context of their articulation. It is here that much of feminist philosophy, with its sweeping vision of the *longue durée* of Western history as a history of pathological phallocentrism, reveals its limitations. For example, recent rereadings of modernity have pointed to its internal complexities and uneven temporalities, arguing that white women and people of color have not been outside of the modern, but have been shaped by, and in turn variously have shaped, its political, cultural, and philosophical meanings (Gilroy 1993; Felski 1995). Rather than endorse a metaphysical vision of woman as invariably and eternally other, feminism can more usefully conceptualize the position of women in terms of a difference within sameness and a sameness within difference, a form of *interference* with the purity of such categories that is variously and contingently actualized. Such a perspective remains more open to the multiple and mutable concerns of feminism than does the appeal to incommensurability and otherness, an otherness that necessarily leaves the realm of the same untouched.

Department of English
University of Virginia

References

Ang, Ien. 1995. "I'm a Feminist but . . . 'Other' Women and Postnational Feminism." In *Transitions: New Australian Feminisms,* ed. Barbara Caine and Rosemary Pringle, 57–73. New York: St. Martin's.

Appadurai, Arjun. 1993. "Disjuncture and Difference in the Global Cultural Economy." In *The Phantom Public Sphere,* ed. Bruce Robbins, 269–95. Minneapolis: University of Minnesota Press.

Barrett, Michèle. 1987. "The Concept of 'Difference.'" *Feminist Review* 26:29–41.

Bhabha, Homi K. 1994. *The Location of Culture.* New York: Routledge.

Bordo, Susan. 1993. *Unbearable Weight: Feminism, Western Culture and the Body.* Berkeley and Los Angeles: University of California Press.

Braidotti, Rosi. 1991. *Patterns of Dissonance: A Study of Women in Contemporary Philosophy.* Cambridge: Polity.

———. 1994. *Nomadic Subjects.* New York: Columbia University Press.

Butler, Judith. 1995. "Contingent Foundations." In *Feminist Contentions: A Philosophical Exchange,* by Seyla Benhabib, Judith Butler, Drucilla Cornell, and Nancy Fraser, 35–57. New York: Routledge.

Chow, Rey, 1993. *Writing Diaspora: Tactics of Intervention in Contemporary Cultural Studies.* Bloomington: Indiana University Press.

Collin, Françoise. 1994. "Plurality, Difference, Identity." *Woman: A Cultural Review* 5(1):13–24.

Connor, Steven. 1992. *Theory and Cultural Value.* Oxford: Basil Blackwell.

Cornell, Drucilla. 1991. *Beyond Accommodation: Ethical Feminism, Deconstruction and the Law.* New York: Routledge.

———. 1993. *Transformations.* New York: Routledge.

———. 1995. "What Is Ethical Feminism?" In *Feminist Contentions: A Philosophical Exchange,* by Seyla Benhabib, Judith Butler, Drucilla Cornell, and Nancy Fraser, 75–106. New York: Routledge.

Davies, Carole Boyce. 1994. *Black Women, Writing and Identity: Migrations of the Subject.* London: Routledge.

Donaldson, Laura. 1992. *Decolonizing Feminisms: Race, Gender and Empire-Building.* Chapel Hill: University of North Carolina Press.

Felski, Rita. 1995. *The Gender of Modernity.* Cambridge, Mass.: Harvard University Press.

Frankenberg, Ruth, and Lata Mani. 1993. "Crosscurrents, Crosstalk: Race, 'Post-coloniality' and the Politics of Location." *Cultural Studies* 7(2):292–310.

Fraser, Nancy. 1995. "Pragmatism, Feminism and the Linguistic Turn." In *Feminist Contentions: A Philosophical Exchange,* by Seyla Benhabib, Judith Butler, Drucilla Cornell, and Nancy Fraser, 157–71. New York: Routledge.

Gasché, Rodolphe. 1994. *Inventions of Difference: On Jacques Derrida.* Cambridge, Mass.: Harvard University Press.

Gilroy, Paul. 1993. *The Black Atlantic: Modernity and Double Consciousness.* Cambridge, Mass.: Harvard University Press.

Grewal, Inderpal, and Caren Kaplan. 1994. "Introduction: Transnational Feminist Practices and Questions of Postmodernity." In *Scattered Hegemonies: Postmodernity and Transnational Feminist Practices,* ed. Inderpal Grewal and Caren Kaplan, 1–33. Minneapolis: University of Minnesota Press.

Harding, Sandra. 1986. "The Instability of the Analytical Categories of Feminist Theory." *Signs: Journal of Women in Culture and Society* 11(4):645–64.

Irigaray, Luce. 1993. *An Ethics of Sexual Difference.* Ithaca, N.Y.: Cornell University Press.

Jones, Ann Rosalind. 1981. "Towards an Understanding of *l'écriture féminine.*" *Feminist Studies* 7(2):264–87.

Loomba, Ania. 1994. "Overworlding the 'Third World.'" In *Colonial Discourse and Post-Colonial Theory,* ed. Patrick Williams and Laura Chrisman, 305–23. New York: Columbia University Press.

McClintock, Anne. 1994. "The Angel of Progress: Pitfalls of the Term 'Post-Colonialism.'" In *Colonial Discourse and Post-Colonial Theory,* ed. Patrick Williams and Laura Chrisman, 291–304. New York: Columbia University Press.

McGowan, John. 1991. *Postmodernism and Its Critics*. Ithaca, N.Y.: Cornell University Press.

Mohanty, Chandra Talpade. 1984. "Under Western Eyes: Feminist Scholarship and Colonial Discourse." *boundary 2* 13(1):333–57.

———. 1991. "Cartographies of Struggle: Third World Women and the Politics of Feminism." In *Third World Women and the Politics of Feminism*, ed. Chandra Talpade Mohanty, Ann Russo, and Lourdes Torres, 1–47. Bloomington: Indiana University Press.

Parry, Benita. 1987. "Problems in Current Theories of Colonial Discourse." *Oxford Literary Review* 9(1):27–58.

Sandoval, Chela. 1991. "U.S. Third World Feminism: The Theory and Method of Oppositional Consciousness in the Postmodern World." *Genders* 10 (Spring): 1–24.

Scott, Joan. 1988. "Deconstructing Equality-versus-Difference: Or the Uses of Poststructuralist Theory for Feminism." *Feminist Studies* 14(1):33–50.

Snitow, Ann. 1990. "A Gender Diary." In *Conflicts in Feminism*, ed. Marianne Hirsch and Evelyn Fox Keller, 9–43. New York: Routledge.

Spelman, Elizabeth V. 1988. *Inessential Woman: Problems of Exclusion in Feminist Thought*. Boston: Beacon.

Spivak, Gayatri Chakravorty. 1987. "French Feminism in an International Frame." In her *In Other Worlds*, 134–50. New York: Methuen.

———. 1988. "Can the Subaltern Speak?" In *Marxism and the Interpretation of Culture*, ed. Cary Nelson and Lawrence Grossberg, 271–313. Urbana: University of Illinois Press.

———. 1989. "Who Claims Alterity?" In *Remaking History*, ed. Barbara Kruger and Phil Mariani, 269–92. Seattle: Bay.

Sypnowich, Christine. 1993. "Some Disquiet about 'Difference.'" *Praxis International* 13(2):99–112.

Taylor, Charles. 1991. *The Ethics of Authenticity*. Cambridge, Mass.: Harvard University Press.

Taylor, Charles, K. Anthony Appiah, Jürgen Habermas, Steven C. Rockefeller, Michael Walzer, and Susan Wolf. 1994. *Multiculturalism*. Princeton, N.J.: Princeton University Press.

Trinh, Minh-ha. 1989. *Woman, Native, Other: Writing Postcoloniality and Feminism*. Bloomington: Indiana University Press.

Young, Iris Marion. 1995. "Together in Difference: Transforming the Logic of Group Political Conflict." In *The Rights of Minority Cultures*, ed. Will Kymlicka, 155–76. Oxford: Oxford University Press.

Young, Robert. 1995. *Colonial Desire: Hybridity in Theory, Culture and Race*. London: Routledge.

Comments and Reply

Comment on Felski's "The Doxa of Difference":
Working through Sexual Difference

Rosi Braidotti, *Department of Women's Studies, University of Utrecht*

> Some differences are playful; some are poles of world historical systems of
> domination. "Epistemology" is about knowing the difference.
> —Haraway 1991, 249

I **would like to start** with a word of thanks for the seriousness and the concern with which questions related to sexual difference are raised in Rita Felski's article. I would also like to thank *Signs* for giving me the chance to elucidate my theoretical position.[1]

My response starts with an observation, which is meant not pedantically but rather for clarity. This debate about difference and diversity is made difficult by problems of conceptual and cultural translation and adaptation of the terms. Thus, Felski's rendition of the debate on sexual difference is for me symptomatic of North American readings of philosophies of difference; they form an integral part of a complex set of interrelations, which Domna Stanton (1980) has rightly defined as the "Trans-Atlantic dis-connection." In order to engage in a serious dialogue with each other, therefore, Felski and I need to make some readjustments in terms of our respective contexts.

As a first example of this kind of difficulty, let me take up Felski's notion of the "prestige of . . . 'high theory'" (74). I would argue that on this point a serious case of dissonance has emerged between Europe and the United States, especially on the issue of the political utility of poststructuralism and sexual difference. From a Continental perspective, it seems at best surprising to state that the only theory that enjoys academic prestige is poststructuralism and sexual difference; Felski also assumes that black and postcolonial theories have no prestige or do not count as "high" theory. This situation may well be the case in American academia, but it does not apply

---

[1] All my thanks also to the staff seminar of the Women's Studies Department at Utrecht University for their useful comments.

[*Signs: Journal of Women in Culture and Society* 1997, vol. 23, no. 1]

to European academic debates, where—the Trans-Atlantic dis-connection being what it is—these theories share in the prestige of all that is imported into Europe from the United States.

Poststructuralism and sexual difference are generally perceived in the Continental tradition to be a radical answer to the decline of modernism, marxism, and postmarxist ideology. They represent an attempt to redefine leftist politics after the historical failure of Marxist-Leninism. Cornel West (1994) has pointed out the importance of assessing the American reception of poststructuralism and deconstruction, which has become associated with an ahistorical and depoliticized formalism, or with an insidious form of neo-universalism.

What I would stress therefore is that in European academia, the movement of thought known as poststructuralism, far from being the prestigious site of high theory—as it seems to be in the United States—has remained a marginal and radical "wing," with barely any institutional pull. Thus, the work of Irigaray, Cixous, Lacan, Deleuze, Derrida, and others, which may appear as dominant from an American academic perspective, is far from being so from a European standpoint.

Consider, for instance, the fact that none of the leading figures of this theoretical generation have achieved their desired institutional success.[2] The situation of feminist academics is even more dramatic: Irigaray has *never* held a tenured teaching position in any institution, and Cixous teaches in a secondary, underprivileged university. This makes their agendas anything but prestigious and influential, but it has the advantage of freeing them for political activity. For instance, Irigaray works extensively as a political advisor to the European Left, especially the Social Democratic parties. Cixous has been active in various areas of cultural action and more recently has worked on antiracism and resistance to anti-immigration laws.

I should also point to the low influence exercised by poststructuralism in European social and human sciences outside France, which can also be attributed to the decreasing influence of French language and culture within the European Union.[3] By contrast, American social and political

---

[2] Derrida was refused chairs at the University of Nanterre, the Sorbonne, and the College de France; Irigaray has not held a teaching position since she was sacked by Lacan in 1974; Deleuze, Lyotard, and Cixous went on teaching at Vincennes/Saint Denis, a university whose degrees are not officially recognized by the French Education Ministry and that is consequently very marginal to the whole French system. Most of the men, however, hold regular jobs in well-endowed, mostly West Coast, universities in the United States.

[3] I have developed this analysis more fully in an essay called "Uneasy Transitions" (Braidotti 1997). See also Wekker and Braidotti 1996.

theories enjoy both prestige and institutional support. A survey conducted on behalf of the European Union by the European Network for Women's Studies has shown the extent to which European women's studies is dominated by topics, themes, and teaching material originating in North America (Braidotti, de Dreu, and Rammrath, in press). It is even true that in a great number of European countries, women's studies courses are institutionally located under "American studies."

In such a context, I would like to recommend that scholars such as Felski make an effort to resist generalizations. I also think they should stop using nationalistic systems of indexation for feminist theories according to their alleged geopolitical origins. This is an inaccurate and reductive way of establishing feminist debates, and it enacts a sort of marketing of ideas that I deeply resist. ("French" feminism was invented the same way, much to the distress of some of the French feminists themselves.)

Even the suggestion — made explicitly by Felski — that thinkers such as Grosz, Cornell, and myself can be conveniently placed in a "second generation" of sexual difference intellectuals, who can then be arranged according to geopolitical distinctions that cover three of the main continents, is objectionable. In my view, we qualify much more readily for the title of nomadic intellectuals, who move in and out of several cultures, political traditions, and languages: we are perfect examples of hybridity and cross-culturalism. Moreover, we all resist systematically the nationalistic metaphors that so often dominate social and political theoretical debates.

In "Post-modern Blackness" (1990), bell hooks points out the paradoxical fact that, given that high theory has become identified with European imports in American debates, it is crucial for black women to get involved in these debates, so as to challenge their Eurocentric bias. What I want to add to this is that this Eurocentric bias emerges when the American receptions of these traveling theories fail to question the aims of their appropriation. In other words, not all that comes from Europe need be Eurocentric, although that bias is written into most American academic adaptations of European social and political theories.

Difference and diversity

Having located the question of sexual difference, I now elaborate on a few theoretical points in response to Felski's article. I focus on her concern that sexual difference may be a self-referential, utopian, monolithic, and therefore universalistic category that eliminates or obscures other differences, notably those of race and ethnicity.

My standpoint on this is simple: sexual difference is primarily a political and intellectual strategy, not a philosophy. Neither *dogma* nor dominant *doxa,* it emerged mostly out of the political practice of Continental feminism in the 1970s as an attempt to move beyond some of the aporias and the dead ends of equality-minded, marxist-based feminism.

As a *praxis,* sexual difference is based explicitly and self-consciously on a number of paradoxes, which are related to the historical contradictions faced by female feminists at the turn of the century, in the global economy. The key terms here are *paradoxes* and *contradictions.* Let me expand on this.

Sexual difference is based on one theoretical and practical paradox: it simultaneously produces and destabilizes the category "woman." This paradoxical reliance on and deconstruction of the female subject fuel the entire political project of contemporary feminism. Working in a broader historical perspective, Joan Scott argues that "the need both to accept and to refuse 'sexual difference' was the constitutive condition of feminism as a political movement throughout its long history" (1996, 3–4).

In my work, I have embedded this paradox within the specific crisis of Western philosophical modernity. I do think that the feminist political project coincides with modernity itself, that is, the moment of loss of the naturalistic paradigm and the emergence of the modern notion of individuality. It also has to do with the investment in the scientific *ratio* and its technological potential.[4] Feminists thus have a double task: on the one hand, they partake in the crisis of classical subjectivity, and they challenge more particularly the equation of individuality with masculinity. On the other hand, they stress the need for a sex-specific redefinition of the subject in such a way as to empower women (by which I refer to the paradoxical entity defined above).

I would speak consequently of sexual difference as a theory that rests on and exploits a number of constitutive contradictions, the answer to which cannot be formal in a logical sense, but practical in the sense of pointing to a solution in the "doing." That particular activity is political practice. Teresa de Lauretis (1990; see also Milan Women's Bookstore Collective 1990) speaks of an "essential difference" between Woman as the classical object of masculine representation and real-life women who are engaged in the project of dismantling the icon, both socially and sexually. Pursuing that further, I have argued that this "essential" difference establishes the groundwork for the contradiction that both links and separates feminists from Woman/woman. The hiatus between, on the one hand, the feminine as the classical "difference" of phallogocentrism and, on the other, the para-

---

[4] I have explored this complex issue in *Patterns of Dissonance* (Braidotti 1991).

doxical difference simultaneously claimed and critiqued by feminists fuels the political project of feminism.

By limiting her reading of sexual difference to rather formal elements of analysis (inner consistency, etc.), Felski misses the point altogether: in my work there is *no question* of autonomous or authentic femininity, as Felski suggests. Feminist affirmation and empowerment of sexual difference indeed go hand in hand with the rejection not only of essentialist identities but also of the dialectics of negation as the logic in the constitution of the subject. For sexual difference theory, resting indeed on the "linguistic turn" but pushing it to its extreme, one "speaks as" a woman, although the subject woman is not a monolithic essence defined once and for all, but rather the site of multiple, complex, and potentially contradictory experiences— also known as signifying markers. These multiple "differences within" can and must be analyzed in terms of power relations: they constitute overlapping variables that cut across any monolithic understanding of the subject: class, race, ethnicity, religion, age, lifestyle, sexual preferences. In other words, one "speaks as" a woman in order to be empowered politically to act as one, according to the terms of the paradox outlined above. It is a way of acknowledging an identity that can then be put to the task of its own emancipation. The political gesture consists in situating oneself at the crest of the contradictions that are constitutive of the social and symbolic position of women and to activate them toward the destabilization of the sociosymbolic system and especially of the asymmetrical power relations that sustain it.

Sexual difference brings into representation the play of multiple differences that structure the subject: these are neither harmonious nor homogeneous, but rather internally differentiated and potentially contradictory. Therefore, sexual difference forces us to think of the simultaneity of potentially contradictory social, discursive, and symbolic effects.

The term *women* may no longer suffice to describe the post-Woman subject who is activated against the grain of phallogocentric femininity. I have even drawn long lists of the many alternative forms of naming that feminists have created in the past ten years for the "subject of feminism." The sheer amount and diversity of the terminology (womanist/cyborg/Black/postcolonial/lesbian/queer/nomadic/women divine, etc.) also confirm the point I am making: that sexual difference can be understood only in terms of multiple differences.

If I have used the term *nomadism* to describe how sexual difference works (I do wonder why Felski has chosen to ignore this aspect of my work), it is precisely because I want to emphasize the dynamic and internally differentiated structure of difference. Sexual difference is not a metaphysical claim to a unitary and sweeping vision of subjectivity, but rather a recognition of their mutually shaping, yet internally contradictory, coexistence of asymmetrical power relations that are predicated along the very axes that shape that subjectivity: sexuality, ethnicity and "race," class, age, and others.

Politically, this means that the terms of possible feminist political coalitions are not to be sought in the categories of "sameness" — be it sisterhood, the "second sex," or some other commonality of oppression. The political focus is shifted instead toward a politics of coalition based on the confrontation of differences among women. Here, issues of race and ethnicity and — especially in Europe — of national identity, nationalism, and religion are of the greatest importance. In this regard, sexual difference can be seen as a critique of emancipationism, or equality-minded feminism.

In contrast to Beauvoir's Hegelian optimism about the possible reversal of the balance of power between the two poles of the sexual dialectics — the masculine and the feminine — Irigaray and other sexual difference theorists argue that the terms of this opposition are *not* reversible, either conceptually or politically.[5] The phallogocentric system constructs its terms in a dissymmetrical power relation, that is, that such terms carry built-in structural inequalities. These cannot be compensated by any direct means: only a change of the overall structure would allow for change. In other words, feminists cannot simply claim or posit radical otherness as a way out of the dialectics of sex. Given the structure of femininity as a site that is systematically constructed as devalued, the political strategy consists in working on the margins of "ex-centricity" that women enjoy from the phallogocentric system. This engenders the strategy of mimesis, to which I will return.

Sexual difference as a political practice is constructed in a non-Hegelian framework whereby identity is not postulated in dialectical opposition to a necessarily devalorized other. There is no negativity involved: rather, it rests on the working through of many differences between, among, and within women. As I have often argued, I see "differences among women" as being constitutive of the category of sexual difference and not exterior or antithetical to it (Braidotti 1994; see also Frye 1996).

Difference and the crisis of European humanism

Contrary to Felski's claim that sexual difference contributes to concealing issues of ethnicity and multiculturalism and therefore to perpetuating the

---

[5] For a more detailed discussion, see Braidotti with Butler 1994.

power and discourse of the Same, I would argue that both "mainstream" and feminist theorists of difference have contributed to laying bare the Christian, white, Euro-centered core of phallogocentrism. In undoing the logic of negation that structures dialectical thought, they have also disassembled the geopolitical specificity of Western discourses and especially of philosophy. Theirs is the philosophical generation that, in proclaiming the "death of Man," also marked the implosion of the crisis of European humanism.

This project of in-depth critique of humanism is an attempt to disengage difference from negativity. Do keep in mind the fact that the notion of "difference" goes to the heart of the European history of philosophy. As a foundational concept, it has been colonized by hierarchical and exclusionary ways of thinking; as such it has played a constitutive role in European fascism and colonialism. It is a concept that functions as a pseudo-universal, predicating its monological unity in a set of binary oppositions — such as male/female, white/black, active/passive — that posit asymmetrical power relations between its terms. Because the history of difference in Europe has been one of lethal exclusions and fatal disqualifications, it is a notion for which critical intellectuals since the poststructuralists have chosen to make themselves accountable.

I think we — critical intellectuals based in Europe — consequently need to *think through* difference, through its imbrication with violence and power, its complicity with totalitarian practices and fascist interpretations. To become accountable for such a history requires means of revisiting it, acknowledging it, and understanding the complicity between "difference" and "exclusion" in the European mind-set. This is a deconstructivist strategy that consists in rereading difference in such a way as to dislodge it from its disastrous history: it is like a repeated attempt at purging this notion of its most poisonous aspects, to sever its links with power and domination. The mimetic strategy de-essentializes differences and reduces them to processes by which power and/as discourse are produced. The aim of this deconstructive process is to disengage difference from its traditional attributes, so that to be "other-than" may stop meaning "being-less-than."

This task is made all the more urgent and necessary in the historical moment known as postmodernity, which, read in terms of the crisis of European humanism, coincides with the shift of geopolitical power away from the North Atlantic in favor of the Pacific Rim and especially Southeast Asia. Gayatri Spivak (1992) raises the suspicion that the many discourses about the "crisis" of Western humanism and more specifically poststructuralist philosophy may actually reassert some universalistic posturing under the pretense of specific, localized, or diffuse intellectual subject-positions.

My line on this is quite different. I think that this shift in geopolitical power becomes both confirmed and theorized in philosophies of difference in terms of the decline of the Euro-centered logocentric system. Philosophers such as Deleuze (1978), Derrida (1997), and Cacciari (1994) have provided critical accounts of the decline of European hegemony. They argue that what makes European philosophical culture so perniciously effective is that it has been announcing its own death for more than one hundred years. Especially since the apocalyptic trinity of modernity—Marx, Nietzsche, and Freud—the West has been thinking through the historical inevitability and the logical possibility of its own decline.

Instead of plunging into nostalgia, it is to the credit of poststructuralists that they take the opportunity of this crisis to challenge the power of logocentric discourse. Especially Derrida and Deleuze denounce the ethnocentric Western habit that consists in passing off Europe as the center of the world, confining everyone else to a huge periphery. They do so by providing an in-depth critique of how the classical notion of "difference" is complicitous with negation and exclusion. They also offer positive counter-practices of difference as something other than "being-less-than." Both "mainstream" and feminist philosophers of difference concentrate their critique on the vision of the subject that constitutes the Norm (the Same). Deleuze summarizes Him effectively as "masculine; white; heterosexual; urbanized; speaker-of-a-standard-language; property-owning; rationalist" (1978, 154). This vision of subjectivity is the poststructuralists' main target of criticism.

On this point, I agree with Cornel West that there is a convergence between the discourse of the "crisis" of the West within poststructuralism and the postcolonial deconstruction of imperial whiteness (1994, 125). They share a common focus that does not erase the dissymmetries between the respective positions but rather lays the grounds for the possibility of an alliance between them. Anthony Appiah (1991) reminds us of the need *not* to confuse the "post" of postcoloniality with the "post" of poststructuralism but to respect instead their specific historical locations. Moreover, feminists are in a very good position to know that the deconstruction of sexism and racism does *not* automatically entail their downfall. Speaking as a feminist antiracist poststructuralist, however, I also wish to stress both the convergence of these lines of critique and their necessary intersection over the issue of political subjectivity, identity, and sexual difference.

In the specific case of the critique of European ethnocentrism, I think a poststructuralist feminist perspective leads us to discuss quite seriously the grounds on which we postulate European identity. Identity is not understood as a foundational issue, based on fixed, God-given essences — of the biological, psychic, or historical kind. On the contrary, identity is taken as being constructed in the very gesture that posits it as the anchoring point for certain social and discursive practices. Consequently, the question is no longer the essentialist one — What is national or ethnic identity? — but rather a critical and genealogical one: How is it constructed? by whom? under what conditions? for which aims? As Stuart Hall (1992) put it: Who is entitled to claim an ethnic or national identity? who has the right to claim that legacy, to speak on its behalf and turn it into a policy-making platform? This interrogation results in the myths of essentialized identity being exposed and exploded into questions related to entitlement and agency that rotate around the issue of cultural identity.

The political phenomenon that is the European Union amplifies these issues: insofar as the European integration project seals the decline of the individual nation states and their regrouping into a federation, it intensifies the question of entitlement to citizenship. The question can then be raised: Can one be European *and* black or Muslim? Paul Gilroy's work (1987) on being a black British subject is indicative of the problem of citizenship and blackness emerging as contested issues. The corollary of this phenomenon is also, however, the emergence of whiteness as a critical category.

Ruth Frankenberg argues that structured invisibility has been the very source of the power of whiteness and has contributed greatly to confusing it with normality (1994, 6). One of the radical implications of the project of the European Union is the possibility of embedding and embodying whiteness, therefore giving a specific location, and consequently historical embeddedness or memory, to whites. Finally, it can racialize our location, which is quite a feat because, until recently in Europe, only white suprema- cists, Nazi-skins, and other fascists actually had a theory about qualities that are inherent to white people. Like all fascists, they are biological and cultural essentialists.

In this regard, my own strategy as a citizen of the European Union is to claim European identity as a site of historical contradictions and to experience it as the political necessity to turn it into spaces of critical resis- tance to hegemonic identities of all kinds. My own choice to rework white- ness in the era of postmodernity is, first, to situate it, denaturalize it, and to embody it and embed it and, second, to nomadize it or to destabilize it, to undo its hegemonic hold. Being a nomadic European subject means to be in transit but sufficiently anchored to a historical position to accept responsibility for it.

I want to argue that the radical theories of difference that have emerged in European philosophy and especially the practice of sexual difference contribute to a critical analysis of the naturalization of difference as a mark of pejoration. This process entails a critique of the ways in which European philosophy contributed to the structured invisibility of the ethnocentrism of white Europeans. It thus pursued a metaphysical illusion of self-representation that concretely resulted in the disembedded and disembodied pursuit of "purity," "objectivity," and "neutrality" as ideals. Philosophy is made especially accountable for the ways in which it contributed both to theorize hierarchical differences and to disqualify large sectors of the population (the many "others") from the exercise of discursive power.

True enough, "race" does not play a central role in these theories of difference, except in the specific case of imperialism, but cultural identity, ethnicity, nationalism, and religion do, as do colonialism, fascism, and anti-Semitism. I have argued therefore that the poststructuralists' critique of the processes by which, in European philosophy, difference has been essentialized, naturalized, and turned into a mark of pejoration echoes the calls for radical embodiment of whiteness and for accountability by whites for their own racialized privileges. I also want to argue that this is not a sufficient but a necessary condition for a dialogue between the poststructuralists and the postcolonial and multicultural perspectives that have emerged especially but not exclusively in feminism.

Mimesis

To these considerations, I would like to add some concrete points of strategy. These points aim to illustrate the political project outlined above. The political subject for sexual difference is not the willful liberal bourgeois subject but rather the so-called split subject, which is far from having been accepted by established European academics. I want to suggest that the resistance to psychoanalytic politics is a result of this vision of the subject clashing with one of the classical assumptions of the philosophical and social sciences, namely, a humanistic vision of the subject as coinciding with his/her consciousness. Butler and Scott (1994) have suggested that another reason for the resistance to the poststructuralist vision of subjectivity is that it arouses the fear of loss of cognitive mastery in those who are comforted by the illusion of possessing it. Let me spell out the defining features of this particular vision of subjectivity.

Beyond the rationalist subject

Sexual difference shares with poststructuralism the critique of the identification of subjectivity with consciousness. It does so by analyzing the latter in terms of a set of power relations that construct the subject but that are blurred and concealed under humanistic rhetoric. What is at stake politically in this is the need to practice feminist subjectivity in such a way as to allow for this inner multiplicity, which is also a way to resist the rationalistic pull toward the closure of fixed identity.

I would like to add to this another, equally challenging insight: in order to practice this open-ended politics of subjectivity, language can no longer be seen as a *means* of communication. It rather functions as the ontological foundation of one's subjectivity. Much ink has been spilled over the word *ontology* in recent feminist theory. I do not think we should let that big word (*ontology*) go to our heads. Why not leave it instead where it belongs in poststructuralist philosophy: as the marker of a foundational site that, being linguistic and historical, is neither one nor forever, but differentiated and differential, partial and in process, not fixed. As such, ontology frames the field of possible political action and a politics of resistance and affirmation.

Feminists as female subjects are not rationalistic entities but a multiplicity split within itself. Each feminist subject is multiple, discontinuous, and internally contradictory. It is linked to a set of social conditions through imaginary or mediated relations, which are both constituted by and constitutive of language. Consequently, the project of changing female subjectivity in the social and the symbolic realms requires in-depth changes that defy both willful emancipationism and utopian revolutions. The affirmation of positive difference is not as simple as a voluntaristic switch of identification. I prefer to describe the project as the patient and often painful process of "working things through."

This means that the emphasis on sexual difference does not necessarily imply a monopoly position, nor does it lead to some sort of neo-universalism. It is rather a radical form of materialism that embeds the subject in his/her specific set of power formations and demands accountability for them. It is about *specific* intellectuals working in situated settings. It is a radical form of politics of location that uses psychoanalysis — Irigaray and not Lacan — as a political weapon.

The unconscious marks the fundamental noncoincidence of the self with his/her consciousness: it is a guarantee of nonclosure. Identity, therefore, is a set of interactions with material and symbolic conditions mediated through language and representation. This implies that no social relations, and certainly not class, race, or gender, are immune from imaginary constructions that differ significantly from one subject to the other. One's interaction with the very locations that structure one's subjectivity — class, race, ethnicity — are not direct but mediated; that is, they contain a sizable "imaginary" component. This nonrationalistic vision of the subject aims at providing a more adequate understanding of contemporary subjectivity; it stresses that there is no unmediated relation to sex, gender, sexuality, class, race, ethnicity, religion, or any other variable. In fact, identity is but a constant process of negotiation among diverse and potentially contradictory variables, which intersect and overlap incessantly. Any one of them can be the hegemonic one for some period of time, but their structure being relational, they constantly shift in relation to each other. As a matter of fact, the singularity of the self, far from being grounded in conventional humanistic assumptions about *the* individual, is paradoxically guaranteed by one's imaginary play with identifications that escape willful control.

The political issue for feminists is how to maintain the openness or non-closure of this vision of the subject while asserting the political will and necessity of alternative social views of female subjectivity. The power of synthesis of an "I" that would guarantee sovereignty over the inner complexities is a mere grammatical fiction that, far from solving the problem, ends up making it worse by projecting over it the illusion of unity or substance. The politics of difference instead borrow from psychoanalysis the profoundly sober — albeit frightening — prospect of a subject whose unity is merely illusory and whose truth resides in the play of the differences, the paradoxes, and the contradictions within oneself.

The subversive power of repetition

The political strategy generated by the practice of sexual difference is *mimesis,* or strategic repetition. This strategy is so central to all sexual difference theorists regardless of their generational or geopolitical location that I am surprised to see that Felski ignores it. Mimesis is a process of inner disentanglement that both precedes and is made possible by a political engagement with processes of social transformation. It is a form of deliberate and self-conscious repetition — mimesis as affirmative gesture — that gives sexual difference its political sting.

Sexual difference as a strategy of empowerment is a form of mimesis insofar as it activates subjects who are conscious of and accountable for the paradox of being both caught inside a symbolic code and deeply opposed to it. Insofar as this paradox is constitutive of feminism, as I argued earlier, it forms the foundation for a radical politics of resistance. This position neither requires the counterassertion of oppositional identities ("Woman" as the future of mankind), nor does it essentialize difference into a new universal.

This strategically enforced form of repetition also acts on one's unconscious identifications with the very identity that one has already rejected at the level of willful political choice. Thus, female feminists single out as the target of their critique the material and symbolic institution of femininity.

Each female feminist, however, is linked to such an institution—albeit by negation—through imaginary relations, which are mediated through language and representation and as such escape rational control. The choreographed repetitions of mimesis, in other words, dislodge the feminist subject from the site of culturally coded Woman. Like all social and symbolic institutions, this Woman (as the Other of the Same) functions like a magnet that draws real-life women in, through both conscious and unconscious interpellations. Insofar as the unfolding of the cultural code is an integral part of the process of construction of one's identity, I argue that mimetic repetition mobilizes and shifts the expectations of femininity as dictated also by unconscious interpellations.[6]

This is an important point, which I connect to the necessity of keeping distinct the levels of conscious volition from that of unconscious desire. I think that the imaginary identifications that constitute the unconscious types of interpellations by which identity unfolds are not only deep and powerful but also unpredictable. They help in following the cultural codes, but they also fuel possible forms of resistance. In fact, the unconscious understood as a guarantee of nonclosure of identity functions primarily through unpredictability and resistance. It can allow, for instance, for forms of nonadherence by women to the social codes of Womanhood as defined in phallogocentrism, in the sense of a deep disidentification, a sort of psychic and symbolic disobedience.

Thus, repetition or strategy mimesis is the process of revisiting and consuming the old, both within and without. What counts as "the old" here is the established definition of the feminine as "the Other of the Same." Mimesis is a process of constant renegotiation of the forms and the contents of female identity, a sort of inner erosion of the feminine by women who are aware of their own implication with that which they attempt to deconstruct. The purpose of this mimetic exercise is not the futility of deconstruction for its own sake but rather the political project of breaking down old social and mental habits and forms of identification. I could summarize this pictorially in the process of peeling off one after the other the successive layers of feminine signification that have been inscribed on our body, in the psychic recesses and the internalized folds of our experience.

To make a difference

Sexual difference as a political practice aims at *making a difference* by opening up the margins of resistance to the dominant views of femininity.

---

[6] With thanks to Carolyn Allen.

Mimesis is a careful use of repetitions that confirms feminists in their para-doxical relation to femininity but also empowers the subversive distance that these women entertain from the same femininity. Crucial to this politi-cal process is the fact that the quest for alternative forms of social represen-tation of women requires the mimetic revisitation and reabsorptions of the established forms of representation of the post-Woman female feminist subjects (for whom the term *woman* no longer need apply). Feminism is the strategy that consists in redefining a social imaginary related to women; it is the strategy of working through the layers of sedimented meanings and significations surrounding the female subject. It activates the imagi-nary as a social and political force.

Let us keep in mind that the difference at stake here is not the "other" of phallogocentrism (which is conceptualized in function of and in relation to a masculine center). Under the heading of "the double syntax," Irigaray (1983, 1985) differentiates this type of otherness (the difference of Woman from Man, also called "the Other of the Same") from what I would call the differences among women (the difference of real-life women from Woman as institution and representation; this is also known as "the other of the Other").

Difference as multiple differences

Sexual difference claims a political subjectivity that is not based on the willful affirmation of radical otherness, as Felski suggests. The politics of sexual difference is a praxis that consists in activating real-life women's difference from the way difference has been institutionalized in the phal-logocentric system as a site of devalued otherness. This praxis rests on a margin of disidentification, that is, of nonbelonging to phallogocentrism, but it is a margin significant enough to open the space to a feminist subject position. The practice of sexual difference rests on the confrontation of multiple differences among but also within women.

In this view, feminist politics consists in activating and disengaging the terms of its constitutive paradox, deconstructing the very term *woman* that gives feminism its political ontology. Thus, when sexual difference femi-nists speak of positive affirmation of the feminine difference, they have in mind a form of empowerment of those spaces of resistance to the reified image of femininity ("the Other of the Same"), which would disengage her from her ancestral obligation both to reflect and to sustain her mas-ter's voice.

Insofar as this political project, in European culture, coincides histori-cally with the decline of classical humanism, it also opens up spaces for alliances or "conversations" between sexual difference and the other axes of differentiation that constitute subjectivity. Mimesis has to do with inner multiplicities or multiple differences: not only does it *not* exclude them, but, on the contrary, it reveals their mutual interdependence and makes it possible and necessary to set them in a dialogue with each other. Sexual difference neither excludes nor synthesizes all other differences, but it historically and conceptually functions in European critical theory as the privileged signifier of difference. Privileged, however, does *not* mean exclusive: in my work, I connect nomadic subjectivity with the political feminist strategy of asserting sexual difference as affirmative mimesis. Mimesis as strategy repetition is also made up of borrowing and lending across cultural, disciplinary, and other boundaries. Consequently, I think that Felski's defense of hybridity, which I share entirely, would profit from and not be antithetical to the strategy of mimetic repetition that is so central to sexual difference.[7]

Political sensibilities

The play of multiple differences in the framework of a theory of subjectivity where embodiment and sexuality are central is indeed a major point of distinction between European and American thinking about sexual difference. In my understanding, sexual difference is primary insofar as sexuality is a central axis of subjectification. But it is not exclusive, nor is it all encompassing.

In other words, to practice sexual difference, one must have a flair for these complexities: a sort of political culture of difference is needed as a support mechanism for what would otherwise be only an intimate project of transformation. This kind of politics assumes, in fact, a complex and split subject who does *not* coincide with his or her conscious self. In this framework, the embodied self plays a particularly important role as the site where subjects are constituted morphologically and socially. The "body" is a crossroads of social and symbolic relations of which sexuality (and sexed identity) is a major axis, but not the only one.

Please keep in mind that for the feminism of sexual difference sexuality as a social and symbolic institution is the main term of reference, as opposed to the Anglo-American "sex-gender" distinction. This seems to me indicative of major differences between Continental European and

[7] I thank Cris van der Hoek for her insightful comments on this and on other parts of this comment.

American philosophical traditions, which are obviously related to larger cultural historical issues. I think feminist scholars involved in the transatlantic dialogue should take at least some of these larger issues into account, especially when it comes to theories of language and consciousness.

I would link the emphasis on sexual difference as a primary—although not exclusive—axis to the importance of sexuality in Continental social and political theory as a whole and to feminism in particular. This aspect has too long a history for me to trace it here, but let me highlight a couple of points that are specially relevant for this discussion.

First, European feminism did not experience anything like the "sex wars" that raged through the U.S. movement, causing not only endless polemics but also vehement polarizations. In my reading, these "sex wars" resulted in a discursive division of labor that is characteristic of contemporary American feminist theory: on the one hand, feminism concentrates on the notion of "gender," in the ubiquitous binary sex/gender couple. On the other hand, sexuality found a nurturing humus in the queer theory movement, which contributes to the critique of "gender" in terms of its heterosexism.

It is of the greatest importance to the transatlantic dialogue on sexual difference to remember that such distinctions, and the organization of discursive and political labor they engender, do *not* apply to Continental feminism.

Which takes me to my second point: European social and political theories have inherited from classical structuralism, notably Levi-Straussian anthropology and structural linguistics, a political theory of sexuality. The primacy of human sexuality as a mythological system, that is, as a political economy, runs through all of the 1950s social theory and enters feminism through the new materialist psychoanalysis of the Lacanians.

As a result, European feminists such as Irigaray traditionally work with a notion of sexuality that encompasses both material and symbolic elements: it is an institution in the materialist and the imaginary sense of the term. Psychoanalysis plays a role in this tradition by providing a materialist theory of the sexual subject and, after the Lacanian intervention, a politics of subjectivity in the framework of advanced capitalism. The dissymmetry between this and the American renditions of the debate could not be greater.

Conclusion

My point is by now clear: sexual difference is neither an unproblematic nor an autonomous category; it is the name we give to a process by which diverse differences intersect and are activated alongside or against each other. It is the process by which subjectivity functions and should be the process by which an adequate form of politics is posited for it.

To illustrate this politics, I would like to take the (I hope) classical feminist axiom "woman is a subject inscribed in power via class, age, race, ethnicity, sexual orientation" and activate it as a set of inner differences that go on multiplying themselves. As in Gertrude Stein's operatic prose, the logocentric gravitational pulls of the sentences would implode under the strain of the repetition: "Woman is a subject is inscribed is in is power is via is of is class is age is race is ethnicity is sexual is orientation is . . ." and so on indefinitely.

What matters ultimately to the politics of sexual difference is repetition. This is the recurrence of the process by which the verb "to be"—which has given phallogocentrism its fundamental ontology—starts whirling off its phallogocentric base. In this de-motion "Being" gets dislodged from its fundamentalist pedestal and loses the dogmatic authority of its essentialist predicates, to expose at last the multiple "differences within." Being thus becomes activated as a force whose function is to stitch together the different moments it enacts but that it does not encompass. The metaphysical weight of Being is reduced to a mere shifter: it drops the pretense of essential continuity on which it erected its imperialist power of signification, to return each subject to the specific multiplicity of one's singularity.

Is this utopian? Only in the sense of the kind of ethical and political drive or longing without which no transformative project can ever get started. In this regard, sexual difference is a hopeful commitment to change, in that it marks an intellectual and affective investment in the desirability of change. Another name for this is political passion.

References

Appiah, Anthony. 1991. "Is the Post- in Postmodernism the Post- in Postcolonial?" *Critical Inquiry* 17(2):336–57.

Braidotti, Rosi. 1991. *Patterns of Dissonance.* New York: Routledge.

———. 1994. *Nomadic Subjects.* New York: Columbia University Press.

———. In press. "Uneasy Transitions." In *Transitions, Environments, Translations: International Feminisms in Contemporary Politics,* ed. Joan Scott, Cora Kaplan, and Debra Keates, 355–72. New York: Routledge.

Braidotti, Rosi, with Judith Butler. 1994. "Feminism by Any Other Name." *differences* 6(2–3):27–61.

Braidotti, Rosi, Ellen de Dreu, and Christine Rammrath. In press. *Women's Studies in Europe,* final report of the European field evaluation, presented at the conference "The Evaluation of Women's Studies in a European Perspective," Coimbra, Portugal, June 1995. Luxembourg: Commission of the European Union.

Butler, Judith, and Joan Scott, eds. 1994. *Feminists Theorize the Political.* New York: Routledge.

Cacciari, Massimo. 1994. *Geo-filosofia dell'Europa.* Milan: Adelphi.

de Lauretis, Teresa. 1990. "Eccentric Subjects: Feminist Theory and Historical Consciousness." *Feminist Studies* 16(1):115–50.

Deleuze, Gilles. 1978. "Philosophie et minorité." *Critique,* no. 369, 154–55.

Derrida, Jacques. 1997. *Cosmopolites de tous les pays, encore un effort!* Paris: Galilee.

Frankenberg, Ruth. 1994. *White Women, Race Matters: The Social Construction of Whiteness.* Minneapolis: University of Minnesota Press.

Frye, Marilyn. 1996. "The Necessity of Differences: Constructing a Positive Category of Women." *Signs: Journal of Women in Culture and Society* 21(4): 991–1010.

Gilroy, Paul. 1987. *There Ain't No Black in the Union Jack.* London: Hutchinson.

Hall, Stuart. 1992. "What Is This 'Black' in Black Popular Culture?" In *Black Popular Culture,* ed. Gina Dent. Seattle: Bay Press.

Haraway, Donna. 1991. "A Cyborg Manifesto." In her *Simians, Cyborgs, and Women: The Reinvention of Nature,* 149–82. London: Free Association.

hooks, bell. 1990. *Yearning: Race, Gender and Cultural Politics.* Toronto: Between-the-Lines.

Irigaray, Luce. 1985. *Speculum of the Other Woman.* Ithaca, N.Y.: Cornell University Press.

———. 1993. *An Ethics of Sexual Difference.* Ithaca, N.Y.: Cornell University Press.

Milan Women's Bookstore Collective. 1990. Introduction to *Sexual Difference: A Theory of Social-Symbolic Practice.* Bloomington: Indiana University Press.

Scott, Joan Wallach. 1996. *Only Paradoxes to Offer: French Feminists and the Rights of Man.* Cambridge, Mass.: Harvard University Press.

Spivak, Gayatri Chakravorty. 1992. "French Feminism Revisited: Ethics and Politics." In *Feminists Theorize the Political,* ed. Judith Butler and Joan W. Scott, 54–85. New York and London: Routledge.

Stanton, Domna. 1980. "Language and Revolution: The Franco-American Disconnection." In *The Future of Difference,* ed. Hester Eisenstein and Alice Jardine, 73–87. Boston: Hall.

Wekker, Gloria, and Rosi Braidotti, eds. 1996. *Praten in het Donker: Multiculturalisme en anti-racisme in feministische perspectief.* Kampen: Kok Agora.

West, Cornel. 1994. *Prophetic Thought in Postmodern Times.* Monroe, Maine: Common Courage. I

Comment on Felski's "The Doxa of Difference":
Diverging Differences

Drucilla Cornell, *Women's Studies, Political Science, and Law, Rutgers University*

want to thank Rita Felski for giving me the opportunity to clarify the central ideas in my work. First and foremost, I am a thinker of sexual difference, but not in Felski's sense. What do I mean by sexual difference? First, I mean that who we are as sexed beings is symbolic, institutional; second, it is a way of being that claims one's own sex outside of the imposed norms of heterosexuality. The first is a point about how to understand gender. The second is a political aspiration that must reform our dreams of how we are to be sexed and to claim our personhood at the same time. I want to begin with my theory of equality, to which Felski briefly refers. In *The Imaginary Domain* (Cornell 1995), I attempted to advocate a new theory of legal equality that would overcome the equality/difference debate that has plagued feminist jurisprudence. My argument was as follows. The basic postulate of political liberalism is that all citizens are to be recognized as free and equal persons. The feminist demand in the great bourgeois revolutions in Western Europe was that women should be included in the moral community of persons constituted by the new democratic governments. As Joan Scott has eloquently described (1996), that basic demand ran afoul of the reality that the person was represented as the white male property owner. The demand to be included in that community had to run up against a paradox. Women were demanding inclusion in a normative political community of persons that by definition excluded them. My attempt to resolve the dilemma posed by the conflation of white masculinity with the purportedly universal person has taken the following form. The juridical person of the early bourgeois government was seemingly "neutered," but of course only "seemingly." Since the characteristics of the person were assumed as given by the equality attributed to citizens, the "sexing" of the representative of the person disappeared. But what do we as feminists do to make the "sexing" of the representative of the person appear? Once we have made it appear, what is our political and, more specifically, our legal demand to the state? Are we to demand the actual "de-sexing" of the idealized person—as if that could be achieved—so that women can be included as equal citizens with the same rights? But then what about the ways in which women are different from men? What about pregnancy and the division of labor in the family?

Perhaps we should instead claim the right to our difference and to the protection of our welfare particularly as mothers. In her book *Only Paradoxes to Offer* (1996), Joan Scott discusses in depth the paradoxes generated over a century of French feminism as generation after generation struggled with the question of what exactly were women's rights. In *The Imaginary Domain,* I argued that we might start to resolve the dilemma by reclaiming the ideal of the person for feminist purposes.

First, I have argued that once we add "sex"—or what I have named "sexuate being"—as a category of political philosophy, we can no longer legitimately represent the person as "neutered." Similarly, we can no longer think of the person as simply given. Sexed beings have a phenomenological existence that puts demands on them. These demands must be addressed in political philosophy, especially in a theory of legal reform. Yet how do we do this without reinscribing the "state of injury" (Brown 1995) imposed by gender hierarchy as the definition of women? We are obviously not born as the full-blown adults that social contract theory models. The concept of sexuate being takes us back to the "prior" point in which human beings become individuated enough to be regarded as capable of the moral capacities attributed to the idealized person of political philosophy.

The person then is no longer represented as just "there." Instead, the person must be respected as part of a project. This project must be available to each one of us as a sexuate being on an equivalent basis. My argument is that without the equal protection of minimum conditions of individuation, we cannot effectively engage in the project of becoming a person. These minimum conditions of individuation can only arise in a space that I have described as the imaginary domain. The minimum conditions of individuation include (1) bodily integrity and (2) access to symbolic forms sufficient to achieve linguistic skills that in turn permit the differentiation of oneself from others.

I like to think of these as ensconced in the imaginary domain because bodily integrity is not used in the way that it has traditionally been used in political philosophy. Again, we do not assume bodily integrity as a given. Instead, the integration of one's own body is understood as a process. The imaginary domain is a heuristic device that allows us to represent the sanctuary needed for any of us to pull ourselves together into that being we think of as a self, or as a person. Since, in my definition, the person is a project undertaken by a sexuate being, I am using person in a particular way. *Per sona* in Latin literally means "shining through." Even though the concept of the mask is the usual association with the word *persona*, I would argue that, in fact, a person is what shines through a mask. For a person to be able to shine through she must imagine herself as whole, even if she knows she can never truly succeed in becoming whole or conceptually differentiate between the mask and the self. A person, in other words, is an aspiration because it is a project that can never be fulfilled once and for all. The person as a sexuate being is implicated in an endless process of working through personae. As sexed beings we are inevitably confronted with this project. In this definition the person is identical neither with the self nor with the traditional philosophical subject.

It should be noted that the appeal to minimum conditions of individuation is universalized. The uniqueness of feminine sexual difference — if one assumes there is such uniqueness — is not taken into account in the elaboration of the conditions themselves. No form of sexuate being can be evaluated as inherently antithetical to personhood since such a devaluation would run counter to the fundamental premise of a politically liberal society that each one of us is to be regarded as a free and equal person.

I   I   I

Although the imaginary domain functions as a heuristic device to help elaborate the space that must be protected prior to the beginning of any conception of proceduralist justice, it also serves to displace the current notion of legal privacy. The equal protection of the imaginary domain gives to the person, and only to the person, the right to represent her or his sexuate being. The argument is that the recognition of the right of self-representation of our sexuate beings works backward. As beings entitled as a matter of right to represent their own sexuate being, women, for example, can no longer be identified in law as a naturalized class whose entitlement and duties flow from this status position. Of course, the idea that the concept of right is constitutive of the person takes us back to Hegel (1967).

If we understand that now the demand for inclusion entails protection of the imaginary domain and minimum conditions of individuation, then we can make a claim to parity that does not turn on any comparison with actual men. For example, in the case of the right of abortion, I have argued that women must have the right to abortion with safe facilities both provided and paid for all the way through the cutting of the umbilical cord (Cornell 1995, chap. 2). If we allow the state to impose on women any prohibition against their right to represent their sexuate being, and in this case to have an abortion, or to make it extremely difficult — that is, deny medical facilities — then we are treating women as things for a greater good and not as persons.

I   I   I

The theory of legal equality I have advocated pits itself against the use of gender as a legal category precisely because the "single axis" for discrimination had been exclusionary of claims made by women of diverse nationalities (African-American, Hispanic, Asian, and Native American women) in the name of the specificity of sexual discrimination and sexual harassment they endured. For example, in *The Imaginary Domain,* I argue that the "braiding cases" that had been denied jurisdiction under our own law would easily be included as making a claim of right under my theory of equality. To be granted jurisdiction is to be given standing to sue. The braiding cases involved situations in which African-American women were discriminated against or harassed because they chose to braid their hair. As Paulette Caldwell has argued (1991), hair braiding is for many black women one representation of the meaning they give to their identification as African-American. For Caldwell personally, the braiding of her hair was an extremely important way of expressing her continuing identification with African tradition. As she elaborates in her essay, hair braiding involves a ritual in which grandmothers braided a young girl's hair on the occasion of her first period. Her own grandmother followed this tradition. For Caldwell, hair braiding was never simply an aesthetic exercise, but also a profound moment of identification both with her own ancestresses and with what being African had meant to them.

Under formal equality hair braiding is not an "immutable characteristic," and therefore it does not fall under the traditional understanding of race discrimination. Indeed, African-American women have themselves been incomprehensible to the doctrine of discrimination since there are divergent standards of legal review under our constitutional law for race and gender. In order, then, to figure out what is the proper legal doctrine under which an African-American woman is to be judged, determinations have to be made as to whether she is one-half African-American, one-half woman, and so on. The absurdity of this dilemma has been pointed to in a series of articles by critical race theorists.[1] Under the theory of equality I advocate, hair braiding is an excellent example of African-American women choosing to represent their own sexuate being as it inevitably implicates both national and racial identification. They would easily be given standing as making a claim of right under my theory of equality.

The feminist purpose of this theory of equality is twofold. First, it serves to extensively critique and replace the single axis model of discrimination that has been so ineffective in recognizing the rights of African-American women, as well as other national differences among women that hardly

---

[1] See Kimberlé Crenshaw (1988).

could be articulated within the framework of Title VII and constitutional law. Another classic example of the failure of formal equality to recognize the specificity of the wrongs imposed on women of color are cases of Latinas who have claimed sexual harassment in the form of being demanded by bosses to speak "dirty" Spanish. Again, such cases frequently have been denied categorization as discrimination because they did not involve race or gender as defined in the model of formal equality that dominates current discrimination law.

Not only have the traditional legal theories of equality excluded women of color — I am reluctant to use the term *women of color* because, as I have argued elsewhere, one of the privileges of being white is that your color is erased so that you appear as the neutralized universal — they also have put gays and lesbians outside the reach of discrimination law. Again, by my concept of right, gays and lesbians easily would have access to the protections of discrimination law because, like all other sexuate beings, they would be granted the right to self-representation of their sexuate being. The basic legal conclusion of my theory of equality is that the state cannot impose the monogamous, heterosexual family because such an imposition violates the right of the person to represent her or his own sexuate being. Thus, it would no longer be a question of "tolerating" gays and lesbians as an acceptable "deviance" from the norm because any norm of the family would be outlawed by my theory of right. Patriarchy, as it necessarily involves the state imposition of the heterosexual, monogamous family as the good family, would be "outlawed" as a violation of the rights of persons. The second purpose of this theory of legal equality is an attempt to address, once again, the dilemma that Scott leaves us with in *Only Paradoxes to Offer* (1996): How can we both demand inclusion and reinterpret that demand away from reference to both white masculinity and to substantive characteristics that legally and paradoxically define us as victims or as other than persons worthy of entitlement?

The way in which women's "difference" is to be taken into account in my theory of equality is that it is to be defined by us in all of our diversity. The law should take a woman's experience into account by giving her the freedom to define what her experience means. The equal protection of the imaginary domain gives to women the right to differentiate themselves and to express their identifications in all their complexities, including their national and linguistic identifications. This theory is based on sameness, not on commonality or likeness, since it stems from the political recognition of all of us as free persons. The sameness always turns us back to the normative standard of what it means to be included in the moral community as a person as an initial matter. To summarize again, inclusion is now defined to contain the protection of the imaginary domain and the minimum conditions of individuation as what it means to be politically identified as a free person.

I   I   I

Does that mean, as Felski suggests, that all differences deserve respect? My answer to that has been as follows: in any theory of legal reform we are addressing the relationship of the individual to the state. There are two legally recognizable limits under my theory of equality as to how persons can express themselves both as sexuate beings and in the other identifications they wish to take on. The first is the obvious one, the prohibition of any form of outright, physical violence. But this limit would be enforced by criminal law. The second is what I call the "degradation prohibition." The degradation prohibition, as I define it, takes us back to what it means to be in the moral community of citizens as an initial matter. By degradation, I mean graded down, treated as less than a person who can represent her or his sexuate being. Obviously, if a gay or lesbian couple is denied access to housing, they are being treated as less than persons because the scope of their rights is being curtailed because of a prohibition against their sexuality that is being enforced by the state.

To emphasize again what I mean by the degradation prohibition and why it is irreducible to offense, let me give an example of the exact kind of complexity to which Felski refers when she questions how a society can legally grapple with identifications that seem to be at war with one another. Several years ago, a conflict arose between the Irish-American Gay, Lesbian and Bisexual Group of Boston (GLIB), who wished to parade openly as a contingent in Boston's St. Patrick's Day Parade, and the parade's organizers, who opposed their entry as openly gay and lesbian.[2] Ultimately, it was legally resolved by the U.S. Supreme Court, which did not allow GLIB to march in the parade. The Court ruled that the inclusion of GLIB violated the parade organizers' First Amendment right to exclude groups whose message they disagreed with. The political argument was over the question of what it means to be Irish. No doubt, for some, being Irish means being white, heterosexual, and Catholic. For others of us, being Irish means rebelling against all forms of unjust hierarchies. I consider myself to be an Irish woman in the latter sense. Under my theory of equality, this conflict would not have been resolved in a court of law. What it means to be Irish ultimately must be struggled with by those to whom it is a meaningful identification. This was not a case of degradation simply because some

[2] Hurley et al. v. Irish-American Gay, Lesbian and Bisexual Group of Boston, 115 U.S. 2338 (1995).

prominent Irish people were offended by the mere suggestion that gays and lesbians could march openly as a contingent in the parade. If they were offended, so be it. The contests over what it means to identify as an Irish person are best left to the streets.

❙ ❙ ❙

I obviously strongly agree with Felski that some theories of equality are better than others. Otherwise, I would not have spent so much time trying to develop one. Better in what sense? First, my argument displaces the equality/difference dichotomy and synchronizes the values of freedom and equality more effectively than other feminist theories of equality that have been defended.[3] What I mean by equivalence does turn us back to the theory of equality I advocate. It does not and cannot stand alone. In that sense I agree with Charles Taylor (1989) that any theory of rights certainly demands some normative framework in which better or worse is given meaning and differences themselves are evaluated.

The minimalist ideal of the imaginary domain, however, is also a reminder of the coercive power of the state that is endlessly deployed in law and the importance of what we traditionally have thought of as sexual freedom, even as it must be reconceived by feminists. I have reconceptualized "sexual freedom" in a platform of legal reform as the right of self-representation of our sexuate being. Its implications are far-reaching, since, as I will defend at great length in my forthcoming book, *At the Heart of Freedom,* the heterosexual, monogamous family could no longer be enforced as the normal family because to do so would violate the equivalent law of persons I advocate.

Second, the egalitarian theory that I advocate extends the reach of equality because it allows for the elaboration of the wrongs done to women of color that have previously remained unarticulable in the law. Again, I would return to the example of both the command to speak "dirty" Spanish and the denial of the right to speak Spanish in workplaces.

Third, my theory of equality is more effective in that it does not connect a theory of rights to any substantive view of women that would negate their entitlement as persons. That is the greatest paradox in Catharine MacKinnon's theory (1989). She positions women as nonpersons and therefore renders incoherent both their claim to full inclusion in the moral community and the critique of their reduction to object status.

I would defend my theory as a better synchronization of the values of freedom and equality than the other theories offered in feminist jurisprudence — and this defense would be pragmatic in the specific sense that it

[3] For a discussion of synchronization, see Cornell 1993a.

defends the value of its position by assuming a framework in which the ideal of the person is already granted as a postulate of practical reason. However, I would also agree with Rey Chow (1993) that any egalitarian theory developed in an engagement with the principles of Western constitutional democracy must be very carefully incorporated in a more worldwide program of human rights.

Before turning to Felski's interpretation of my reading of Lacan, I want to make a last comment on my theory of equality. The idea of minimum conditions of individuation clearly recognizes the legitimacy of Felski's argument that we are always engaging with a situation from which we differentiate ourselves. That is why throughout *The Imaginary Domain* I use the word *individuation* and not *the individual* or *autonomy*. I am in complete agreement with Charles Taylor's description of self-identification that Felski quotes. Taylor remarks, "Defining myself means finding what is significant in my difference from others" (1991, 35–36; quoted in Felski, 86). The theory of difference that Felski advocates is Hegelian, which is fine by me. Both Taylor and I come out of a long engagement with Hegel. The central idea of the imaginary domain—that is, that one is a person only as individuated and as protected in the process of individuation—is clearly Hegelian in its inspiration. Lacan was also deeply influenced by Hegel, and therefore it is not surprising that his incorporation of philosophical insight with psychoanalysis attracted me.

My engagement with Lacan was also inspired by the need to try to develop an explanation of the hold of patriarchy in Western democracies that at least superficially recognize women as equal citizens. Why is it so difficult for feminism to sustain itself as a movement and transmit its lessons to the next generation so that we can build on what we have achieved in the past rather than be fated to engage in the same battles over and over again? For instance, why can't we win the right of abortion and never have to talk about it again? My engagement with Lacan was also driven by my own desire to find a more adequate analysis of how race is engendered and how the meaning of "color" is perpetuated through unconscious fantasies that become the underpinnings of a symbolic order.

As I argued in *Transformations* when I engaged with the work of the anthropologist Gananath Obeyesekere (1990), my fundamental reason for relying on psychoanalysis is that we need to have an understanding both of how symbolic systems come to hold sway and of how they are governed inevitably by social fantasies. Of course, the very phrase "governed by fantasy" means that they cannot be firmly grounded and therefore are always open to transformation. I recognize that Lacan may seem like an unlikely ally in my argument that the barriers to transformation can never be *absolutely* effective in their erection. My argument in a series of books, starting with *Beyond Accommodation* (Cornell 1991), has been that Lacan's own analysis of the unconscious is incompatible with his defense of the phallus as a transcendental signifier. Thus, his claim to the absoluteness of the barrier to the symbolization of feminine sexual difference is deconstructed by his own insight. My argument in *Beyond Accommodation* was that phallogocentrism, because of it own logic, *cannot homogenize itself.* I strongly disagree with Felski's interpretation of my work as defending phallogocentrism's "homogenizing" force. For a true Lacanian, a woman who thinks she "is" beyond accommodation to patriarchical norms, let alone advocates a feminism that seeks to be beyond "accommodation," would be considered delusional — psychotic in the clinical sense. My alliance with Lacan, then, is about what he has right about the unconscious, *not* about his own philosophical defense of the positioning of the phallus as a transcendental signifier.

Let me return to my effort to rethink the eroticization of race. As I argued, in "What Takes Place in the Dark," in *Transformations* (Cornell 1993b), the conception of the "inessential woman" (Spelman 1988) lets white women off the hook too easily. In that essay I wanted to demonstrate that the relationship between African-American women and white women was a relationship of inequality and had to be addressed as that. As such, then, white women could not simply neutralize their own whiteness or their position of privilege in their relationships with African-American women. Felski seems not to note this persistent, if not relentless, argument on my part, that it is this inequality and privilege that has prevented solidarity among women of different nationalities, cultures, and linguistic traditions. To show the economy of the asymmetrical positioning of African-American and white women, as in part engendered by the eroticization of meanings of color, I have turned to Lacan's understanding of linguistics and particularly his linguistic analysis of the unconscious.

Lacan, following Saussure but also Hegel, argues that meaning and systems of representation only come to gain significance through the articulation of differential relations between signs and the elements of the signs themselves. It is the differential relationship between letters and words that supports the congelation of meaning we think of as a form of life. Meaning, in other words, is an established set of differential relationships. The "arising" of meaning out of differential relationships also allows for the gaps that open up the space for the possibility of transformation. Lacan's statement, that the signifier is privileged over the signified, means that there is no ontologically distinct order, for example, of race and gender, that can be separated from signifiers. The differential relation between the elements of the signs and the signs themselves means that each term needs another term to be understood and that term needs another and so on.

This on and on, or horizontal, process, in which meaning continually tries to create new meaning is what Lacan refers to as metonymy. Metonymy relies on the endless re-creation of the context that results in the intrajuxta-position of one term to another through contiguity. For Lacan, contiguity is itself a linguistic relation and is not based on any real relation between objects. Objects connected by metaphoric transference are also clearly in a linguistic relation. But, because for Lacan metaphor operates vertically, the transferential relationship is often erased in the congelation of meaning in which the substitution implied by the transference is taken for reality. The term that has been substituted easily falls below the bar of consciousness, thus continually producing the material of the unconscious. The substitu-tion process is identified by Lacan with the principle of condensation. In other words, metaphor, through the potential erasure implicit in substitu-tion, can make the replaced signifier disappear into the unconscious. The unconscious has no ontological status. The unconscious "is" only the signi-fiers that have disappeared because the process of condensation has erased the past in which they were pushed under.

I　I　I

I use a "real life" example to try to make what I know seem to be abstract arguments become vivid as a different way of analyzing race and gender. The example comes from a union drive in which I was involved. This story goes back twenty years or so to the time when I was a full-time union organizer. The solidarity between the workers broke down because one of the white women on the organizing committee developed a sexual rela-tionship with an African-American man who was a partner of one of the African-American women, who was also a leading activist in the factory. The African-American women on the committee asked me to give the white woman notice that if she continued to behave in this manner — fla-grantly having sex with this man in the parking lot — there would be conse-quences for her. There had already been consequences for the union drive. Ultimately, there was a serious scuffle between this white woman, who would not desist in her sexual activity with the African-American man, and several African-American women. The scuffle took place in the parking lot before all of our eyes. To see to it that I would not intervene and thus get hurt, I was escorted to my car and guarded by two women until the inci-dent had played out. The white woman left her job the next day. She was a member of a Marxist-Leninist organization to which I also belonged and justified her action in part because it expressed her adherence to "third world leadership." Obviously, the African-American women did not regard her action as a righteous political statement. She was a student at Stanford, and for her, the job and the success of the union drive was not a crucial matter of survival. But it was for the other women.

Those of us who remained after her departure worked to put our union drive back together. For me, it demanded a confrontation with the way in which my own sexual imago had been colored as white. The demand on the part of the African-American women was the recognition of the eroticization of privilege. The "white girl" is fantasized — obviously only by some black men — as the one who is desirable precisely because she is the woman of the Man. Femininity is modeled on this whitened desirable object, which, of course, has little to do with actual "white girls" but instead depicts how they exist in the imaginary of our culture. But this imaginary in which this "desired female" is represented is only too real. In *The Bluest Eye,* Toni Morrison portrays the rage at "white" dolls as hardly being child's play. The white "doll" is the other by which the black female child is judged as not desirable in her blackness: "I destroyed white baby dolls. But the dismembering of dolls was not the true horror. The truly horrifying thing was the transference of the same impulses to little white girls. The indifference with which I could have axed them was shaken only by my desire to do so. To discover what eluded me: the secret of the magic they weaved on others. What made people look at them and say 'Awwwww,' but not for me?" (Morrison 1970, 22).

Our organizing committee read *The Bluest Eye* together, and for me it was a moment of revelation of the "white skin privilege" inherent in who is marked as a desirable object, a "doll." Of course, as feminists, none of us would easily admit to embracing the desirability of the doll, the one who gets the "Awwwww." Who wants to be a "doll"? And yet on some unconscious plane, what white heterosexual woman has not sought safety and protection behind that "Awwwww"? In order for the solidarity to be remembered, those of us on our committee who were white had to confront the racialization of prettiness, color, and value. Since that time, I have never been able to "see" myself as other than white.

The demand on us was to understand the differential eroticized articulations through which "white" and "black" are given meaning. The relationship between African-American and white women exists as an asymmetrical relationship in which what is held in common can be recognized only by struggling with and against the asymmetrical positioning of white and black women. To understand white and black in this, the Lacanian manner helps us understand how the condensation of meaning creates a fundamental asymmetry that is inseparable from the way in which racial inequality is not only symbolized but also justified on a day-to-day basis. It would make it a mockery to assume that the experience of black and white women would be the same. But an understanding of this asymmetrical relationship would also deny that color can be reduced to a set of positive characteristics separate from the chain of signifiers in which it is given meaning. In other words, there are not just "white" and "black" women who are just there and can be reduced to their whiteness and blackness as if color could signify separately from the matrix of desire in which it is given meaning. What it means to be "white," in other words, can be grasped only in a relationship of privilege, not of difference, within the asymmetrical articulation of white and black womanhood. Lacan's insight into the linguistic "nature" of the unconscious can elaborate a different understanding of the asymmetrical positioning of African-American and white women, particularly as this coloration plays out in the way we are rendered visible and eroticized.

As a lifetime activist, I have been one of the "multitudes of women" engaged in cultural activity—"the artists, the revolutionaries, the mothers, the teachers"—and therefore have argued strongly against the idea that we are, again to quote Felski, "really nothing more than the passive vehicles of phallocentrism" (76). Here I believe that Felski collapses my position with that of Catharine MacKinnon, whom I critique (Cornell 1991). Unlike MacKinnon, I have insisted that part of the desirability of a psychoanalytic feminism is that it separates the masculine and the feminine from actual men and women. Indeed it separates, and necessarily so, patriarchal and phallic institutions from the lives of actual men. The phallic "ideal" is unattainable, as I have argued so many times, and in so many places, and does not exist, and yet because it is idealized, it is still sought after in representations of masculinity. But in spite of their phantasmatic underpinnings, the dynamics of castration are only too real. As Frantz Fanon has argued eloquently (1963), the rape of a people's "women" as a public enactment of castration is a mark of imperialist domination. An obvious example within the United States is lynching. In this horrifying ritual, castration is not only symbolized but also played out on the dead body of the hanged African-American man, whose penis is stuffed in his mouth. This is metaphor becoming living "theater" in the most horrific sense.

In spite of my critique of Felski's interpretation of my own reading of Lacan, I have come to see it as a legitimate and important question whether or not Lacan and Lacanianism inescapably privileges, and in spite of itself ontologizes, the divide between idealized masculinity and the feminine other.[4] Again, I want to stress idealized masculinity because of Lacan's insight into how and why the cultural organs of patriarchy are in no real sense in the interest of most men. In *Beyond Accommodation*, I use Beckett's

---

[4] Judith Butler has pushed me to confront the ontologizing of sexual difference in Lacan. See Butler 1995.

Happy Days to allegorize the suffering articulated by Beckett, an Irishman, of living with oneself as castrated from the standpoint of an idealized and unreachable masculinity. In my life, as a union organizer, I saw only too many times how the gap between an idealized masculinity and the failure to live up to it when deeply internalized norms of what it meant to be a man collapsed before economic disaster led to intense psychic suffering and, on certain tragic occasions, to suicide.

In spite of my criticism of Lacan, I have returned continually to him, at least up until *The Imaginary Domain,* not only to explain a linguistic basis of the unconscious and the role of fantasies as a work of culture, but also to explain the continuing bar on the articulation and affirmation of feminine sexual difference. Of course, in a deconstructive reading of Lacan, the bar is not "real," but just because it is not real does not mean that it does not have power or cannot operate.

The utopian aesthetic project which I continue to affirm wholeheartedly is a feminism involved in an endless struggle to rearticulate and reaffirm both the divergent and not-yet-dreamed-of ways of setting forth lives as sexuate beings. This project insists that feminism has an aesthetic dimension, but also that this aesthetic dimension is inseparable from the way in which "qualities" are given to women. The theory of equality gives to women of all nationalities and "races" the right to represent their own meaning of their racial, national, and sexual identification. The symbolic aspect of feminism implicates renaming and reshaping our form of life. A symbolic project is inseparable from any materialist feminism because how the world comes to be materialized is in language (Butler 1993). Within the legal world, an obvious example is the renaming of obsessive behaviors that previously were considered the way of the world — sexual harassment and date rape are two examples. But in the work of artists, cultural workers, mothers, teachers, union organizers, and activists of every sort, there is also this attempt to rename, resymbolize, and reimagine the world.

As I have already argued, I not only recognize but also insist on a feminist analysis that clearly sees that any actual specificity that is given to feminine sexual difference is inherently and necessarily racialized, nationalized, and linguistically conditioned. It is in Morrison's *Sula* that I find best described my own version of utopia, which would start with the turning of the world upside down:

"Oh, they'll love me all right. It will take time, but they'll love me." The sound of her voice was as soft and distant as the look in her eyes. "After all the old women have lain with the teen-agers; when all the young girls have slept with their old drunken uncles; after all the black men fuck all the white ones; when all the white women kiss all the black ones; when the guards have raped all the jailbirds and after all the whores make love to their grannies; after all the faggots get their mothers' trim; when Lindbergh sleeps with Bessie Smith and Norma Shearer makes it with Stepin Fetchit; after all the dogs have fucked all the cats and every weathervane on every barn flies off the roof to mount the hogs . . . then there'll be a little love left over for me. And I know just what it will feel like." (1973, 145–46)

My argument is that the feminine within sexual difference must be affirmed rather than repudiated if there is to be "a little love left over" for a woman "with glory in her heart." I begin with the basic Derridian insight that one cannot simply neutralize dichotomies. For if we repudiate the feminine, we end by reinstating its evaluation as the degraded other that no person would want to be. Of course, what it means not to repudiate the feminine, and to affirm it, can be determined, discussed, and contested only within the specifics of any historical struggle.

The heart of my response to Felski is reflected in the title *Divergent Differences*. If I have a criticism of Felski, it is that she pigeonholes many of the thinkers whom she addresses. I did not recognize my own interpretations of the other thinkers she discussed in her essay.

For example, I read Chandra Mohanty's article "Under Western Eyes: Feminist Scholarship and Colonial Discourse" (1984) differently than Felski. Mohanty brilliantly demonstrates the way in which the representation of "third world women" completely eclipses the national and linguistic specificity of those women. She also effectively argues that this representation is grounded in the projection of these "third world women" as a kind of absolute other. As Mohanty argues throughout her essay, the "third world woman" is identified as the victim, as the one who needs help, as opposed to the "freer" "first world woman." Of course, the words *third* and *first* already imply a hierarchy. This representation erases the specificity of the actual national struggles and also erases the accomplishments, dignity, and history of feminism in other parts of the world as they have developed and made a contribution not only to feminist theory but also to feminist politics throughout history.

To develop my point, I want to take the example of Puerto Rico. Puerto Rico has a unique political history with the United States because of its continual standing as a commonwealth. The political struggle of Puerto Ricans for national and linguistic identity is inseparable from this "unique" relationship with the United States. Indeed, the United States also has been deeply and profoundly influenced in its engagement with the Spanish language and its place in our political culture with Puerto Rico, as it has not with other Hispanic cultures, precisely because of this relationship.

Even the category "Hispanic" misrepresents many of the people in South America, because, of course, the Spanish language was brought there and imposed on the native populations at the time of imperialist invasion. If one identified Puerto Rican women as "third world," it would clearly erase their unique struggle within, and against, the United States and for their cultural and linguistic identity. "Third world women" are not just represented outside of their national context, they are also subjected to fantasies of themselves that undermine their historical accomplishments. Of course, this undermining, which translates itself into a view of the people, is inseparable from what I have called the symbolic underpinnings of imperialist domination.

Mohanty's work exemplifies the kind of work we need in order to expand the reach of the field of representation in which women can articulate their national and linguistic differences. Of course, there may be many times in which it will make sense for there to be unions and alliances of South American peoples and indeed of cultures and national identities that we think of as Hispanic. Nothing in Mohanty's work denies the desirability of such alliances, or the generalizations on which they may be based, in a particular political context any more than her article out of hand implies any critique of overarching theories of imperialist domination.

Felski reads a different theoretical ambition into Mohanty's work other than the one I find there. Felski, at least to some extent, is addressing straw women. Thus, I did not find it surprising that I did not agree with her interpretations of the work of either Ien Ang or Rosi Braidotti.

I do not have much to write about Madonna. But I do want to remember Eva Perón. Eva Perón was a relentless fighter for the rights of women's suffrage in Argentina. She was determined that under her rule with Perón, women would be given the right to vote. They were. The year she died, twenty-one women were elected and seated for Parliament for the first time. We now have a makeup kit called "Evita." Her political accomplishments are not given credit in either the movie with the "icon" or in the advertisement that tries to convince women that we cannot live without lipstick. The makeup kit is an only-too-vivid reminder of how "third world women" are remembered . . . as . . . sexual objects that can be reduced to the components of a made-up face. Where could Eva Perón be "truly remembered"? Only in the imaginary domain. Certainly not in Hollywood.

References
Brown, Wendy. 1995. *States of Injury: Essays on Power and Freedom in Late Modernity.* Princeton, N.J.: Princeton University Press.

Butler, Judith. 1993. *Bodies That Matter.* New York: Routledge.

———. 1995. "For a Careful Reading." In *Feminist Contentions: A Philosophical Exchange,* by Seyla Benhabib, Judith Butler, Drucilla Cornell, and Nancy Fraser, 127–43. New York: Routledge.

Caldwell, Paulette. 1991. "A Hair Piece: Perspectives on the Intersection of Race and Gender." *Duke Law Journal,* April, 365–96.

Chow, Rey. 1993. *Writing Diaspora: Tactics of Intervention in Contemporary Cultural Studies.* Bloomington: Indiana University Press.

Cornell, Drucilla. 1991. *Beyond Accommodation: Ethical Feminism, Deconstruction, and the Law.* New York: Routledge.

———. 1993a. "Pragmatism, Recollective Imagination, and Transformative Legal Interpretation." In her *Transformations: Recollective Imagination and Sexual Difference,* 23–44. New York: Routledge.

———. 1993b. "What Takes Place in the Dark." In her *Transformations: Recollective Imagination and Sexual Difference,* 170–94. New York: Routledge.

———. 1995. Introduction to her *The Imaginary Domain: Abortion, Pornography and Sexual Harassment,* 3–27. New York: Routledge.

———. In press. *At the Heart of Freedom: Sex, Equality and the Enactment of Personhood.* Princeton, N.J.: Princeton University Press.

Crenshaw, Kimberlé. 1988. "Race, Reform, and Retrenchment: Transformation and Legitimation in Anti-discrimination Law." *Harvard Law Review,* vol. 101 (May).

Fanon, Frantz. 1963. *The Wretched of the Earth.* New York: Grove.

Hegel, Georg W. F. 1967. *The Philosophy of Right,* trans. T. M. Knox. London: Oxford University Press.

MacKinnon, Catharine. 1989. *Toward a Feminist Theory of the State.* Cambridge, Mass.: Harvard University Press.

Mohanty, Chandra Talpade. 1984. "Under Western Eyes: Feminist Scholarship and Colonial Discourse." *boundary 2* 13(1):333–57.

Morrison, Toni. 1970. *The Bluest Eye.* New York: Penguin.

———. 1973. *Sula.* New York: Knopf.

Obeyesekere, Gananath. 1990. *The Work of Culture: Symbolic Transformation in Psychoanalysis and Anthropology.* Chicago: University of Chicago Press.

Scott, Joan. 1996. *Only Paradoxes to Offer: French Feminists and the Rights of Man.* Cambridge, Mass.: Harvard University Press.

Spelman, Elizabeth V. 1988. *Inessential Woman: Problems of Exclusion in Feminist Thought.* Boston: Beacon.

Taylor, Charles. 1989. *Sources of the Self: The Making of the Modern Identity.* Cambridge, Mass.: Harvard University Press.

———. 1991. *The Ethics of Authenticity.* Cambridge, Mass.: Harvard University Press. I

Comment on Felski's "The Doxa of Difference": The Uses of Incommensurability

Ien Ang, *Research Centre in Intercommunal Studies, University of Western Sydney*

R ita Felski's powerful critique of "the doxa of difference" (in this volume) addresses one of the most urgent and complex political predicaments of our time. The predicament can be described in deceptively simple terms: How are we to live together as the twentieth century draws to a close? "We" and "together" are the key sites of contestation here. In this postmodern world of multiplying claims to difference and proliferating pluralisms, any overarching sense of "we" has become fundamentally problematic and contentious. The emergence of what Cornel West has called "the new cultural politics of difference" has bred a profound suspicion of any hegemonizing, homogenizing, universalizing representation of "us" and nourished a strong resistance against modes of political mobilization on the basis of such representations, especially among those who used to be silenced or rendered invisible by them. In this climate, the very idea of living "together" becomes hugely daunting. Can togetherness be more than a coincidental and involuntary aggregation of individuals and groups being thrust into the same time and space, an uneasy and reluctant juxtapositioning of different bodies and identities forced to share a single world even if their respective imaginative worlds are worlds apart? What are the possibilities of constructing transcultural imagined communities in this era of rampant cultural differentiation and fragmentation? How, in short, can we live with difference?

Felski's intervention is motivated by a desire to reinstate the importance of "the seemingly obsolete issue of equality" (73), to avert the increasing fragmentation of the discarded "sisterhood" of the second wave into a proliferating and mutually exclusionary array of differences, and to rescue the possibility of women of different backgrounds to share a sense of commonality/community. She wants, in short, to reclaim the importance of "identity" (or sameness) in the face of what she perceives as an almost absolutist reign of "difference" in contemporary feminism. She does not want to do this, however, by recourse to a claim of natural or ontological similarity of all women (as in the old, essentialist notion of sisterhood) but by emphasizing its rhetorical quality and contextual usefulness. That is, she argues for a "*pragmatic* analysis of the contingent political utility adhering to either side of [the equality/difference] dialectic for specific groups of women" (88). In methodological terms, this amounts to the pronounce-ment of a mode of analysis that eschews abstract philosophical general-ization in favor of a theoretical conjuncturalism stressing the primacy of contextual specificity and strategic pragmatism. "Both the construction of commonality among subjects and the assertion of difference between sub-jects are rhetorical and political acts, gestures of affiliation and disaffiliation that emphasize some properties and obscure others. It is only in such con-tingent terms that their value can be assessed" (87).

In these general terms, I have no quarrel with Felski's perspective. I too believe that politics can proceed only if we are willing to settle our differ-ences in favor of a common goal, a shared project. I too am worried about the fact that we seem less and less capable of pursuing such common goals, of envisaging such shared projects. I too, in fact, think that theories of hybridity, however problematic, are crucial in our attempts to overcome the doxa of difference. As she puts it: "Metaphors of hybridity and the like not only recognize differences *within* the subject, fracturing and complicat-ing holistic notions of identity, but also address connections *between* sub-jects by recognizing affiliations, cross-pollinations, echoes, and repetitions, thereby unseating difference from a position of absolute privilege" (82; emphasis added). In other words, by recognizing the inescapable impurity of all cultures and the porousness of all cultural boundaries in an irrevoca-bly globalized, interconnected, and interdependent world, we may be able to conceive of our living together in terms of "complicated entanglement" (83), not in terms of insurmountable differences.

Unlike Felski, however, I do not believe that there are no longer cultural incommensurabilities in such a hybridized world. On the contrary, I be-lieve that acknowledgment and acceptance of moments of incommensura-bility are crucial if we are to make the most, politically and theoretically, of the condition of complicated entanglement in which we find ourselves. But I should add that my notion of incommensurability does not refer to an absolute and permanent incompatibility of totalized and mutually exclusive discursive universes (as Felski interprets it); rather, it points to the limits of and the partiality involved in all forms of communication and affiliation across lines of cultural division (Ang 1995). These limits operate as the (often unconscious) backdrop of our efforts to construct planes of commonality: we can only enter into dialogue with one another on the assumption that we can understand and comprehend each other, but to the extent that full mutual understanding (which would amount to full mutual identification and sameness) is impossible, the common discursive worlds we construct through our dialogues will always be necessarily partial. Incommensurability then pertains to the residue of the irreducibly particular that cannot, ultimately, be shared. It does not imply an absolute impossibility of communication, but relates to the occasional and interspersed moments of miscommunication (or breakdown of communication) that always accompany communicative interchanges between differently positioned subjects. Ironically, such moments of incommensurability, while generally not acknowledged as such, are precisely what propel us to go on communicating, forever chasing for an ultimate fullness of understanding and complete commonality that are never achieved. This does not mean that such effort to go on communicating is useless — indeed, our complicatedly entangled lives make it impossible for us *not* to go on communicating as we willingly or unwillingly negotiate over the partial understandings and incomplete commonalities we continue to produce. I will return to the centrality of negotiation in a moment. First, however, I want to elaborate on the cultural and political significance of the moments of incommensurability I have just discerned as lurking behind any communicative transaction.

I have to say that I am developing these ideas out of a sense of frustration precisely with the realization of incommensurable realities in my own life. Felski is right, of course, to say that black and white feminists can argue with each other because their discourses are shaped by overlapping conceptual frameworks and discursive regimes and because they use overlapping vocabularies and repertoires of meaning, and it is because I do position myself and am sufficiently proficient in the "language game" of cultural studies that I am able to intervene in feminist and critical debates on identity and difference, race and ethnicity, power and culture. In this regard I am "the same" (in the sense of having a common resource base) as my "white" friends and colleagues, and it is a sameness I cherish and value highly. But profound moments of incommensurability make themselves felt whenever I attempt to share my experiences with racism, for example. Time and again I have found myself in the uncomfortable position of realizing that I cannot bridge the gulf of difference separating me and my white counterparts, no matter how willingly they engage in the conversation (which is not, I should say, all that often when it comes to the personal politics of "race"): there is always a residual personal truth, the irreducibly particular experiential knowledge of being the object of racialized othering, which I cannot share and the impact and repercussions of which they cannot ever fully understand.

I do not intend to claim the authority of "experience" here, nor do I claim that the experience of racism is unmediated by a whole variety of discourses and social positionalities (it is precisely because of such mediations that those subjected to racist abuse can respond in so many different ways, from denial to self-hatred to political radicalism, although I would argue that there is always pain involved).[1] What I want to argue is that while racism can very easily be a shared theme for discussion about which we, sharing overlapping theoretical and conceptual vocabularies, can develop shared political understandings (and as something to be "against"), how we are each subjectively positioned very differently (and potentially antagonistically) in relation to the phenomenon is a much more difficult insight to share, perhaps precisely because it would necessitate an acknowledgment of the structural, historically entrenched asymmetry that places us on divergent sides of the polarity.[2] The subjective knowledge of what it means to be at the receiving end of racialized othering—whatever it means to individual people of color—is simply not accessible to white people, just as the subjective knowledge of what it means to be a woman—whatever it means to individual women—is ultimately inaccessible to men. To claim otherwise would be tantamount to a form of incorporation of the (nonwhite) other within the (white) self without confronting the otherness of the other. In short, the overlap in our frameworks, discursive regimes, and repertoires of meaning may indeed be more or less considerable, but it is never complete, and it is at those instances when the overlap falls away that moments of incommensurability occur.

Felski objects to the notion of incommensurability because it "does not allow for disagreement, critique, or persuasion because there are no common terms that would allow one argument to latch onto and address another" (83). But I hope to have clarified that our lives together do present us with moments when no common terms are available over which we can agree or disagree; these are moments that go beyond rational argument, and they mark areas of experience (which of course are historically constructed) that are, in some fundamental way, unspeakable, expressable only circuitously. Paul Gilroy, for example, has pointed to the unspeakability of the terror of the slave experience in the Americas, whose painful expression is articulated in the affective intensity of black music, which, in Gilroy's view, "provides an enhanced mode of communication beyond the petty power of words—spoken or written" (1993, 76). Gilroy goes on to note that this mode of communication, which is essentially phatic and not discursive, "challenges the privileged conceptions of both language and writing as preeminent expressions of human consciousness" (74). In a similar

[1] For a nonessentialist theorization of "experience," see Scott 1992.
[2] I have discussed this further in Ang 1995.

way, the complex mixture of pain, humiliation, rage, and shame taking hold of me after each seemingly mundane incident of racist name-calling ("go back to your own country!") is impossible to explain to those who have not had similar experiences, because words fail to capture the depth of those feelings. Yet often no discursive explanation is needed to establish a sense of "recognition" among other people of color (and other minoritized subjects) who *have* had similar experiences, who "know" what you are talking about without so many words.

No doubt the identifications occurring in the latter instance are no less of an imaginary nature than any other identificatory mirroring, and the resulting affirmation of "oppressed" commonality is a matter not simply of pregiven ontological sameness but of rhetorical and political construction. Furthermore, it is not my intention here to castigate white people for not "getting" it—far from it. What I would like "them" to do, however, is to *recognize* that they don't (quite) "get" it, to accept the fact that whether or not one is "white" in the (Western) societies we live in does make a fundamental difference to our experiential worlds (even though, importantly, we might share a whole lot of things as well) and that our respective experiential worlds are not easily reconcilable and mutually translatable into one another's discursive registers. Felski argues that such a "recourse to incommensurability" would be politically damaging and defeatist because it "legitimates . . . the inaccessibility of [the political concerns of women of color] to white women, who are thereby relieved of any need to engage with them" (83–84). I would suggest, however, that this does not have to be so: indeed, why should political affiliation and solidarity not be possible without the postulation of a fully shared world? A solidarity that is based on the statement: "I cannot know what it feels like to be racially abused, but I know it hurts you"—what Jodi Dean (1996) calls "a solidarity of strangers." Acknowledgment of incommensurability does not have to result in political paralysis, but it can be the starting point for common political pursuits if we accept that politics does not have to be premised on the construction of a solid, unified "we"—as in most conventional conceptions of politics including, as Dean (1996) shows, identity politics—but on the very fragility, delicacy, and uncertainty of any "we" we forge.

Indeed, in my view, Felski's "complicated entanglement" resides precisely in the uneasy and ongoing *tension* between incommensurability and commensurability, sameness and difference, togetherness and separateness. Robert Young's description of hybridity, partially quoted by Felski, is illuminating here: hybridity "operates according to the form of logic that Derrida isolates in the term 'brisure,' a breaking and a joining at the same time: difference and sameness in an *apparently impossible simultaneity*" (Young

1995, 35; my emphasis). In other words, insofar as hybridity "is not the third term that resolves the tension between two cultures . . . in a dialectical play of 'recognition'" (Bhabha 1994, 113–14), it does not, as Felski suggests, erase incommensurability but, rather, encapsulates it. "Complicated entanglement" means that the ultimate unassimilability of cultural differences necessarily remains unresolved in what Felski astutely calls "the logic of both/and" (82). This is why *negotiation* is the central term for what politics is about and why we need to elaborate with much greater sophistication what *negotiation* can mean in our efforts to create conditions in which we can learn to live with the apparently impossible simultaneity of incommensurable realities.

Let me close with an example from Australia, where I work and live. As is well known, the colonization of the island-continent by white Europeans from 1788 onward was accompanied by massive violence against and dispossession of the indigenous population. Thus, a fundamental incommensurability lies at the heart of modern Australian history and culture: what for white Australia has been the fortuitous "settlement" of the country, for indigenous people can only be seen as a tragic "invasion." For two centuries, this incommensurability was denied as the white occupation of the land was legitimized through the invention of *terra nullius,* the notion that the land was not inhabited before the Europeans came. In 1992, this colonial principle was officially overturned (in the so-called Mabo decision) as the High Court recognized that the land was never "empty" and acknowledged the right to "native title" for Aboriginal and Torres Strait Islander groups throughout the country. Needless to say, this recognition was received with great apprehension in many parts of white Australia, especially among those who felt that it damaged their material interests in the land, such as mining companies and farmers. The historic significance of this development cannot be overstated: in its (belated, reluctant) recognition of the injustice of the previous virtual annihilation of indigenous presence, it also, as a logical consequence, acknowledges the existence of ultimate incommensurable Aboriginal and white perspectives on Australian history, which are now to be seen as in complicated entanglement with one another.

I would argue that this discursive recognition of incommensurability has been overwhelmingly empowering for indigenous people, as it is precisely the "apparently impossible simultaneity" constructed by it that has turned the need for "reconciliation" between indigenous and nonindigenous Australians into one of the most urgent and prominent issues in contemporary Australian national life. "Reconciliation" is called for as historically constructed and inherited differences are ultimately unerasable, while we still have to live together, now, and in the future. For indigenous Australians, as Gatjil Djerrkura (1997), chairman of the Aboriginal and Torres Strait Islander Commission, puts it, "reconciliation means respect for our cultures, recognition of our prior occupancy of this land and regard for the rights that result from that history." That this is not going to be easy is clear from further developments. The Mabo judgment was followed in December 1996 by another one (the so-called Wik decision), in which the High Court declared, contrary to general expectations, that pastoral leases did not automatically extinguish native title; that native title rights and the rights of the lease-holding pastoralists could legally "coexist"; and that the pragmatic terms of this "coexistence" should be negotiated. The very notion of "coexistence" signifies an acceptance of two distinct, partially incommensurable realities that need to be "reconciled." But those opposed to the judgment responded angrily that such "coexistence" would breed an "uncertainty unacceptable for the system of land tenure and for economic activity and future investment" (*Weekend Australian* 1997, 16); they demanded a speedy removal of that "uncertainty" through the wholesale legislative "extinguishment" of native title on pastoral leases. From this perspective, as Djerrkura (1997) observes, "reconciliation seems to be an asset to be traded, or perhaps a favour to be granted or withheld." In other words, the very meaning of "reconciliation" is hotly contested and prone to incommensurability: its importance for indigenous Australians in their search for dignity and justice (the affective dimension of which may never be fully grasped by white Australians) is matched by its meaning as a political nuisance and economic liability by their opponents. That is, the idea of "reconciliation," proposed today as the common goal for the Australian nation as a whole to come to terms with a dark episode of its past, can only produce a fragile, vulnerable "we," which needs to be constantly nurtured and nourished if it is to survive. Opponents of indigenous rights want to get rid of the discomfort of incommensurability that comes with the recognition of "coexistence": they refuse to accept the "uncertainty" that comes with the embracement of "reconciliation." But we must learn to live with the fact that uncertainty is inherent in the operation of the logic of the both/and encapsulated in the idea of reconciliation and that ongoing negotiation is the (small) price we have to pay to make it work.

Incommensurability means that because we are products of distinct, sometimes conflicting, nonreconcilable but complicatedly entangled histories, the task of sorting out our differences will always be a difficult, never-ending, and partial negotiatory process; accepting (rather than rejecting) its consequences may be the only hope we have for a common hybridized future no longer determined by totalizing, universalizing, all-assimilating truths.

References

Ang, Ien. 1995. "I'm a Feminist but . . . 'Other' Women and Postnational Feminism." In *Transitions: New Australian Feminisms*, ed. Barbara Caine and Rosemary Pringle, 57–73. New York: St. Martin's.

Bhabha, Homi. 1994. *The Location of Culture*. London: Routledge.

Dean, Jodi. 1996. *Solidarity of Strangers: Feminism after Identity Politics*. Berkeley, Los Angeles, and London: University of California Press.

Djerrkura, Gatjil. 1997. "Giving Wik Its Worth," *Sydney Morning Herald*, January 23.

Gilroy, Paul. 1993. *The Black Atlantic: Modernity and Double Consciousness*. London: Verso.

Scott, Joan W. 1992. "'Experience.'" In *Feminists Theorize the Political*, ed. Judith Butler and Joan W. Scott, 22–40. New York and London: Routledge.

Weekend Australian. 1997. "Editorial." *Weekend Australian*, January 4–5.

Young, Robert. 1995. *Colonial Desire: Hybridity in Theory, Culture and Race*. London: Routledge. I

Reply to Braidotti, Cornell, and Ang

Rita Felski, *Department of English, University of Virginia*

would like to thank Ien Ang, Rosi Braidotti, and Drucilla Cornell for their courteous and comprehensive responses to my article (in this volume).

My main point of disagreement with Ang, as her reply recognizes, focused on the issue of "incommensurability." This term was used originally by philosophers of science such as Thomas Kuhn to describe differences between competing scientific theories that could not be resolved by appealing to the facts because what counted as a fact was already predetermined by the theory-paradigm. The idea of incommensurability was enthusiastically taken up in the social sciences as a way of talking about historical and cultural differences, but in rather ambiguous and even contradictory ways. Some theorists have interpreted *incommensurability* as referring to a clash of rival frameworks that share no common points of reference or compari-

Thanks to Allan Megill for helpful discussions about incommensurability.

son. In other instances, incommensurability is understood as referring to the coexistence of paradigms that may be comparable at various points but that cannot be synthesized into an ultimate unity where all disagreements are resolved.[1]

Some of Ang's original formulations led me to think that she was using incommensurability in the first sense, which is the one I find theoretically and politically problematic. Her response suggests, however, that she is using incommensurability in yet another sense, to refer to instances of miscommunication that arise from the irreducible particularity of social experience. Incommensurability, in other words, is less about the incompatibility of frameworks or paradigms, as in Kuhn's usage, than about the incomprehensibility of particular experiential knowledges, knowledges that in fact may not be fully expressible in language.[2] Thus, Ang describes certain emotionally charged areas of experience as in some fundamental sense unspeakable, noting that "words fail to capture the depth of those feelings" (131).

Assuming that I have understood Ang's argument correctly, I do not disagree with her claim that the positions of white women and women of color are "incommensurable" in this specific sense. Clearly, as a white woman I cannot share or fully understand the "irreducibly particular experiential knowledge of being the object of racialized othering" (129). There will, in this sense, always be fundamental differences of perspective and, arguably, conflicts of interest among women arising from their specific positions in the social world. My point was simply to argue that if interpretative frameworks were nothing more than the products of contrasting and mutually incomprehensible experiential knowledges, there would be no possibility of individuals ever recognizing or condemning an injustice they had not themselves directly experienced. For example, Ang's anecdote about racist name-calling invokes a phenomenological experience of pain and humiliation engendered by everyday encounters with racism, which cannot be fully grasped by those who do not routinely have such encounters. But it also invokes a truth claim and a moral imperative (this personal experience is symptomatic of pervasive and systematic racist structures; such structures are unjust), which speak to shared epistemological and

---

[1] For a useful survey of the debates on incommensurability, see Bernstein 1989, 1992.

[2] Ang's usage thus differs from Kuhn's not only in focusing on experiences rather than paradigms but in equating incommensurability with incomprehensibility. Within a Kuhnian model there is no necessary connection between these two terms. For example, a scientist may fully understand a rival paradigm that is nevertheless incommensurable with her own. Similarly, individuals who work within the same paradigm are not precluded thereby from misunderstanding each other.

moral frameworks and are thus in principle accessible to those "outside" the experience.

Any account of the politics of discourse surely needs to engage with both of these aspects of the communicative act if it is to be persuasive. For this reason, I find myself very much in sympathy with the more dialectical tone of Ang's response, which acknowledges both the possibility and necessity of communication between differently positioned subjects and the inevitable limits of any such communicative acts. As she writes, "we can only enter into dialogue with one another on the assumption that we can understand and comprehend each other, but to the extent that full mutual understanding (which would amount to full mutual identification and sameness) is impossible, the common discursive worlds we construct through our dialogues will always be necessarily partial" (128). This strikes me as exactly right, as does her assertion that political affiliation cannot and should not rely on the postulation of a fully shared world.

Drucilla Cornell chooses in her response to focus on her most recent book, *The Imaginary Domain,* which had not yet been published when I sent my paper to *Signs* in 1995. Her reply prompted me to read the book, which does indeed develop a feminist theory of legal equality. I am very much in agreement with most of Cornell's arguments in *The Imaginary Domain,* including her defense of a limited concept of universality in the legal domain and her turn to a Kantian-inspired notion of practical reason. The book strikes me as an important and valuable contribution to feminist theory, which in fact does speak to a number of the issues I raised in my article. Cornell's reliance on the work of liberal theorists such as John Rawls, however, does mark a dramatic shift away from the poststructuralist tenor of her previous writings.

On the issue of Lacan, my point was not that Cornell endorses Lacan's homogenization of culture, but that her own insistence on the importance of social transformation seems at odds with the premises of a Lacanian framework. Of course, she is right to point out that the central role of fantasy and the unconscious in psychoanalysis does allow for slippage across the masculine/feminine divide. For example, my original reference to the monolithic portrayal of masculinity within Lacanian theory was somewhat misleading. The phallus, as we now all know, is not the penis, and some feminist theorists, including Cornell, draw from Lacan a recognition of the sham of patriarchal authority and the internal fissures within masculinity. Yet this recognition remains a highly abstract one, which cannot adequately explain the dramatic power differentials between men of different races and classes. Furthermore, it also collapses the social into the psychic in problematic ways. For example, male ambivalence toward traditional norms of phallic masculinity and men's espousal of the feminine need not prevent them from wielding significant power, given the increasingly feminized, therapeutic, consumer-oriented logic of late capitalist culture.[3]

On the issue of race, my point was not to keep a tally of how frequently sexual difference theorists mention race (this kind of moralistic point-scoring would be inappropriate and hypocritical on my part) but to raise the question of whether racial hierarchies *in principle* can be adequately theorized through a psychoanalytical framework. Undoubtedly, images of racial difference contain an imaginary, often an explicitly erotic, component, but I simply do not think that the politics of race, which necessarily involves the economics of race, can be fully apprehended through the vocabulary of fantasy and desire. In this regard, there remains a fundamental disagreement (dare I say incommensurability?) between feminists such as Cornell who believe that psychoanalysis can provide an adequate basis for a critical social theory and feminists such as myself who do not.[4] I agree, of course, with the view that racial difference is formed hierarchically and relationally, but it is not clear to me why theorists of race need to turn to Lacan for this elementary insight.

Rosi Braidotti is right to point out that the prestige of poststructuralism is primarily an American rather than a European phenomenon, but I find the rest of her introductory comments to be unfair and contradictory. My original observation that sexual difference theorists are "writing in Europe, Australia, and the United States" simply records the fact that sexual difference theory is a transnational rather than a national phenomenon. Note that I do not identify any individual theorist with a particular country, nor do I at any point read sexual difference theory through a nationalist framework. On the contrary, it is Braidotti herself who continually reduces theoretical positions to geopolitical distinctions. She begins by reading my position as symptomatic of "North American readings of philosophies of difference" (93) and refers repeatedly to American misunderstandings of European culture in responding to my arguments. As someone who was raised in England, who has spent most of her adult life in Australia, and whose intellectual training is in European literature and critical theory, I am surprised to find myself (mis)represented in this way as the voice of American feminism. Similarly, Braidotti reifies a monolithic notion of

[3] Maria Angel and Zoe Sofia (1996) have argued recently that Lacanian theory cannot adequately explain the symbolic logic of late capitalist consumer culture, which is increasingly organized around oral and excremental, rather than phallic, metaphors.

[4] For a wide-ranging critique of the psychotherapeutic ideologies underpinning recent feminist theories of sexual difference and the body, see Bray 1997.

"European feminism" or "Continental theory" as *the* ultimate context and justification for her own work, even though, as she acknowledges, poststructuralism is by no means a dominant European intellectual framework. The diverse feminisms emanating from Europe in fact have included extended critiques of the race and class biases of sexual difference theory, most obviously, but by no means exclusively, in Britain.

Braidotti's comments are lengthy and raise numerous issues; as I was asked to keep my response short, I can only respond to a couple of them. She wonders why I fail to address the concept of nomadism in her work (my article in fact does note, very briefly, my reservations about the term). Let me expand on those reservations. As I acknowledge in my original article, all metaphors in some sense are problematic and open to critique, but the figure of the nomad does seem particularly fraught as a celebratory image for either feminist or postcolonial theory, for obvious reasons. The problems are summarized clearly by Irene Gedalof:

> There is of course the suggestion of class privilege that allows for the purely joyful and voluntary mobility of the nomad as high-flying academic, which has little in common with the forced, or at least more uncomfortable and complicated, trajectories of migrants, exiles, and others who travel without tenure. But I would also argue that Braidotti's figuration emerges from an unexamined race- and nation-inflected privilege as well. Put simply, it is so much easier for white westerners to refuse the limits of fixed racial or national identities, when "whiteness" and "westernness" continue to function as the invisible, unmarked norms that don't seem to fix identity at all. (1996, 193)

In relation to Braidotti's comments on difference and the crisis of European humanism, my original article noted some of my reservations about the postmodernist discourse of "crisis," which reinscribes grand historical narratives at the very moment that it appears to be questioning them. In my own view, poststructuralist theory is neither necessary for nor antithetical to political struggles around either gender or race. Sometimes poststructuralist ideas are integrated effectively into arguments attentive to historical and cultural specificity, and sometimes they are not. As I originally argued, I do not think that the form of poststructuralism known as sexual difference theory has been able to achieve such context specificity, primarily because of its excessive reliance on the work of Lacan.[5] For example, the concept of mimesis as subversive repetition is of little use unless it is an-

---

[5] On this point, see Nancy Fraser's (1992) excellent discussion.

chored in a multidimensional social theory that can provide meaningful criteria for evaluating which forms of repetition are "subversive" and which are not. I have yet to see such an account and, consequently, find Braidotti's claim that sexual difference theory is "a radical form of materialism that embeds the subject in his/her specific set of power formations" (103) to be misleading.

References

Angel, Maria, and Zoe Sofia. 1996. "Cooking Up: Intestinal Economies and the Aesthetics of Specular Orality." *Cultural Studies* 10(3):464–82.

Bernstein, Richard J. 1989. *Beyond Objectivism and Relativism*. Oxford: Basil Blackwell.

———. 1992. *The New Constellation: The Ethical-Political Horizons of Modernity/Post-Modernity*. Cambridge, Mass.: MIT Press.

Bray, Abigail. 1997. "Corporeal Feminism and the Ill Logic of (Dis)embodiment." Ph.D. dissertation, Murdoch University, Australia.

Fraser, Nancy. 1992. "The Uses and Abuses of French Discourse Theories for Feminist Politics." *Theory, Culture and Society* 9(1):51–71.

Gedalof, Irene. 1996. "Can Nomads Learn to Count to Four? Rosi Braidotti and the Space for Difference in Feminist Theory." *Women: A Cultural Review* 7(2):189–201.

Confounding Gender

Gender is an a priori qualifying of one's intending, affecting not merely
what one perceives but what one is, partly as a fact of one's life and partly
as an issue dominating the meaning of one's life.
— Smith 1992, 55

It is not possible to live 24 hours a day soaked in the immediate awareness
of one's sex. Gendered self-consciousness has, mercifully, a fleeting nature.
— Riley 1988, 96

At the moment of political shock, Chinese women become degendered,
and join everyone else as "Chinese."
— Chow, 1991, 95

The natural attitude

Last summer at a family gathering, my mother asked what I would be
working on during my sabbatical. "Gender," I responded. "You mean
gender bias?" she asked helpfully. "No, gender," I said. There ensued
an awkward silence, then my sixteen-year-old nephew quipped, "There are
men and there are women. What more is there to say? Short book."

Both the awkward silence and my nephew's untroubled response can be
understood as manifestations of what Harold Garfinkel called the "natural
attitude" toward gender. The natural attitude encompasses a series of "unquestionable" axioms about gender, including the beliefs that there are two
and only two genders; gender is invariant; genitals are the essential signs
of gender; the male/female dichotomy is natural; being masculine or feminine is natural and not a matter of choice; all individuals can (and must)
be classified as masculine or feminine — any deviation from such a classification being either a joke or a pathology. According to Garfinkel, the beliefs constituting the natural attitude are "incorrigible" in that they are held
with such conviction that it is nearly impossible to challenge their validity
(1967, 122–28).

I would like to thank Nancy Theriot, Susan Griffin, Philip Alperson, and several *Signs*
reviewers for their helpful comments on earlier versions of this article.

[*Signs: Journal of Women in Culture and Society* 1997, vol. 22, no. 3]

Slip slidin' away

While the nature of gender remains a matter of pure self-evidence for those within the grips of the natural attitude, it has become a highly contested concept within feminist theory. In the past decade, gender has become the central analytic concept in women's studies and indeed has been the focal point for the development of new interdisciplinary programs (gender studies) in colleges and universities across the United States. Although originally a linguistic category denoting a system of subdivision within a grammatical class, feminist scholars adopted the concept of gender to distinguish culturally specific characteristics associated with masculinity and femininity from biological features (male and female chromosomes, hormones, as well as internal and external sexual and reproductive organs). Early feminist scholars used gender to repudiate biological determinism by demonstrating the range of variation in cultural constructions of femininity and masculinity. In more recent works, others use gender to analyze the social organization of relationships between men and women (Rubin 1975; Barrett 1980; MacKinnon 1987); to investigate the reification of human differences (Vetterling-Braggin 1982; Hawkesworth 1990; Shanley and Pateman 1991); to conceptualize the semiotics of the body, sex, and sexuality (de Lauretis 1984; Suleiman 1985; Doane 1987; Silverman 1988); to explain the distribution of burdens and benefits in society (Walby 1986; Connell 1987; Boneparth and Stoper 1988); to illustrate the microtechniques of power (de Lauretis 1987; Sawicki 1991); to illuminate the structure of the psyche (Chodorow 1978); and to account for individual identity and aspiration (Epperson 1988; Butler 1990).

Discussions of gender in history, language, literature and the arts, education, the media, politics, psychology, religion, medicine and science, society, law, and the workplace have become staples of contemporary feminist scholarship. As research on gender proliferates, so does the tendency to assume that the meaning of gender is unproblematic. Different scholars use gender in markedly different ways, however. Gender has been analyzed as an attribute of individuals (Bem 1974, 1983), as an interpersonal relation (Spelman 1988), and as a mode of social organization (Firestone 1970; Eisenstein 1979). Gender has been defined in terms of status (Lopata and Thorne 1978), sex roles (Amundsen 1971; Epstein 1971; Janeway 1971), and sexual stereotypes (Friedan 1963; Anderson 1983). It has been conceived of as a structure of consciousness (Rowbotham 1973), as triangulated psyche (Chodorow 1978), and as internalized ideology (Barrett 1980; Grant 1993). It has been discussed as a product of attribution (Kessler and McKenna 1978), socialization (Ruddick 1980; Gilligan 1982), disciplinary practices (Butler 1990; Singer 1993), and accustomed stance (Devor 1989). Gender has been depicted as an effect of language (Daly 1978; Spender 1980); a matter of behavioral conformity (Amundsen 1971; Epstein 1971); a structural feature of labor, power, and cathexis (Connell 1987); and a mode of perception (Kessler and McKenna 1978; Bem 1993). Gender has been cast in terms of a binary opposition, variable and varying continua, and in terms of a layering of personality. It has been characterized as difference (Irigaray 1985a, 1985b) and as relations of power manifested in domination and subordination (MacKinnon 1987; Gordon 1988). It has been construed in the passive mode of seriality (Young 1994), and in the active mode, as a process creating interdependence (Levi-Strauss 1969, 1971; Smith 1992), or as an instrument of segregation and exclusion (Davis 1981; Collins 1990). Gender has been denounced as a prison house (Cornell and Thurschwell 1986) and embraced as inherently liberating (Irigaray 1985b; Smith 1992). It has been identified as a universal phenomenon (Lerner 1986) and as a historically specific consequence of modernity's increasing sexualization of women (Riley 1988).

Should this multiplicity of meaning be a source of concern to feminist scholars? Can one concept encompass such a vast terrain? Does deployment of gender as an analytic category enhance our understanding of the various modes of oppression that circumscribe women's lives? A number of feminist scholars have recently raised questions about the utility of gender as an analytic category, although the multiplicity of meanings of the term has not been the focal point of their critique. Susan Bordo has identified two currents fueling the emergence of a new "gender skepticism" (1993, 216). One current flows from the experiences of women of color and lesbian feminists who have suggested that the "multiple jeopardy" characteristic of their lives raises serious questions about the validity of gender generalizations. If gender is always mediated by race, class, ethnicity, and sexual orientation, then an analytic framework that isolates gender or construes gender in terms of an "additive model" is seriously flawed and may serve only to mask the numerous privileges of white, heterosexual, middle-class feminists who have the luxury of experiencing only one mode of oppression (King 1988; Spelman 1988; Higginbotham 1992; Brewer 1993). The other current flows from postmodern criticism that depicts gender narratives as totalizing fictions that create a false unity out of heterogeneous elements. In addition to calling into question the binary opposition that fixes men and women in permanent relations of domination and subordination, postmodern critics have also challenged the "ground" of the sex/gender distinction. If gender was devised to illuminate the social construction of masculinity and femininity and naively took the sexed body as given, then it has little to offer in a postmodern world that understands the body, sex, and sexuality as socially constructed.

Acknowledging the importance of the issues raised by women of color, lesbian feminists, and postmodern feminists, several feminist scholars have offered a defense of feminist uses of gender, suggesting that a sophisticated conception of gender can incorporate the central points made by these critics. In an important and influential essay, Joan Scott defines gender as a concept involving two interrelated but analytically distinct parts. "Gender is a constitutive element of social relationships based on perceived differences between the sexes, and gender is a primary way of signifying relationships of power" (1986, 1067). In explicating gender as a constitutive element of social relationships, Scott emphasizes that gender operates in multiple fields, including culturally available symbols that evoke multiple representations; normative concepts that set forth interpretations of the meanings of symbols; social institutions and organizations; and subjective identity (1067–68). According to Scott, gender is a useful category of analysis because it "provides a way to decode meaning and to understand the complex connections among various forms of human interaction" (1070). Noting that gender is always contextually defined and repeatedly constructed, Scott cautions that gender analysts must not replicate the mistakes of early feminist accounts that credited gender as a universal causal force. On the contrary, gender analysts must seek a "genuine historicization and deconstruction of the terms of sexual difference" (1065). Scott demonstrates that problematic theoretical assumptions informing radical feminism, Marxist feminism, and psychoanalytic feminism gave rise to a variety of misapplications of gender as an analytic category, resulting in ahistorical analyses, oversimplified and reductive explanations, universal generalizations impervious to change in history, exclusive fixation on the "subject," and restrictive foci on the family or the household. Such flaws need not be endemic to gender analysis, however. Indeed, Scott argues that a self-critical deployment of gender analysis has provided and could provide meaningful explanations of historically and culturally specific relations obtaining between individual subjects and modes of social organization. If feminist scholars examine "how things happened in order to find out why they happened" (1067), their analytic investigations will enable them to reverse and displace the binary and hierarchical construction of gender, refuting the naive belief that gender "is real or self-evident or in the nature of things" (1066).

Sandra Harding has also advanced a defense of gender as an analytic category. "The fact that there are class, race, and cultural differences between women and between men is not, as some have thought, a reason to find gender difference either theoretically unimportant or politically irrelevant. In virtually every culture, gender difference is a pivotal way in which humans identify themselves as persons, organize social relations, and symbolize meaningful natural and social events and processes" (1986, 18). The very pervasiveness of gender requires systematic feminist analysis. Thus, Harding argues that feminists must theorize gender, conceiving of it as "an analytic category within which humans think about and organize their social activity rather than as a natural consequence of sex difference, or even merely as a social variable assigned to individual people in different ways from culture to culture" (17). Recognizing that gender appears only in culturally specific forms in no way mitigates the force of gender analysis. On the contrary, gender as an analytic category illuminates crucial cultural processes. "Gendered social life is produced through three distinct processes: it is the result of assigning dualistic gender metaphors to various perceived dichotomies that rarely have anything to do with sex differences (gender symbolism); it is the consequence of appealing to these gender dualisms to organize social activity, dividing necessary social activities between different groups of humans (gender structure); it is a form of socially constructed individual identity only imperfectly correlated with either the reality or the perception of sex differences (individual gender)" (17–18). According to Harding, feminist investigations of gender symbolism, gender structure, and individual gender challenge the basic presuppositions of the natural attitude, thereby helping to dispel essentialized identities, while creating the possibility of a politics grounded in solidarities that cross the divisions of race, class, age, ethnicity, and sexual orientation.

The defense of gender as an analytic category advanced by Scott and Harding suggests that the concerns of gender skeptics can be incorporated into a sophisticated conception of gender. Their defense also tends to mute concern about the multiplicity of meanings accorded gender in contemporary feminist scholarship, for they provide a coherent account of the intricate connections linking psyche to social organization, social roles to cultural symbols, normative beliefs to "the experience" of the body and sexuality. Indeed, they suggest that feminist research into such connections can undermine the mistaken beliefs informing the natural attitude. Thus their defense also provides a bridge linking feminist scholarship to feminist politics outside the academy. Feminist research designed to confound gender provides the analytic tools to loosen the strictures of the natural attitude and the oppressive social relations that the natural attitude legitimates.

Are Scott and Harding correct about the potential of gender as an analytic category? Can gender be deployed as an analytic tool that escapes (or dispels) the natural attitude? Can attention to the historicity of gender enable feminists to avoid universal causal claims, grand narratives, and totalizing accounts? How does the use of gender as an analytic category fit in with a thoroughgoing understanding of the social construction of the body?

To explore these questions, this article investigates four efforts to theorize gender: Steven Smith's *Gender Thinking* (1992), Judith Butler's *Gender Trouble* (1990), R. W. Connell's *Gender and Power* (1987), and Suzanne Kessler and Wendy McKenna's *Gender: An Ethnomethodological Approach* (1978). These four works are the most ambitious efforts that I have found to theorize gender in ways that connect psyche, self, and social relations. They also represent some of the major methodological approaches (phenomenology, postmodern deconstruction, dialectical materialism, ethnomethodology) currently vying for the allegiance of feminist scholars. Each of these accounts casts itself as a systematic, feminist analysis of gender. Each examines the multiple domains of gender, ranging across cultural symbols, normative concepts, social institutions, and subjective identities. Each conforms to Scott's directive to focus on *how* in order to explain *why* gender works. Each starts from the premise that the body is socially constituted and culturally mediated. And each advances arguments that challenge fundamental presuppositions of the natural attitude. Emerging from and drawing upon different methodological traditions, each advances a markedly different account of gender. Yet, despite the diversity and richness of these accounts, each also constructs a tale of gender that is markedly unsettling.

I argue that despite important differences in their approaches to and their conceptions of gender, these works construct a narrative that implicates gender in "the ideology of procreation."[1] In so doing, these texts illuminate presuppositions that replicate rather than undermine the natural attitude. That such troubling presuppositions surface in accounts of gender that grow out of markedly different theoretical projects should be of concern to feminist scholars, for the presuppositions that structure this narrative of gender stand in stark contrast to the emancipatory project of feminist scholarship. Excavating the assumptions in these works, then, can help to identify the danger points in certain deployments of gender, dangers that arise in a subtle shift from using gender as analytic tool to attributing to gender explanatory force.[2] Interrogating the conceptual tools of

[1] Michele Barrett defines the "ideology of procreation" as conceptions of sexuality that construe sexual behavior only in relation to reproduction (1980, 62–77).

[2] I have learned a great deal from each of these insightful texts. Each helps clarify many assumptions about gender that surface in other works. I have selected these four texts, in part, because they illuminate a conflation of analytic category and explanation that is charac-

feminist scholarship can help feminist scholars avoid these potential pit-falls. I offer this analysis in an effort to mark the dangers that lurk in certain uses of gender as a mode of explanation, rather than as an analytic category. Before turning to that task, I explore the meaning of gender as an analytic category and introduce a number of conceptual distinctions that may help make feminist claims about gender less confounding.

Mapping the conceptual terrain

What does it mean to use gender as an analytic category? Neither Scott nor Harding explicitly addresses this question, but both seem to use the term in a semitechnical sense drawn from the philosophy of science. In this sense, an analytic category can be understood as a heuristic device that performs both positive and negative functions in a research program (Lakatos 1970). As a positive heuristic, gender illuminates an area of inquiry, framing a set of questions for investigation. Although it need not involve any explicit methodological commitment, gender as analytic tool identifies puzzles or problems in need of exploration or clarification and provides concepts, definitions, and hypotheses to guide research. By demonstrating in their own work the intricate interrelations of symbol systems, normative precepts, social structures, and subjective identities subsumed under gen-der's rubric, Scott and Harding invite other scholars to probe these diverse domains to discover how culturally specific gender relations are created, sustained, and transformed. The very notion of a positive heuristic is tenta-tive, suggesting a trial-and-error method of problem solving requiring the collective efforts of multiple scholars to advance the field. But the notion of a "negative heuristic" developed by Imre Lakatos suggests a shared set of assumptions so central to a mode of analysis that they cannot be jetti-soned (1970, 132). Given gender's original meaning in feminist discourse and the frequency with which feminist scholars reiterate this goal, the neg-ative heuristic of gender analysis could be "to contest the naturalization of sex differences in multiple arenas of struggle" (Haraway 1991, 131). The use of gender as an analytic category, then, would be intimately bound up with challenges to the natural attitude.

The terminology developed within feminist discourses on gender

---

teristic of many other feminist works. The recurrent attribution of explanatory force to gen-der in these markedly differing accounts suggests a need to interrogate the concept more thoroughly to see how to avoid this problematic move. In an article of this length, I cannot demonstrate that the narrative of gender that I trace in these four works is representative of a much larger current in contemporary feminist scholarship, although I believe this is the case. In my own reading of contemporary feminist research, I have found that many works present in compressed form the narrative of gender that these works develop in greater detail.

certainly suggests the centrality of efforts to challenge the natural attitude. Feminist scholars have introduced a number of important distinctions to illuminate the complexity of gender: sex, sexuality, sexual identity, gender identity, gender role, gender-role identity. Virtually all scholars working in the field employ some of these distinctions, although all scholars do not use the terms in the same way. Sex, for example, can refer to the biological features such as chromosomes, hormones, internal and external sexual and reproductive organs, or to acts romantically characterized as lovemaking. Gender identity typically refers to the individual's own feeling of being a man or a woman, but this "feeling" may be defined in a rudimentary sense as having a conviction that one's sex assignment at birth was "anatomically and psychologically correct" (Stoller 1985, 11) or more expansively as a patterned subjectivity that bears some relation to cultural conceptions of masculinity or femininity.[3] Although usage varies from text to text, most feminist scholars would grant that there are important conceptual differences between sex construed in biological terms; sexuality understood to encompass sexual practices and erotic behavior; sexual identity referring to designations such as heterosexual, homosexual/gay/lesbian/queer, bisexual, or asexual; gender identity as a psychological sense of oneself as a man or a woman; gender role as a set of prescriptive, culture-specific expectations about what is appropriate for men and women; and gender-role identity— a concept devised to capture the extent to which a person approves of and participates in feelings and behaviors deemed to be appropriate to his or her culturally constituted gender.[4] This terminology provides the analytic vocabulary that enables feminist scholars to challenge the natural attitude. Consider the distinction between gender identity and gender-role identity, for example, which admits of the possibility that one can have a clear sense of oneself as a woman (or a man) while being thoroughly disaffected from and refusing participation in prevailing conceptions of femininity (or masculinity). This distinction breaks any connection between masculinity/ femininity and sexed bodies, interpreting masculinity and femininity as culture-specific abstractions notoriously plagued by gender symbolism that mark a chasm between romanticized ideal and lived experience, attributed and actual, propaganda and practice.

[3] It should be noted that "identity" can also mean markedly different things. It can mean a psychological sense of "who I am," a sociological notion of a person qua agent prior to assuming specific social roles, a Foucauldian concept that captures an array of regulatory practices that produce the internal coherence of the subject, a philosophical concern with the individuation and unity of a person in the face of change, or a narrative construction the individual develops to make sense of his or her life.

[4] In developing these distinctions, I am drawing from Barrett 1980, 42–79, and Kessler and McKenna 1978, 7–11.

Once feminists introduce conceptual distinctions that differentiate sex, sexuality, sexual identity, gender identity, gender role, and gender-role identity, then critical questions emerge: What do these phenomena have to do with one another? How are they related? How do their complex interrelations pertain to gender as lived experience? The natural attitude postulates sex as the determinant of gender identity that flows naturally into a particular mode of heterosexuality and that mandates certain rational gender roles embraced happily by individuals with uniformly positive gender-role identities. In keeping with the negative heuristic of gender as an analytic category, feminist scholars have challenged each of these posited relations. Drawing upon linguistics, historical analysis, structuralism, deconstruction, Freudian and Lacanian psychoanalysis, phenomenology, existential and cognitive psychology, as well as dialectical materialism, feminists have advanced a variety of accounts not only of the relations that obtain among these diverse domains but also of how such complex social processes are naturalized. In the following section I examine four feminist accounts of the "facticity" of gender, which move from use of gender as an analytic category to an explanation of gender as lived experience.

Complementarity models: Gender within a functionalist frame

Gender initially existed as a grammatical category. Some attention to linguistics then may help illuminate the concept's appeal to feminist scholars. Etymologically, gender derives from the Latin, *genus,* via old French, *gendre,* roughly translated as "kind" or "sort." Designated "the most puzzling of grammatical categories, . . . genders are classes of nouns reflected in the behavior of associated words" (Corbett 1991, 1). Gender is puzzling for linguists precisely because it is *not* universal or invariant. In some languages, gender is central and pervasive, while in others it is totally absent. Corbett's examination of more than two hundred languages revealed that "the number of genders is not limited to three; four is common, and twenty is possible" (1991, 5). As the proliferation of genders in specific languages makes clear, gender need not have anything to do with sex. "In some languages, gender marks the distinction masculine/feminine/non-sexed; but in other languages the divisions animate/inanimate, human/non-human, rational/non-rational, male human/other, strong/weak, augmentative/diminutive, male/other, female/other function exactly as does the division into male/female" (30). As the etymology suggests, grammatical gender is based on a wide range of "kinds" including "insects, non-flesh food, liquids, canines, hunting weapons, items whose lustrous surfaces reflect light. . . . The worldview of the speakers determines the categories" (30–32). Given the enormous range of grammatical genders, the determining criterion of gender is agreement: genders are distinguished syntactically by the agreements they take. In some languages, adjectives and verbs show agreement, in others, adverbs, numerals, and even conjunctions agree; but, in all cases, agreement is the way in which the genders are reflected in the behavior of associated words (5).[5]

Gender's conceptual appeal for feminists is closely tied to its versatility in linguistics. As a linguistic construction, the cultural origins and historicity of gender are unmistakable. Gender's relation to the belief systems of determinate peoples frees it from the specter of biological determinism. Moreover, linguistic gender is not inherently enmeshed in binary opposition. Yet there is another facet of gender's linguistic legacy that should give feminists pause. If feminists were to draw an explicit analogy from grammatical gender, they would define genders as categories of persons constituted in and through the behavior of associated others, emphasizing that the relevant behavior involves concord or harmony. Although this aspect of the grammatical heritage is seldom addressed explicitly in feminist accounts of gender, notions of agreement, harmony, and complementarity surface obliquely and problematically in numerous feminist accounts of gender. Indeed, a close reading of some of the most intricate and sophisticated recent accounts of gender reveals that notions of agreement or complementarity form the secret core of the authors' efforts to explain gender and to use gender to explain other social relations. Explanations of this sort situate gender in a functionalist frame. Within this frame, gender is depicted as a cultural construct devised to promote particular social functions that bear a marked resemblance to the presuppositions of the natural attitude.

Perhaps the most explicit version of this view can be found in Steven Smith's phenomenology of gender, *Gender Thinking* (1992). A philosopher steeped in the phenomenological tradition, Smith argues that an accurate analysis of gender must begin with an explication of the "life world," the fundamental structures of consciousness: "The first false move . . . is the identification of gender with sex, or sex-as-socially constructed, or sex role, when in fact ordinary talk of 'feminine' and 'masculine' is not necessarily or even most often about any of these things but instead has to do typically with intentional qualities and indeed, ideals" (xiv). Thus Smith seeks to illuminate how gender operates in the life world.

[5] It would be fascinating to explore the relations between agreement in adjectives, verbs, and adverbs in languages in which gender corresponds to sex for some insights into the origins of gender symbolism. Did the linguistic agreement reflect demeanors and roles ascribed to men and women in traditional societies? Have certain descriptions, actions, and qualifications of actions come to seem sex specific due to grammatical agreement?

Defining gender as a "conventional formation of a plastic humanity," Smith describes "gendering as a cultural process: a cultivation of human nature determined by the vicissitudes of early childhood and the customs of one's community" (15). Rather than invoking the metaphor of cultivation to imply growth or development, Smith uses the term to convey the imposition of certain constraints on human potential. Thus he suggests that gendering "qualifies" our humanity. Indeed, it is one of two critical social forces that shape human potential. "Humanity is a generic nature that stands in two chains of mutually qualifying categories, one physical (which includes sex) and the other intentional (which includes gender)" (23). Physical and intentional constraints admit of a range of differentiation, hence the phenomenon of individuality, but according to Smith, there are "limits to our plasticity, to the range of differentiations possible" (27). On Smith's view, "There are observable human phenomena that give definite shape to our openness" (25), and sex is perhaps the most powerful of these limits. "The sexes have the status of physical fact, almost always instantly and unproblematically ostensible" (46). Although he refers to "the sexes" as almost unproblematically ostensible, Smith acknowledges that culture shapes what is perceived as a body. Through "embodiment," "the community stipulates what counts as a male/female body, what life will be like in a male/female body in relation to other bodies, what norms (and latitudes) of character and conduct are associated with these bodies, and who is male and female" (91). When culture takes up the task of molding human nature, then, its aim is to enhance its own construction of what is naturally given, to mark sex differentiations through language, character, and roles. For this reason, gender always entails a "dual reference to sex and character for purposes of description and evaluation" (36).

For Smith, language is paradigmatic of the cultural desire to mark sex differences. "In grammar, genders are *sex-related* systems of syntactical concord. . . . Human genders also work as systems of concord insofar as distinctive ways of speaking and acting are assigned to persons of different sexes" (43; emphasis added). Smith's claim that grammatical gender is exclusively sex related enables him to suggest that the core content of the human gender system is not chosen but given. "Human gender schemes possess centers of meaning in (what are taken to be) sexed bodies" (44). Thus, cultural constructions of masculinity and femininity are not arbitrary. They are rooted in sex, which in turn has its own "center of meaning rooted in reproduction: woman as egg producer; man as sperm producer" (46). Starting with an overly restrictive account of grammatical gender, Smith links gender to sex to reproduction, and hence, to heterosexuality.

"Confronting sex differences makes me realize that I need a partner to reproduce. . . . A gendered being teams with other gendered beings" (71).

Smith's claim that gender merely marks differences and meanings given by sexed bodies does not rest comfortably with his acknowledgment of how much work gendering involves. He notes that "we are continually subjected to gender attributions in all phases of our lives and that this gendering scheme has more orienting force for most of us, most of the time, than any other human differentiation" (36). Gender involves a "fundamental shaping of selfhood" that produces not only differences in "attunement and appreciativeness" but "a normative solicitation of our intentions" and "an already granted permission to think, feel, act, and appear in ways that everyone does not and cannot" (53, 55, 184). Lifelong subjection to such gendering makes the experiences of the genders partly incommensurable. Smith suggests that gender both "marks the limit of comprehension" between men and women and yet gives these gendered beings a reason to live together: "Gender's normative force consists of nothing other than its ability to answer the life-interpreting question of how intenders should live together" (53, cf. 56). Gender creates sex-specific experience and cognition, makes men and women mysteries to each other, and thereby inculcates a desire for cohabitation. For it is the culturally constructed incommensurability that enables men and women to regard each other as complementary (80). Hence, genders constitute "generic realities . . . complementary kinds of a kind" (49, cf. 52).

Why does culture engage in the double effort to differentiate bodies through embodiment and gendering? If the center of sexual meaning is unproblematically reproduction, why is this double effort necessary? Smith's response is reminiscent of Lévi-Strauss. "Culture and gender are both normative organizations of intention binding the group together" (68). Gender as "a culturally-engineered central meaning with a culturally-influenced physical base" is necessary because certain "functions (e.g., childbearing and fighting) are necessary and require that our lives be substantially adapted to them" (69, cf. 73). Underlying the cultural creation of complementarity is the species demand for survival. "Since men and women have significantly different reproductive risks and opportunities in evolutionary terms, their guiding sex-related emotions must be sex-differentiated, that is, there must be different female and male sexual natures" (124). In a somewhat bizarre inversion of sociobiological premises, Smith suggests that species reproduction requires sexual differentiation; therefore culture creates that differentiation in order to insure the perpetuation of the species but masks its role by attributing the original difference to sex itself. Hence, "heterosexuality's postulated union of male and female specializations is the basic premise of the gender system" (80). Returning to the theme of concord, Smith concludes his analysis by legitimating the cultural creation of difference with an appeal to a classical conception of the "natural." "Gender dualizing is humanly natural, if nature means that which satisfies conditions of harmonious adjustment. The adjustment in question is humans to themselves. Because humanity is a social reality, it has to be balanced within itself; the category of complementarity is bound to be invoked in the self-interpretation of beings who form their own environment. . . . Reciprocal dependency may take a number of forms, but duality is a preferred principle for elaborating such forms because of the nature of the problem of balancing" (247–48).

From a feminist perspective, the shortcomings of Smith's account of the intricate connections between sex, sexuality, gender, and gender role are numerous. He develops an enormously complex phenomenological analysis of "gender thinking" only to vindicate the natural attitude. Like Lévi-Strauss, Smith accepts a conception of culture as an elaborate mechanism devised to create interdependence and cooperation in the reproduction of the species. Yet culture's mission in inducing complementarity makes sense only if one presupposes an atomistic, asocial, or even antisocial conception of human nature, a conception with strong ties to capitalist ideology, but little validity as universal description. Smith tries to mask the inadequacy of his conceptions of culture and human nature by repeated references to sex construed in terms of "natural kinds," but none of the typical correlates of sex conform to the demands of that classification. A natural kind refers to a category that exists independent of the observer and that can be defined in terms of an essence, a set of properties common to all members of the kind. Feminist scholarship has repudiated the notion of any sexual essence precisely because "there are no behavioral or physical characteristics that always and without exception are true only of one gender" (Kessler and McKenna 1978, 1). Chromosomes, hormones, sperm production, and egg production, all fail to differentiate all men from all women or to provide a common core within each sex. "No matter how detailed an investigation science has thus far made, it is still not possible to draw a clear dividing line even between male and female" (Devor 1989, 1). If one moves from the natural sciences to the social sciences, efforts to identify behavioral differences that conform to the definition of a natural kind have again ended in failure. Attitudinal and behavioral "sex differences" attributed to men and women are mired in gender symbolism. Indicators of "biologically based femininity" typically include interest in weddings and marriage, preference for marriage over career, interest in infants and children, and enjoyment of childhood play with dolls, while indicators of "biologically based masculinity" include high activity levels, self-assurance, and a preference for career over marriage (Devor 1989, 11–15; see also Connell 1987, 167–90; Tavris 1992). Psychological inventories of masculinity and femininity have fallen prey to the misogynist tendency to define socially valued traits as male (logical, self-confident, ambitious, decisive, knows way around world) and less valued characteristics as female (talkative, gentle, sensitive to others' feelings, interest in appearance, strong need for security) (Devor 1989, 32). Even with all the cultural bias built into such studies, they have not been able to differentiate clearly men and women in the cultures that produced the inventories. "'Normal femininity' of the psychological test variety may actually be a rare commodity. In one study of college-aged females, only 15% of the heterosexual sample tested as feminine on a widely accepted sex role inventory. The remaining 85% scored as either masculine or as some combination of masculine and feminine" (15). Differences cast in terms of averages, tendencies, and percentages do not meet the criteria of a natural kind. Nor do such cultural characterizations of masculinity and femininity constitute clear manifestations of "complementarity." If gender is to be judged by the standard Smith sets for it, the creation of reciprocal dependence, then a great deal of contemporary evidence (divorce rates, out-of-wedlock births, levels of domestic violence, numbers of "deadbeat dads") suggests that it fails dismally in its mission.

The main virtue of Smith's account is that it illustrates so graphically how gender, a category specifically devised to avoid biological determinism, covertly invokes the very biological ground it set out to repudiate. Smith's account, like the natural attitude itself, operates within the confines of a base/superstructure model of the sex/gender distinction (Connell 1987, 50; Laqueur 1990, 124). Within this model, the body is assumed to provide the raw material that culture can refine in various but limited ways. Gender is assumed to be "hard-wired," at least in part. The presumed naturalness (understood as the absence of force or coercion) of gender turns on that presumption of hardwiring. Thus, discussions of gender seldom move far beyond presuppositions concerning inherent sex differences. R. W. Connell has attempted to explain this recurrent problem in feminist accounts of gender by suggesting that in contemporary Western culture "the notion of natural sex difference forms a limit beyond which thought cannot go" (1987, 66). Similarly, Holly Devor describes biological determinism as the dominant cognitive schema in North America, that is, as the conceptual structure that organizes social experience on the basis of shared understandings (1989, 45–46). Mary Poovey (1988), Ludmilla Jordanova (1989), and Thomas Laqueur (1990) have provided fascinating accounts of the emergence of the base/superstructure model of gender since the seventeenth century. According to Laqueur, "It is a sign of modernity to ask for a single, consistent biology as the source or foundation for masculinity and femininity" (1990, 61). Whatever the cause of this tendency toward biological determinism, it is an impossible ground for feminist accounts of gender. As Smith's account makes clear, appeal to a biological ground traps gender in "the ideology of procreation," construing women in terms of an essential maternal role mandated by culture and nature — a role undifferentiated by race, ethnicity, age, class, sexual orientation, or any mode of individuality.

Is there any escape from the base/superstructure model of the sex/gender distinction? Must feminist scholars incorporate functionalist assumptions about culture in their conceptions of gender? Although references to limits beyond which thought cannot go and dominant cognitive schemas suggest quite pessimistic responses to these questions, attempts to locate the base/superstructure model of gender in the politics of modernity offer more optimistic possibilities. If this problematic conception of gender is rooted in modernity, then a postmodern feminist strategy specifically devised to abandon all binary oppositions should afford a conception of gender that escapes the traps of biological determinism. An examination of Judith Butler's complex and innovative analysis of gender in *Gender Trouble* (1990) may be instructive, then, revealing the prospects for a feminist conception of gender beyond the functionalist frame.

Judith Butler's *Gender Trouble* sets out to explain how the "naturalness" of sex, sexuality, and gender are "constituted through discursively constrained performative acts that produce the body through and within the categories of sex" (x). She cautions at the outset that "'being' a sex or a gender is fundamentally impossible" (19). The binary oppositions male/female and masculine/feminine are incompatible with the continuous variability of human characteristics, constructing a false opposition between the sexes and an artificial coherence within each term of the binary. Stereotypical genders, then, must be understood as "ontological locales that are fundamentally uninhabitable" (146). Rejecting the "old dream of symmetry," Butler argues that gender must be understood, not as a noun, nor as a set of attributes, but as a "doing," a performance that constitutes the identity that it purports to be (24).

According to Butler, gender is the process that constructs the internal coherence of sex, (hetero)sexual desire, and (hetero)sexual practice within the modern subject. It is the mechanism that produces a notion of a "presocial body" shaped by culture. And, it provides the standard of intelligibility for persons that informs both the naturalistic paradigm and the authentic-expressive paradigm of the self. "Gender is the discursive/cultural means by which 'sexed nature' or 'a natural sex' is produced and established as 'prediscursive,' prior to culture, a politically neutral surface on which culture acts" (7). Gender performs this work of naturalization through the "stylized repetition of actions through time" (141). The natural attitude is produced through the repetition of words, acts, and gestures. The sheer weight of these repetitions leads the actor to believe in the "naturalness" of the body and of heterosexuality and to act in conformance with "nature's dictates." Gender functions, then, as a regulatory fiction, "a fabrication, a fantasy instituted and inscribed on the surface of bodies" (136). Becoming gendered is a laborious process, bringing the self into belief in the natural attitude is arduous; yet the intensity of effort and the power relations that produce this effect are hidden by the very naturalization at the core of the gendering process.

Butler's account reverses the direction of causality presumed by the natural attitude: "gender designates the apparatus of production whereby sexes are established" (7). But Butler insists that gender itself is the effect of specific formations of power, of institutions, practices, and discourses that establish and regulate its shape and meaning. What are the practices that produce gender? Butler identifies phallogocentrism and compulsory heterosexuality as the discursive sites that produce gender. "The heterosexualization of desire requires and institutes the production of discrete and asymmetrical oppositions between 'feminine' and 'masculine' understood as expressive attributes of 'female' and 'male'" (17). Like Smith, Butler appeals to the cultural creation of complementarity qua heterosexuality as the ultimate explanans of gender. Her route to this conclusion, however, is markedly different, relying upon a critical rereading of Freud and Lacan.

The incest taboo plays a central role in psychoanalytic accounts of the individual's relation to culture/civilization. It has been advanced as an explanation of the cost that civilization exacts from individuals in return for life-enhancing artifacts, as an explanation of the primary repression through which the individual enters culture, and as an explanation of the formation of gender identity. Butler suggests that the incest taboo itself naturalizes heterosexuality and masculine sexual agency. Through a close reading of Freud's discussion of the sexual dispositions that frame the oedipal conflict, Butler demonstrates that the incest taboo that fuels the oedipal conflict makes no sense without a prior prohibition of homosexuality. On Butler's reading, Freud's "polymorphous perversity" itself turns on a truncated conception of bisexuality. "The conceptualization of bisexuality in terms of *dispositions,* feminine and masculine, which have heterosexual aims as their intentional correlates, suggests that for Freud *bisexuality is the coincidence of two heterosexual desires within a single psyche.* . . . Within Freud's thesis of primary bisexuality, there is no homosexuality, and only opposites attract" (60–61; emphasis in original). The absence of homosexuality in Freud's account attests to the power of culture's original prohibition. Culture produces two prohibitions that regulate the shape and meaning of sexuality: the first is the taboo against homosexuality and the second is the incest taboo. "The prohibitive law both produces sexuality in the form of 'dispositions' and appears disingenuously at a later point in time to transform these ostensibly 'natural' dispositions into culturally acceptable structures of exogamic kinship" (64). Butler notes that the law qua prohibition is also productive: it creates that which it prohibits. Thus homosexuality and bisexuality cannot be understood as either "before" or "outside" culture, for they too are constructed within the terms of the constitutive discourse. "If the incest taboo regulates the production of discrete gender identities, and if that production requires the prohibition and sanction of heterosexuality, then homosexuality emerges as a desire which must be produced in order to remain repressed. In other words, for heterosexuality to remain intact as a distinct social form, it requires an intelligible conception of homosexuality and also requires the prohibition of that conception in rendering it culturally unintelligible" (77).

Butler's account of the formation of gender identity illustrates the complex relations of prohibition, production, and naturalization. Drawing on Freud's notion of melancholia, a process of identification through which the ego incorporates attributes of a lost loved one to minimize the pain of the loss, Butler construes gender identity as a kind of melancholia. The incest taboo's prohibition of the maternal body triggers an identification with the prohibited object. Abjuring the language of internalization, Butler suggests the process of identification is better understood as a mode of incorporation or "encrypting." As a technical psychological term, incorporation refers to an "antimetaphorical activity [that] literalizes the loss on or in the body and so appears as the facticity of the body, the means by which the body comes to bear 'sex' at its literal truth. The localization and/or prohibition of pleasures and desires in given 'erotogenic' zones is precisely the kind of gender-differentiating melancholy that suffuses the body's surface" (68). The incest taboo's prohibition produces gender identity as a process that minimizes loss through identification's complex disavowal of loss. The systematicity of this disavowal erodes the conditions of metaphorical signification resulting in encrypting, a literalizing fantasy that deadens the body, even as it masks its genealogy, producing a body experienced as "natural fact." Becoming a gender is becoming naturalized. The taboo against homosexuality in conjunction with the taboo against incest differentiate bodily parts and pleasures on the basis of gendered meanings, as melancholia deadens some organs to pleasure and brings others to life (68–70).

Butler's psychoanalytic account accords primacy to compulsory heterosexuality both as an explanation of culture's production of complementarity and as an explanation of gender's production of a naturalized body. Where Smith endorses cultural mechanisms that "harmonize" human relations and foster social integration, Butler denounces the modes of power that produce homosexuality as necessary, yet prohibited; within culture, yet marginalized. Butler is careful to note that homosexual/heterosexual is itself a problematic discursive formation, a binary relation premised upon a false opposition and a fraudulent unity within each term of that binary. Indeed, in criticizing Monique Wittig's radical disjunction between homosexuality and heterosexuality, Butler insists that there are "structures of psychic homosexuality within heterosexual relations, and structures of heterosexuality within gay and lesbian sexuality and relationships" (121).[6] And in criticizing Lacan, Butler cautions against totalizing conceptions of identity that follow from too efficacious and univocal a conception of the Law. She calls instead for a recognition that "multiple and coexisting identifications produce conflicts, convergences, and innovative dissonances within gender configurations which contest the fixity of masculine and feminine placements with respect to the paternal law" (67). The very possibility of such multiple identifications is central to Butler's strategy for confounding gender. Arguing that power can never be escaped, only redeployed, Butler endorses parody as a tactic designed to subvert "the real" or the "sexually factic." Strategies of subversive repetition can dispel belief in the illusions of the "natural" body/desire/sexuality, thereby rendering gender incredible (141, 146).

As a postmodern critic, Butler's genealogy of gender is designed to probe what is left out of discursive formations that construe sex/gender/ desire as natural. She points out that homosexuality as a legitimate mode of sexuality is omitted from naturalistic accounts. Given the pervasiveness and persistence of the natural attitude, it makes sense to attribute its production to powerful cultural forces. In Butler's analysis, gender as performativity becomes the cultural force that produces belief in the naturalness of heterosexuality. Gender is no longer an analytic tool used to illuminate a variety of asymmetries in culture but, rather, the process that

---

[6] In the third chapter of *Gender Trouble,* Butler develops an analysis of Wittig's corpus, suggesting that certain problematic assumptions concerning the disjuncture between heterosexual and homosexual surface in Wittig's major theoretical essays (1980, 1981, 1985, 1992).

naturalizes and justifies a particular asymmetry. The "effect of compulsory heterosexuality," gender reproduces a "natural" heterosexual world.

Why does gender act as such a helpful handmaiden of her progenitor (rather than as a rebellious adolescent)? Butler's response is telling: "Because gender is a project which has cultural survival as its end, the term strategy better suggests the situation of duress under which gender performance always and variously occurs. Hence, as a strategy of survival within compulsory systems, gender is a performance with clearly punitive consequences" (139). Butler's first formulation casts gender in the service of cultural survival. This does not explain why gender performs its designated cultural function, it merely redescribes the function. The second formulation, gender as a strategy of survival within a compulsory system, suggests that gender must perform its function to avoid punishment, a punishment presumably imposed by culture. But why does culture insist upon heterosexuality? In a discourse that explicitly eschews any sociobiological explanation, the options seem to be limited to either a simple notion that culture is a self-replicating system (begging the question of the origin of the cultural preference for heterosexuality) or a Freudian notion that renunciation of homosexual desire is the sublimation that civilization demands. The first option follows from Butler's characterization of gender as performativity, yet it has conservative implications Butler is unlikely to embrace. Butler defines performativity as repetition of words, acts, gestures. This definition is virtually indistinguishable from J. G. A. Pocock's conception of tradition, "an indefinite series of repetitions of an action," introduced both to vindicate the authority of tradition and to eliminate unhelpful and potentially destabilizing queries about origins (1973, 237). Such a conservative project is diametrically opposed to Butler's stated objectives as a genealogist. If Butler's account of gender is not to fall prey to a static conception of cultural self-replication, then her appeal to "cultural survival" must be interpreted in a Freudian vein. Sexuality is offered as the explanans of culture.

Butler's analysis drives a wedge between sex and sexuality, thereby avoiding biological determinism. The belief that sexuality "follows" from sex can be understood only as a relation of political entailment. But what is required to understand culture as "following" from compulsory heterosexuality? Can all of culture's complex domains plausibly be construed as emanating from or mandated by compulsory heterosexuality? Butler tends to conflate culture with phallogocentrism, thereby privileging the Symbolic system over science, industry, engineering, or other more palpable cultural constructs. Phallogocentrism captures feminist concerns about male domination in history and culture, but it does so at an exacting cost.

For by construing culture in terms of a Symbolic system that itself privileges the Phallus, Butler perpetuates women's invisibility, underestimating their role as cocreators of culture and miring them in victimization. Phallogocentrism fails to provide a sufficiently exhaustive account of culture. Moreover, it indulges a form of anthropomorphism that sustains discussions of what might be called the "cunning of culture,"⁷ the ingenious means by which culture insures its own survival through the production of organizational practices and structures independent of the needs or intentions of individuals. Such a reification makes culture appear at once omniscient, seamless, and unassailable, a markedly unhelpful point of departure for those aspiring to feminist transformation. There is also a certain irony in Butler's positing of compulsory heterosexuality as the explanans of culture. Foucault cautioned against the trap of conceiving sex (qua sexuality) as the secret of being, suggesting that such beliefs implicate the subject in ever deeper modes of subjugation. It is unlikely that Butler's Foucauldian gesturing toward sexuality as the secret of culture can escape that trap.

What does Butler's discursive construction of gender leave out? By interpreting gender in terms of the cultural production of heterosexual desire and psychoanalytic production of gender identity, Butler's account makes gender too much a matter of the self—a self that appears peculiarly unmarked by race, class, or ethnicity. Her account privatizes gender, restricting the utility of the concept. Butler's conception offers little prospect for unraveling gender symbolism or for addressing gender structures beyond the psyche. The operation of gender in social, political, and economic institutions disappears as the psychodrama of the desiring self is played out. This occlusion of gender as an organizational feature of social life that is itself mediated by race and class may explain why Butler's reliance on parody as a transformative mechanism rings so hollow. While parody might help subvert the naturalization of desire, it is unlikely to make inroads against the economic and political forces that circumscribe women's lives.⁸

⁷ I am extrapolating from the notion of the "cunning of reason." For a full explication of this concept see Tucker 1974, 269–95.

⁸ Judith Grant has questioned the subversive potential of parody: "One cannot simply subvert gender rules by inverting them. . . . Lots of people rebel, but it does not always get taken up as a rebellion. . . . Truly transformative rebellion involves several interpretive moments" (1993, 177–78). Butler herself has moved away from optimism about parody. In *Bodies That Matter*, Butler analyzes drag as "hyperbolic conformity" to gender imperatives that can "reveal the hyperbolic status of the norm itself," but goes on to note that "these norms, taken not as commands to be obeyed, but as imperatives to be 'cited,' twisted,

Butler's postmodern account of gender succeeds in escaping biological determinism, but it still proffers a functionalist explanation of gender. Moreover, in positing heterosexuality as the explanans of culture, Butler's account of gender comes far too close to Smith's for comfort, for allusions to compulsory heterosexuality do nothing to dispel the ideology of reproduction that sustains the natural attitude. Despite the virtuosity of Butler's account of gender as performativity, it does not provide a conception of gender that breaks definitively from the problematic presuppositions of the ideology of procreation.

R. W. Connell's *Gender and Power* (1987), which blends strains of Marxism, existentialism, and poststructuralism in developing its account of gender, is richly deserving of close examination. Connell advances a "systematic social theory of gender" that strives to account for the historicity of gender; the dynamic role of gender in economic, political, sexual, and psychological domains; and the relation between personal agency and social structure in gender formation and reproduction, as well as the turbulence and contradictions pertaining to gender as lived experience. Attuned to the problems associated with conceptions of gender that construe women as perennial victims, Connell develops a "practice-based" theory of gender attentive to both the constraining power of gender and the myriad struggles people engage in against those constraints. In addition, Connell provides a cogent critique of all modes of biological determinism. Noting that the body is never experienced without cultural mediation, he defines gender in terms of the cognitive and interpretive practices that "create, appropriate, and recreate reproductive biology" (79).

According to Connell, gender as a social practice is more than a mere marking of the human body, "it is the weaving of a structure of symbols which exaggerate and distort human potential" (79). Repudiating various versions of mind/body dualism, Connell insists that "the practical transformation of the body in the social structure of gender is not only accomplished at the level of symbolism. It has physical effects on the body, the incorporation is a material one" (87). Connell is also careful to point out that the social practices constituting gender bear no direct relation to what might be considered "functional" for human reproduction. The patterns of posture, movement, dress, adornment, body shape, body image, sexuality, intonation, speech, skilling, and de-skilling associated with cultural constructions of masculinity and femininity may not be at all conducive to reproduction. Arguing that the "logic" that drives gender is autonomous,

queered, brought into relief as heterosexual imperatives, are not, for that reason, necessarily subverted in the process" (1993, 237).

Connell rejects all theories that attempt to derive gender from natural differences, biological reproduction, the functional needs of society, or the imperatives of social reproduction. Indeed, he insists that functionalist arguments must be viewed with extreme suspicion: they serve only to mask the power underlying these cultural symbolizations in order to justify inequitable distributions of social burdens and benefits.

In developing his account of the historicity of gender, Connell delineates a conception of human practices in relation to social structures informed by the works of Marx and Sartre. On this view, practices are the daily actions of human beings who appropriate and transform nature in order to satisfy their needs and in the process transform themselves, producing new needs and new practices. Practices are inherently dynamic transformations of the natural world that open up new possibilities as well as new risks and pressures. Practices can also become solidified, entrenched, and institutionalized, creating a degree of intractability in the social world that limits the freedom of future practices. Connell defines social structure in terms of such limits. A social structure is a pattern of constraint on practice inherent in social relations. Operating through the complex interplay of power and institutions, "'structure' specifies the way practices (over time) constrain practices" (95). Although structures mark the fixity of the social world, the sedimentation of past practices that limit present action, the dimension of collective life that exists beyond individual intention, they are not impervious to change. "Practice can be turned against what constrains it; so structure can deliberately be the object of practice. But practice cannot escape structure, cannot float free of its circumstances" (95). According to Connell, gender can best be understood as an interrelated set of social structures that define men and women in terms of their reproductive role and organize social life around sex and sexuality. On this view, gender is far more than an attribute of an individual or a characteristic of a social collectivity, it is the active process that reduces people to, and conceives social life in terms of, reproductive function, thereby constraining individual potential (97, 140, 245).

Taking issue with feminist accounts that construe gender structure in terms of a monolithic male domination, Connell argues that gender must be conceived in terms of very specific structures tied to particular social practices of labor, power, and cathexis. He insists that gender is not an "ideological addendum" to social structures rooted in race or class but, rather, an autonomous structure constitutive of these fields. As a constraint upon labor, gender structures the allocation of particular types of work, the organization of domestic activity, the division of paid versus unpaid labor, the segregation of labor markets, patterns of production and consumption, wage levels, opportunities for employment and promotion, and even the conditions and terms of labor exchange. Within the domain of power, gender structures authority, control, and coercion, establishing hierarchies in public and private sectors, creating a virtual male monopoly on institutional and interpersonal violence, and promoting particular modes of domestic and sexual asymmetries. Defining cathexis in terms of practices constructing emotionally charged relations with others, Connell notes that gender structures identities of desiring subjects and designation of desirable objects, patterns of desire, and sexual practices, as well as terms and conditions for sexual exchange.

Connell notes that these diverse gender structures exist in complex interrelationship but insists that it is a mistake to characterize that relationship as either a logical or systemic unity. Even the notion of a "historical unity" tends to convey more coherence and internal consistency than may exist, masking tensions, uneven developments, and internal contradictions among these structures that can precipitate crises crucial to their transformation. Connell prefers the term *historical composition* to capture the human agency that creates the imperfect and incomplete orderliness linking diverse gender structures. As a historical composition, gender is "a linking concept. It is about linking other fields of social practice to modal practices of engendering" (140). Its central tools are the principles of separation, division, and unequal integration (97).

Human agency is essential to the creation and transformation of gender, yet the natural attitude sees gender as fixed by nature. Connell suggests that the apparent fixity of gender structures is maintained by "sexual ideology." Describing his approach to sexual ideology as "more akin to the sociology of knowledge than to contemporary theories of discourse," Connell suggests that ideology must be understood as "a practice, ontologically on a par with other practices and equally involved in the constitution of social interests" (244–45). Connell identifies two fundamental practices constitutive of sexual ideology, naturalization and cognitive purification. Naturalization collapses social structure into nature in order to legitimate social practices and insulate them from change. "Naturalization is not a naive mistake about what biology can or cannot explain. At a collective level, it is a highly motivated ideological practice which constantly overrides biological facts" (246). Cognitive purification involves the production of ideological representations devoid of any of the messy complexity of lived relations. Shallow stereotypes, romantic narratives, and "squeaky clean" sociobiological images of women as nurturers and men as providers, are the stock-in-trade of cognitive purification.

Gender and Power presents a remarkably insightful and systematic analysis of gender. Like Smith and Butler, Connell moves from a description of gender as analytic category to an account of gender as an active process structuring multiple domains of social life. He offers a modest justification for his approach: "This framework is serviceable for understanding current history" (97). He might also have said that his theory accounts for virtually every feminist usage of gender over the past several decades and relates them in a multilayered whole.

At the level of conceptualization, however, there is some slippage in his theorization of gender. For Connell, gender is the process that relates all the rich and varied levels of human activity to biological reproduction. It is an active force that makes people think constantly in terms of sex. And it is precisely this reductionism that enables gender to constrain so many dimensions of social organization. Yet, when Connell so deftly identifies the gender structures operative in the domains of labor and power, it is not at all clear that they gain their force by dragging the mind back to reproductive biology. Do women really earn less because they are capable of bearing children? Does gender make us think so? Is job segregation in clerical work, fast-food industries, secondary education, or nursing really related to women's gestational ability? Are women subjected to domestic violence because of their reproductive role?

Connell notes that "the practices of sexual reproduction are often quite remote aspects of social encounters in which gender is constructed and sustained" (81). But if this is so, how does gender work? Connell introduces Sartre's distinction between a practico-inert series and an intentionally mobilized group to explain gender's operative mechanisms. According to Sartre, a series is a mode of collective unity structured by external social or material circumstances, or what might be called the "logic of the situation." Because the commonality that unites the series is imposed by external objects or the actions of others, seriality is passive, implying no conscious awareness on the part of those who make up the series. Sartre used the example of people waiting for a bus to illustrate his conception of the series: they have certain things in common by virtue of their situation, even though they may not be consciously aware of any common ties. In contrast, a group is a collection of persons who consciously acknowledge a bond uniting them, whether it be a collective identity, a common project, or shared values.

According to Connell, sex can be understood as a series. The biological differentiation of men and women in reproduction imposes an external logic upon individuals on the basis of a parallel situation. Thus women share a passive commonality by virtue of their reproductive capacity, as do men. In keeping with Sartre's description of seriality as practico-inert (i.e., a product of human action that constrains), Connell notes that construing sex as a series does not imply any awareness of the postulated commonality, any incorporation of the seriality into one's identity, or any identification with those others who share the situation. By describing gender in terms of a Sartrean group, Connell suggests that gender's task is to create a conscious awareness of reproductive capacity as the basis for solidarity. "To construct the social category 'man' or 'woman,' with a common identity and interest, requires a negation of the serial dispersion characteristic of the array of parallel situations constructed by biological categories. This is done in practices that create and assert the solidarity of the sex (or of a group within it)" (81, cf. 137). For gender to accomplish its mission, then, it must negate the passive experience of the body and create a notion of commonality embraced by members of the group, thereby mobilizing women and men as distinctive groups. But how can gender simultaneously negate the biological ground of the series and mobilize reproductive biology as the basis of a shared identity? And if certain social expectations about the sexed body constitute sex as a practico-inert series, structuring the logic of situation in terms of reproduction, how does gender differ from those initial social expectations?[9] The sex/gender distinction seems to collapse into a vortex of reproduction.

Sartre conceives of the group as a collection of persons whose conscious awareness of shared characteristics serves as the basis for united action, for the initiation of a collective project. But Connell's conception of gender cannot begin to carry men and women that far, for he explicitly acknowledges the deficiencies of any construction of men and women as internally undifferentiated categories. And he is keenly aware of the social cleavages rooted in race, class, ethnicity, age, and homophobia that preclude any collective identification, much less collective action. Thus the group/series explanation of how gender accomplishes its work founders both in its account of sex as series and in its account of gender as group. And despite Connell's numerous caveats, it appears to accord primacy to reproduction in cultural constructions of sex, as well as gender.

The limitations of Connell's attempt to define gender as a process linking diverse fields of social relations to reproductive biology also surface in his discussion of sexual ideology. It is not at all clear how gender differs from sexual ideology. Both are described as cognitive and interpretive practices, as symbolizations that naturalize social constructions and impose

[9] Without addressing Connell's use of Sartre's conception of seriality, Iris Young presents cogent reasons for treating gender as a series, not as a mechanism for transcending seriality (1994).

untenable sex distinctions on men and women. Is gender, after all, a matter of belief more than a structure of social forces? In what precise ways does it differ from sexual ideology? Connell uses sexual ideology to discuss literature, film, and modes of cultural production that do not fit into his categories of labor, power, and cathexis. But if we are to take seriously his discussions of the role of beliefs in constituting social practices and his rejection of simplistic base/superstructure models, what is the purpose of the distinction between gender and sexual ideology? In devising a conception of sexual ideology "akin to the sociology of knowledge," Connell is able to discuss the role (conservative vs. radical) of intellectuals in ideological production and to introduce a conception of social interests (male hegemonic) served by naturalization. Both of these moves allow Connell covertly to introduce functionalist premises that he had explicitly renounced earlier in his analysis.

Connell offers several functionalist speculations about why belief in gender persists despite all the philosophical arguments and scientific evidence that demonstrate the defects of the natural attitude. "There is a logic to paradoxes such as gross exaggerations of difference by social practices of dress. . . . They are part of a continuing effort to sustain the social definition of gender, an effort that is necessary precisely because the biological logic, and the inert practice that responds to it, cannot sustain gender categories" (81). But if gender is doing its cultural work successfully, what explains the perceived necessity to shore up gender? Connell's account is startling: "The solidarity of the heterosexual couple is formed on the basis of some kind of reciprocity rather than on the basis of common situation or experience. . . . Sexual difference is in large part what gives erotic flavor to relationships. It is emphasized as a means of heightening and intensifying pleasure, hence, the systematic exaggeration of gender differences" (113). Despite the enormous complexity of Connell's account, despite his repeated cautions against functionalist explanation, the complementarity thesis undergirds his analysis. It provides the fundamental explanation of why gender persists.

Connell's book is remarkably sensitive to heterosexism, but the notion that "sexual difference" heightens erotic pleasure depends on heterosexist presuppositions. Eve Kosofsky Sedgwick (1990) has pointed out that the heterosexual/homosexual opposition allows equivocation in the meaning imputed to "homo"/sexual. As one moves from notions of one sex, to same sex, to selfsame, to sameness, an enormous range of differences is elided. And this elision sustains Connell's assumption that there is greater difference, hence greater potential erotic pleasure, across genders than within genders. "The new calculus of homo/hetero . . . owes its sleekly utilitarian feel to the linguistically unappealable classification of anyone who shares one's gender as the 'same' as oneself, and anyone who does not share one's gender as Other" (Sedgwick 1990, 160). But Sedgwick points out that even the most cursory examination of human beings will reveal that being of the same gender cannot guarantee "similarity" anymore than being of "opposite" genders can guarantee difference. Moreover, the belief that the gender of one's sexual partner is the crucial difference determining pleasure (rather than differences pertaining to positions, acts, techniques, zones or sensations, physical types, symbolic investments, relations of power, etc.) does not withstand serious scrutiny. Thus, there appears to be a suppressed procreationist premise in Connell's allusion to the best means to heighten erotic pleasure. Once again, the "cunning of culture" seems to insert a pro-creationist agenda into an explanation of gender.

Connell's attempt to describe gender as a reductionist process linking divergent social fields to sexual reproduction does not adequately account for all the modes of injustice women experience, although it certainly identifies a wide range of feminist concerns. Ultimately it founders on the complementarity thesis as the rationale for the cultural imposition of gender. No longer in the service of species or cultural survival, Connell's appeal to complementarity serves hedonistic ends. Gender is posited as a mechanism for heightening the intensity of pleasure. But whether the function attributed to gender is the production of heterosexuality or erotic pleasure, functionalist explanation leads feminists to a dead end, for feminists theorizing gender within a functionalist frame cannot escape the spectre of biological determinism or the ideology of reproduction. Once again an insightful deployment of gender as analytic category slips into problematic claims about gender as explanans.

In a remarkable and insightful approach to the study of gender, Suzanne Kessler and Wendy McKenna attempt to bracket ontological claims about gender in order to explore gender attribution, the instantaneous process by which one person classifies another as a man or a woman. Their explicit goal in *Gender: An Ethnomethodological Approach* (1978) is to explain how gender attribution works. Their exposition of how the process operates does, however, sustain certain speculations about the larger question "why."

Kessler and McKenna begin their investigation by noting several factors concomitant to gender attribution: the urgency that governs gender attribution in daily life (people feel they need to know whether they are interacting with a man or woman, boy or girl), the conviction that every individual can be categorized as a man or a woman, and the uneasiness that surrounds "ambiguous" cases. Linking the "need" to classify people by gender to the natural attitude, Kessler and McKenna provide a comprehensive demonstration that the assumptions informing the natural attitude are systematically flawed. Yet, they note that the fact that the natural attitude rests upon a number of mistaken beliefs in no way mitigates its hold. On the contrary, each time particular beliefs informing the natural attitude are refuted, new ones seem to replace them. Thus, they note that the absence of any physical or behavioral grounds for a dichotomous classification of men and women has led to the emergence of a new "scientific" concern with gender identity, the individual's psychological sense of being a male or a female, as a firmer foundation for a "fixed dichotomy." "Transsexual is a category constructed to relieve ambiguity, to avoid the kinds of combinations (male genitals and female gender identity) that make people uncomfortable because they violate basic rules about gender. Since genitals can now be changed, gender identity is now seen as a less flexible criterion; thus marking the triumph of surgeons over psychotherapists in the rush to restore gender to unambiguous reality" (120).

What fuels this incessant replenishing of the natural attitude? Kessler and McKenna argue that sexual dimorphism is not given in nature, but imposed upon nature by the perceiver. "Gender is a social construction, a world of two sexes is the result of the socially shared, taken-for-granted methods which members use to construct a world" (vii). The perceiver's expectation that there are two genders leads to the perception of two genders by forcing all perceived phenomena into the posited dichotomous categories. Anomalies are hidden and ambiguities masked, allowing the perceived phenomenon to conform to and thereby confirm the validity of the original expectation. According to Kessler and McKenna, the selective perception that sustains gender attribution in daily life also shapes the socially accredited perceptions of scientists, whose work is then taken as incontrovertible proof of the validity of the perceptual categories.

> Scientists construct dimorphism where there is continuity. Hormones, behavior, physical characteristics, developmental processes, chromosomes, and psychological qualities have all been fitted into dichotomous categories. Scientific knowledge does not inform the answer to the question, "What makes a person a man or a woman?" Rather it justifies (and appears to give grounds for) the already existing conviction that a person is either a man or a woman and that there is no problem differentiating between the two. Biological, psychological, and social differences do not lead to our seeing two genders. Our seeing two genders leads to the "discovery" of biological, psychological, and social differences. (163)

Kessler and McKenna's goal is to discern how gender attributions are made, for once a person has been classified as a man or a woman, his or her actions and intentions are interpreted on the basis of culturally specific gender expectations that have pervasive life consequences. In accordance with the modernist assumption that biology provides the foundation for masculinity and femininity, most people believe that the genitals provide the ultimate criterion for gender attribution. But Kessler and McKenna point out that, in daily practice, attribution is almost always made in the absence of any information about genitals. Sex assignment at birth typically follows from the delivering physician's inspection of genitalia, but in social interactions, the decision to categorize another as male or female seldom turns on such direct inspection. The recent emphasis on gender identity as the ground for the dichotomous classification of men and women makes gender identity a possible basis for gender attribution. But, gender identity, as the psychological sense of being a man or a woman, is not immediately perceptible. Kessler and McKenna note that the only way to ascertain someone's gender identity is to ask the individual a direct question, and such queries are not typically made prior to gender attribution.

How, then, is gender attributed? Kessler and McKenna argue that gender attribution depends upon cues given by the perceived that facilitate categorization on the basis of socially constructed, gender-specific norms. The dimensions of the presentation of self that provide cues for gender attribution include: modes and content of speech; styles of dress, adornment, posture, and movement; and the construction of a narrative history that conforms to gender stereotypes (126–28). For gender attribution that depends exclusively upon visual encounters, "tertiary sexual characteristics"—nonverbal behaviors such as facial expressions, movement, body posture—are the predominant gender markers. Kessler and McKenna introduce the term *cultural genitals* to characterize these culturally specific appearances that sustain inferences about gender. Gender attribution is dependent upon "genital attribution," but genital attribution "takes place irrespective of biological genitals on the basis of 'cultural genitals'—that are assumed to be there" (153–54). People believe that sound inferences about biology can be made on the basis of stylized gender cues and this belief fixes gender symbolization in the body. "The relationship between cultural genitals and gender attribution is reflexive. The reality of 'gender' is proved by the genital which is attributed and at the same time the attributed genital only has meaning through the socially shared construction of gender attribution" (155).

Kessler and McKenna insist that gender categories are culturally specific. In order to demonstrate that dichotomous classification is not the only

alternative, they discuss the *berdache* — a person who receives social sanction to become a gender other than that to which he or she was originally
assigned — as a third gender recognized by certain Native American
peoples. How, then, are culturally specific gender categories constructed?
Since psychology treats gender as a "way of seeing," Kessler and McKenna
review psychoanalytic, social learning, and cognitive development theories
for clues to the construction of gender categories. They argue persuasively
that none of these approaches can explain adequately either the individual's
acquisition of gender categories or the social construction of gender categories. They turn instead to the idea of a cognitive schema to explain the
organizing expectations that shape perception. "A categorizing scheme is
not dependent on any particular cue, nor is it a rule followed by robots.
Rather it is a way of understanding . . . a method of applying information"
(158, cf. 161). In keeping with their ethnomethodological approach, they
suggest that these categorizing schemas arise from the incorrigible propositions of specific cultures, bracketing questions concerning the origins of
the incorrigible propositions themselves. Unfortunately, such a bracketing
removes from consideration some of the difficult questions about the nature of, and possibilities for change in, categorizing schema and severely
limits Kessler and McKenna's prescription for escaping the life-constrain-
ing force of dichotomous gender.

Kessler and McKenna suggest that the key to transforming gender lies
in changing our incorrigible propositions. They suggest that this can be
done by "confronting the reality of other possibilities (e.g., the berdache),
as well as the possibility of other realities" (164). Enhancing awareness of
other cultures could then serve to liberate people from the natural attitude.
In addition, they suggest marshaling logical arguments and empirical evidence to demonstrate the deficiencies in incorrigible beliefs as a means of
dispelling them. Kessler and McKenna recognize, for example, that the
complementarity thesis undergirds sociobiological accounts of gender. A
clear understanding of gender attribution should therefore help dispel the
erroneous belief that gender differentiation saves the species from extinc-
tion by enabling sperm producers and egg producers to recognize each
other. They demonstrate that gender attribution is based upon cultural
genitals that can provide no certainty whatsoever about who might be a
suitable reproductive partner. Thus gender fails in its "evolutionary mission," a failure so significant that it should be sufficient to undermine sociobiological claims. Despite the lucidity of their argument, the reliance upon
rational argument to expunge such errors confronts a problem. If incorrigible beliefs are as impervious to evidence as their definition suggests, this
strategy is doomed to failure. And if categorizing schema routinely screen

out anomalies to the extent that Kessler and McKenna claim, then it is unlikely that culture-bound individuals will be able to perceive the evidence that other cultures afford. The very presuppositions of ethnomethodology undermine the possibility of freeing people from gender by an appeal to evidence, for that evidence is theoretically constructed within a particular cultural frame, and, according to Kessler and McKenna, "Ultimately there is no way to determine the truth of theoretical formulations. Theories may be more or less useful, aesthetically pleasing, or 'in vogue,' but their claim to truth is, in some sense, a matter of faith in basic assumptions" (100). And reason is no match against faith.

What is important about Kessler and McKenna's conception of gender is not merely their insightful account of the mechanics of gender attribution, but their subtle shift of gender's terrain. Gender moves from a stylization of the body to a category of the mind. It is, in an important sense, an immaterial substance — an intangible idea with palpable consequences, an a priori category that structures the phenomenal world. The notion of cognitive schema that is invoked in this work is seriously undertheorized. It is not clear whether such a mental category has more in common with Hume's notion of a "habit of the mind," with Kant's conception of a "category of the mind," or with cognitive psychology's version of "prototype theory." Each of these acknowledges the active role of the knower in constructing the object of knowledge, but they differ in their accounts of the origins of such categories, the role of tradition, reason, and language in structuring these categories, and in their assessments of how coherent, ubiquitous, and persistent such categorizations may be. Feminists who describe gender as a lens (Bem 1993), a way of seeing, or a cognitive category may not mean to invoke the full force of the Humean or Kantian conceptions, but they should proceed with extreme caution. Hume, for example, links "habits of the mind" to constant conjunction of empirically observable phenomena, suggesting that where the eye perceives two things occurring together, the mind imposes a "necessary connection." Extrapolating the Humean model to gender produces an account that locks cultural constructions of masculinity and femininity to sexed bodies with a degree of necessity that it is nearly impossible to break. Similarly, Kantian categories of the mind constitute the condition of rationality. If gender is construed as a category of the mind, then no thinking subject can escape its grip. For those who would eradicate gender-based injustice, there are dire implications in the displacement of gender from external world to internal, mental terrain. It is not at all clear that one can alter gender construed as cognitive schema. Moreover, the mind as a site of political action raises unsavory images of political intrusion and abuse. Within a social constructionist frame, cognitive schema may serve merely to mark the social constitution of consciousness. But if this is what is meant, then culture resurfaces in this discourse without any clear explication of why particular cultures cause dichotomous perceptions of gender. Biological determinism may be avoided in this account, but the natural attitude remains entrenched, as the cunning of culture structures the basic categories of the mind.

The problematics of gender as explanans

Gender as an analytic category illuminates a range of questions for feminist investigation and provides a framework for those investigations that challenges androcentric assumptions. A sophisticated understanding of gender as a theoretical tool can enable feminists to identify important issues pertaining to social institutions and relations, as well as individual identity, that can be researched within particular cultures and subcultures at particular historical moments. Developing conceptual distinctions that differentiate sex, sexuality, sexual identity, gender identity, gender role, and gender-role identity can enable feminist scholars to deploy gender as an analytic device, engaging questions that confound the natural attitude and thereby contribute to progressive feminist politics.

If feminist scholars are to use gender as an analytic category that fosters emancipatory projects, however, there are crucial pitfalls to avoid. The foregoing analysis of a number of feminist efforts to theorize gender locates one danger in the construction of a narrative that links gender to the cunning of culture operating in the interests of reproduction. These efforts to explain the function of gender replicate problematic assumptions of the ideology of procreation, rather than dispelling the natural attitude. Despite repeated references to cultural specificity, these accounts suggest a universal and invariant role for gender. Race, class, and ethnicity disappear from these accounts as the cunning of culture produces species survival, compulsory heterosexuality, heightened sexual pleasure, or categories of the mind.

I have tried to show that in each of these works the effort to theorize gender involves a subtle shift from an account of "how" gender operates under specific historical conditions to a universal claim about "why" gender performs a particular social function. In this shift, gender is transformed from an analytic category into a causal force. The heuristic tool is displaced as gender is accorded an ontological status. It is described as the *cause* of certain beliefs about the world; the *force* that molds a plastic humanity, produces naturalized bodies, or imposes sexual dimorphism; the *determinant* of identity; the *process* that structures labor, power, and cathexis; or the *mental category* that structures a form of dichotomous perception. The distortion involved in the move from analytic category to causal force becomes apparent when the causal claims are subjected to critical scrutiny. Whether gender is advanced to explain the cultural production of heterosexual desire, the psychoanalytic production of individual identity, the power asymmetries in social life, or the structure of perception, close examination of these claims reveals that the imputed causality is unfounded. Although gender as analytic category can be invaluable to feminist scholarship in illuminating certain facets of social existence, it is a grave error to attribute explanatory force to gender.

Feminist analysis is not strengthened when gender is conflated with universal explanans. On the contrary, ersatz explanation is dangerous. It proffers a false security, suggesting that issues in need of interrogation and analysis are already understood. Constructing a functionalist narrative of gender that appears to possess universal validity occludes cultural specificity and historical variability, according gender an intransigence that is markedly unhelpful to feminist projects. Rather than tracing the instability of gender as a cultural category, marking the fault lines, and searching for points at which feminist interventions might be possible, gender as universal explanans aggregates various forms of difference, disadvantage, and domains of social life under one vague, reproductive rubric, masking the specificity of problems and impairing the identification of possible solutions. There is no question that women experience systematic disadvantages in male-dominated societies, forms of injustice that constrain their opportunities and life prospects. But gender can *explain* these disadvantages only by definitional fiat.

As a mode of explanation, functionalism has been faulted for insensitivity to history, a teleology that conflates putative function with genetic cause, a tendency to mask power, and a conservative propensity to legitimate the status quo. None of these features of functionalism sits well with the liberatory impulse of feminist scholarship and feminist politics. Functionalist explanations of gender are particularly worrisome because they accord gender an intractability that renders transformative strategies either inconceivable, utopian, or impracticable. According gender a functional role in relation to reproduction also lends cultural constructions of gender unwarranted legitimacy. I have already noted that gender as universal explanans occludes the mediations of race, class, and ethnicity, and, in so doing, works against a feminist politics that tries to build solidarities across the divisions of race, class, and ethnicity. To the extent that gender as universal explanans shifts feminist politics toward issues of self, psyche, and sexuality, it structures a politics that is insufficiently inclusive. As Chandra Mohanty has pointed out, feminist strategies that privilege privatized gender fail to engage Third World women who locate their politics in a collective struggle against racism, sexism, colonialism, imperialism, and monopoly capital (Mohanty, Russo, and Torres 1991, 2–38).

The problematic accounts of gender discussed in this article suggest that gender as universal explanans poses grave threats to the potential benefits of gender as analytic category. If feminist scholars are to confound gender and the natural attitude, rather than be confounded by gender, it will be helpful to enrich our conceptual terminology, taking advantage of crucial distinctions such as sexed embodiedness, sexuality, sexual identity, gender identity, gendered divisions of labor, gendered social relations, and gender symbolism, rather than collapsing such diverse notions into the single term *gender.* Feminist scholars must also steadfastly resist the tendency to treat gender as universal explanans, to construe it as causal force in domains as disparate as psyche, self, and social relations. Universal claims about the invariability of gender and unwarranted assumptions about the cunning of culture securing gender's psychic and social functions are self-defeating, for they signify the persistence of the natural attitude in feminist discourses, a fundamental failure to escape its grip.

Department of Political Science
University of Louisville

References

Amundsen, Kirsten. 1971. *The Silenced Majority.* Englewood Cliffs, N.J.: Prentice Hall.

Anderson, Margaret. 1983. *Thinking about Women.* New York: Macmillan.

Barrett, Michele. 1980. *Women's Oppression Today.* London: Verso.

Bem, Sandra. 1974. "The Measurement of Psychological Androgyny." *Journal of Clinical and Consulting Psychology* 42:155–62.

———. 1983. "Gender Schema Theory and Its Implications for Child Development." *Signs: Journal of Women in Culture and Society* 8(4):598–616.

———. 1993. *Lenses of Gender.* New Haven, Conn.: Yale University Press.

Boneparth, Ellen, and Emily Stoper, eds. 1988. *Women, Power and Policy: Towards the Year 2000.* New York: Pergamon.

Bordo, Susan. 1993. *Unbearable Weight: Feminism, Western Culture, and the Body.* Berkeley and Los Angeles: University of California Press.

Brewer, Rose. 1993. "Theorizing Race, Class and Gender: The New Scholarship of Black Feminist Intellectuals and Black Women's Labor." In *Theorizing Black Feminisms,* ed. Stanlie M. James and Abena Busia, 13–30. New York: Routledge.

Butler, Judith. 1990. *Gender Trouble: Feminism and the Subversion of Identity.* New York and London: Routledge.

———. 1993. *Bodies That Matter.* New York and London: Routledge.

Chodorow, Nancy. 1978. *The Reproduction of Mothering.* Berkeley: University of California Press.

Chow, Rey. 1991. "Violence in the Other Country." In Mohanty, Russo, and Torres 1991, 81–100.

Collins, Patricia Hill. 1990. *Black Feminist Thought.* New York: HarperCollins.

Connell, R. W. 1987. *Gender and Power.* Stanford, Calif.: Stanford University Press.

Corbett, Greville J. 1991. *Gender.* Cambridge: Cambridge University Press.

Cornell, Drucilla, and Adam Thurschwell. 1986. "Feminism, Negativity, Intersubjectivity." *Praxis International* 5(4):484–504.

Daly, Mary. 1978. *GYN/ECOLOGY.* Boston: Beacon.

Davis, Angela. 1981. *Women, Race and Class.* New York: Random House.

de Lauretis, Teresa. 1984. *Alice Doesn't: Feminism, Semiotics, Cinema.* Bloomington: Indiana University Press.

———. 1987. *Technologies of Gender.* Bloomington: Indiana University Press.

Devor, Holly. 1989. *Gender Blending: Confronting the Limits of Duality.* Bloomington: Indiana University Press.

Doane, Mary Ann. 1987. *The Desire to Desire.* Bloomington: Indiana University Press.

Eisenstein, Zillah. 1979. *Capitalist Patriarchy and the Case for Socialist Feminism.* New York: Monthly Review Press.

Epperson, Sharon. 1988. "Studies Link Subtle Sex Bias in Schools with Women's Behavior in the Workplace." *Wall Street Journal,* September 16.

Epstein, Cynthia Fuchs. 1971. *Woman's Place.* Berkeley: University of California Press.

Firestone, Shulamith. 1970. *The Dialectic of Sex.* New York: William Morrow.

Friedan, Betty. 1963. *The Feminine Mystique.* New York: Norton.

Garfinkel, Harold. 1967. *Studies in Ethnomethodology.* Englewood Cliffs, N.J.: Prentice Hall.

Gilligan, Carol. 1982. *In a Different Voice.* Cambridge, Mass.: Harvard University Press.

Gordon, Linda. 1988. *Heroes of Their Own Lives: The Politics and History of Family Violence.* New York: Viking.

Grant, Judith. 1993. *Fundamental Feminism.* New York: Routledge.

Haraway, Donna. 1991. "'Gender' for a Marxist Dictionary: The Sexual Politics of a Word." In her *Simians, Cyborgs and Women,* 127–48. New York: Routledge.

Harding, Sandra. 1986. *The Science Question in Feminism.* Ithaca, N.Y.: Cornell University Press.

Hawkesworth, Mary. 1990. "The Reification of Difference." In her *Beyond Oppression,* 17–46. New York: Continuum.

Higginbotham, Evelyn Brooks. 1992. "African-American Women's History and the Metalanguage of Race." *Signs* 17(2):251–74.

Irigaray, Luce. 1985a. *Speculum of the Other Woman,* trans. Gillian Gill. Ithaca, N.Y.: Cornell University Press.

———. 1985b. *This Sex Which Is Not One,* trans. Catherine Porter. Ithaca, N.Y.: Cornell University Press.

Janeway, Elizabeth. 1971. *Man's World, Women's Place.* New York: Delta.

Jordanova, Ludmilla. 1989. *Sexual Visions: Images of Gender in Science and Medicine between the 18th and 20th Centuries.* Madison: University of Wisconsin Press.

Kessler, Suzanne, and Wendy McKenna. 1978. *Gender: An Ethnomethodological Approach.* New York: Wiley.

King, Deborah. 1988. "Multiple Jeopardy, Multiple Consciousness: The Context of a Black Feminist Ideology." *Signs* 14(1):42–72.

Lakatos, Imre. 1970. "Falsification and the Methodology of Scientific Research Programmes." In *Criticism and the Growth of Knowledge,* ed. Imre Lakatos and Alan Musgrave, 91–195. Cambridge: Cambridge University Press.

Laqueur, Thomas. 1990. *Making Sex: Body and Gender from the Greeks to Freud.* Cambridge, Mass.: Harvard University Press.

Lerner, Gerda. 1986. *The Creation of Patriarchy.* New York: Oxford University Press.

Lévi-Strauss, Claude. 1969. *The Elementary Structures of Kinship.* Boston: Beacon.

———. 1971. "The Family." In *Man, Culture and Society,* ed. H. Shapiro, 340–58. London: Oxford University Press.

Lopata, Helena Z., and Barrie Thorne. 1978. "On the Term 'Sex Roles.'" *Signs* 3(3):718–21.

MacKinnon, Catharine. 1987. *Feminism Unmodified.* Cambridge, Mass.: Harvard University Press.

Mohanty, Chandra, Ann Russo, and Lourdes Torres, eds. 1991. *Third World Women and the Politics of Feminism.* Bloomington: Indiana University Press.

Pocock, J. G. A. 1973. *Politics, Language, and Time.* New York: Atheneum.

Poovey, Mary. 1988. *Uneven Developments.* Chicago: University of Chicago Press.

Riley, Denise. 1988. *Am I That Name? Feminism and the Category of "Women" in History.* Minneapolis: University of Minnesota Press.

Rowbotham, Sheila. 1973. *Women's Consciousness, Man's World.* London: Penguin.

Rubin, Gayle. 1975. "The Traffic in Women: Notes on the 'Political Economy' of Sex." In *Toward an Anthropology of Women,* ed. Rayner Reiter, 157–210. New York: Monthly Review Press.

Ruddick, Sara. 1980. "Maternal Thinking." *Feminist Studies* 6(2):342–67.

Sawicki, Jana. 1991. "Foucault and Feminism: Toward a Politics of Difference." In Shanley and Pateman 1991, 217–31.

Scott, Joan. 1986. "Gender: A Useful Category for Historical Analysis." *American Historical Review* 91:1053–75.

Sedgwick, Eve Kosofsky. 1990. *Epistemology of the Closet.* Berkeley and Los Angeles: University of California Press.

Shanley, Mary, and Carole Pateman, eds. 1991. *Feminist Interpretations and Political Theory.* University Park: Pennsylvania State University Press.

Silverman, Kaja. 1988. *The Acoustic Mirror.* Bloomington: Indiana University Press.

Singer, Linda. 1993. *Erotic Welfare: Sexual Theory and Politics in the Age of Epidemic.* New York: Routledge.

Smith, Steven G. 1992. *Gender Thinking*. Philadelphia: Temple University Press.

Spelman, Elizabeth. 1988. *Inessential Woman*. Boston: Beacon.

Spender, Dale. 1980. *Man Made Language*. London: Routledge & Kegan Paul.

Stoller, Robert. 1985. *Presentations of Gender*. New Haven, Conn.: Yale University Press.

Suleiman, Susan Rubin, ed. 1985. *The Female Body and Western Culture*. Cambridge, Mass.: Harvard University Press.

Tavris, Carol. 1992. *The Mismeasure of Women*. New York: Simon & Schuster.

Tucker, R. W. 1974. "The Cunning of Reason in Hegel and Marx." *Review of Politics* 18(3):269–95.

Vetterling-Braggin, Mary, ed. 1982. *"Femininity," "Masculinity," and "Androgyny."* Totowa, N.J.: Littlefield Adams.

Walby, Sylvia. 1986. *Patriarchy at Work*. Minneapolis: University of Minnesota Press.

Wittig, Monique. 1980. "The Straight Mind." *Feminist Issues* 1(1):103–11.

———. 1981. "One Is Not Born a Woman." *Feminist Issues* 1(2):47–54.

———. 1985. "The Mark of Gender." *Feminist Issues* 5(2):1–14.

———. 1992. *The Straight Mind and Other Essays*. Boston: Beacon.

Young, Iris Marion. 1994. "Gender as Seriality: Thinking about Women as a Social Collective." *Signs* 19(3):713–38.

Comments and Reply

Comment on Hawkesworth's "Confounding Gender": Who Needs Gender Theory?

Wendy McKenna, *Department of Psychology, Barnard College*
Suzanne Kessler, *Department of Psychology, Purchase College, SUNY*

We welcome this chance to reply to Mary Hawkesworth's article. It is always more agreeable to respond to a critique that is embedded in a complimentary analysis. We will use this opportunity to reflect on our own writings in the context of the substantial gender theorizing that has occurred in the past twenty years but will limit our remarks to some general points and to Hawkesworth's critique of our work. We will leave it to the other authors to respond to her discussion of their theories.

At the outset, we want to clarify the source of certain terms and concepts that we employed and that those who cite us sometimes confuse. Harold Garfinkel, the sociologist who coined the term *ethnomethodology* (1967), appropriated Alfred Schutz's description of the "natural attitude" for studying the commonsense understanding of social actions (1964), including the action of "doing" gender. Garfinkel (not us) introduced the term *cultural genitals*. We refined and developed these concepts and tried to make Garfinkel accessible to a wider audience. We took the concept of "incorrigible proposition" from ethnomethodologists Hugh Mehan and Houston Wood (1975) (who credit Douglas Gasking).

The essence of Hawkesworth's critique is that the four theoretical accounts of gender she discusses provide no method for practical improvement in the *lived* experience of women. The problem, she believes, is that these feminist theories are grounded in a functional framework that "cannot escape the spectre of biological determinism or the ideology of reproduction" (167). In addition, she fears that functionalist narratives "suggest a universal and invariant role for gender" (172) and that such claims "are self-defeating, for they signify the persistence of the natural attitude [of gender] in [our] discourses" (174). Hawkesworth also alleges that gender theories, including ours, transform gender "from an analytic category into a causal force" and that gender is "accorded an ontological status" as process, force, determinant, or mental category (172).

Hawkesworth is concerned that functional accounts are grounded in biology and reproduction. Even if we accept that human reproduction involves the joining of a sperm cell and an egg cell, and that individuals might produce one or the other or neither, but not both, we can still ask questions. We can ask, (1) In what sense is the reproductive function necessary? and (2) If it is necessary, are there other possible ways to serve that same function besides present gender arrangements? We explicitly say on the last page of the last chapter of our book "that 'sperm carriers' and 'egg carriers' are as much of a construction as 'male' or 'female' (but) we all have to make a decision to take something for granted . . . otherwise it would be impossible to get out of bed in the morning. Our decision has been to stop here; others may wish to go on" (Kessler and McKenna 1978, 169). For example, there could be ten genders, with only two of them serving the reproductive function (a small part of the time). To imagine such an arrangement is not difficult; to have it become more than theoretical is extremely hard. However, that is true of all social and political change.

Theorizing what function gender may perform does not transform gender into a *causal* force. We clearly say that incorrigible propositions in the natural attitude structure perception, leading us to see two, and only two, genders. We clearly do *not* say that gender *causes* the structure of perception (or anything else). What we were attempting to do, in the ethnomethodological tradition, was to describe the interpretive practices that permit us to "see" and "do" gender, not to identify the gender-related causes of any particular set of cultural circumstances. Gender is not a mental category (in an ontological sense). Mental schemas (categories) result in seeing gender as an ontological category.

Functional analyses, especially if they are not grounded in obligatory reproduction, do not have to be "blinding" and do not have to imply a view of gender that is invariant or universal. We certainly do not claim that gender is invariant or universal, and we provide ample evidence from other cultures and from children in our own culture that there are many possible ways to experience gender. The gendered world that is produced might just as easily not be produced. Ethnomethodologists claim that while "critics are arguing about the nature of the best theory of the social world . . . ethnomethodology is concerned with the possibility that the social world can be theorized at all" (Sharrock and Anderson 1986, 105).

Hawkesworth herself has a (partial) functional interest. She feels we

should have addressed why particular cultures "cause" (her word) dichotomous perceptions of gender. Theorizing why particular cultures have dichotomous gender categories is an interesting and important academic
pursuit, but change is possible without a consideration of "why." Consider
the greater efficacy of behavioral psychotherapies for some problems compared to psychoanalytic therapies. Psychoanalytic theories provide richer
accounts of life-as-experienced than do behavioral theories, but if the priority is concrete change, then sometimes a blueprint for such change can
come from a good description of "what is" and "how it is sustained," without an answer to the question "why."

Hawkesworth critiques our notion of cognitive schema as seriously undertheorized. To some extent, we agree with her. We do not say what kind
of mental category gender is, and the map we provide is rather sketchy.
However, it was never our intention to uncover a "gender attribution
schema," which, when followed precisely, would allow anyone to determine or display a particular gender. Although we write about how gender
attributions are made, it would not be correct to say, as Hawkesworth
does, that it was our goal. Our goal was to show that gender attribution
is a *constructive* process, by describing possible ways it could be done.

Whatever type of cognitive schema gender may be understood as in a
specific culture (and we leave it to others to theorize about that), we do
not agree with Hawkesworth's complaint that "it is not at all clear that one
can alter gender construed as cognitive schema" (171). In a related point,
she worries that a focus on the "internal" is not sufficiently inclusive and
that the transformative strategies implied by our analysis (and the others')
are "utopian or impracticable" (173). By splitting the world this way, she
is naturalizing "internal" and "external," treating them as concrete locations
just as others have naturalized and concretized gender. The first step in
transformation comes from understanding that there are other possibilities, whether one divides them into "internal" (the possibility of a different
incorrigible proposition) or "external" (the possibility of increased access
to effective contraceptives for women).

Hawkesworth is correct in stating that we claim that in order to transform gender it is necessary to transform incorrigible propositions about
gender. She says it will not work, that "reason is no match against faith"
(171). We strongly disagree. As teachers we have seen the potency of "reason" time and again in the classroom, if reason can be read to mean understanding that it could be otherwise. Kate Bornstein calls gender a cult
(1994), but even in cults there are crises of faith. The success of theoretically based "transformative strategies" in creating these crises, even when
they are only implied, as in our work, is not trivial. We note here that

Hawkesworth discusses the four theories in *reverse* historical order and does not deal with the influence (direct or indirect) of each theory on the next, although she claims that history cannot be ignored.

When we wrote our book it was, in part, to demonstrate the problems with traditional social science work on gender and sex. The social construction of gender was a radical idea. A nonbiologically based conception of the body was not part of "women studies" discourse. Contrary to what Hawkesworth writes, the field of *sex differences* (not gender) "illuminat[ed] the social construction of masculinity and femininity and naively took the sexed body as given" (143–44). Once the body became problematized as part of the analysis, "gender studies" was born. Gender needed to be made problematic; it needed to be seen — as an appearance. Only then could theorists concern themselves with where it comes from and what functions it serves. In the almost twenty years since our book was published, things have changed to the extent that our work-as-critique now serves as theoretical ground for others to critique. It could have been otherwise.[1]

We agree with Hawkesworth that practical change is of paramount importance. But her questions about gender theory could as easily be applied to academic discourse in general. What is the use of theorizing about anything? How will this redistribute power? The short answer is, it may not, and gender theory might not be the place to look for transformative strategies about women's lives. However, we know that describing the natural attitude illuminates other possible realities. Social constructionists Bruno Latour and Steve Woolgar wrote that "the set of statements considered too costly to modify constitute what is referred to as reality" (1979, 243). When one comes to deeply acknowledge that truth, one is forced to confront one's own participation in this possible world and can begin to accept that change is not against what is called "nature."

References

Bornstein, Kate. 1994. *Gender Outlaw: On Men, Women, and the Rest of Us.* New York: Routledge.

Garfinkel, Harold. 1967. *Studies in Ethnomethodology.* Englewood Cliffs, N.J.: Prentice Hall.

---

[1] The initial reaction to our book was minimal. Few people in the mid-1970s were likely to imagine that, in the 1990s, there would emerge a "transgender movement" due, in part, to a compelling argument of socially constructed gender categories. The many transsexuals who wrote thanking us for articulating a version of gender that they could live with testifies to the power of good theorizing.

Kessler, Suzanne, and Wendy McKenna. 1978. *Gender: An Ethnomethodological Approach*. New York: Wiley.

Latour, Bruno, and Steve Woolgar. 1979. *Laboratory Life: The Social Construction of Scientific Facts*. Beverly Hills, Calif.: Sage.

Mehan, Hugh, and Houston Wood. 1975. *The Reality of Ethnomethodology*. New York: Wiley.

Schutz, Alfred. 1964. "The Phenomenology of the Social World." In his *Collected Papers*. The Hague: Martinus Nijhoff.

Sharrock, Wes, and Bob Anderson. 1986. *The Ethnomethodologists*. Chichester: Ellis Horwood Ltd. ∎

Comment on Hawkesworth's "Confounding Gender"

Steven G. Smith, *Department of Philosophy, Millsaps College*

I **am grateful** to Mary Hawkesworth for this chance to pursue the analysis of gender at what I take to be the very heart of the thought, that is, the *confrontation* between two families of arguments and motives: on the one hand, a critique of gender keyed to a rejection of the descriptive and normative validity of gender identifications, and, on the other hand, an appreciation of "positive gender thinking" in its most cogent forms. To conceive gender adequately, one must stage this confrontation in one's mind and not terminate it — neither with "Now we're clear of gender's claims!" nor with "That's a gender program we can live with!" The matter asks to be put this way, I think, not only because we stand at a certain crossroads of discussion but also because any idea of a physically conditioned humankind constitutes in itself a crossroads of concrete determinacy and freedom.

I would like first to offer cautions against a number of oversimplifications that often hamper gender criticism, Hawkesworth's included, and then delve into issues raised by the claim that my argument in *Gender Thinking* (Smith 1992) is phenomenological.

1. For the ordinary forms of gender thinking that are most familiar to us, it is axiomatic that humans are virtually always either "women" or "men," that sexual reproduction mandates some sort of partnership (hence "complementarity") between these "sexes," and that the "sexes" have important "gender" concomitants in human character (although the instancing of gender is partly independent of the instancing of sex). Such is the dogmatic platform for a gender order. But these gender axioms set up a range of *questions* — compelling questions about embodiment and

relationships, notably—and allow for a range of discussible *theses* on the nature of human life, even theses on the human inadequacy of femininities and masculinities. Much in our culture grows out of these questions and theses that we would not jettison even if we could. (I am thinking especially of the interesting gender icons in art and literature.) Gender criticism should not assume that the axioms of gender merely limit thinking, as though gender were always the figure of the crudest, most repressive schoolyard sex typing. Gender does often work this way. But an insensitive rejection of the gender axioms likewise blocks thinking about the meanings of sex. Positive gender thinking is "problematic" not only in the sense that its evidences and arguments are flawed; it is also *about* problems, ultimately about the same problem that properly concerns critical gender thinking, namely, how humans can best live with sex.

The apparent "pure self-evidence" and "unquestionableness" of ordinary assumptions about gender is at least sometimes an artifact of gender critics' way of tackling the question. Skepticism about gender is puzzling to people who (with much justification) feel sure that sexual reproduction is bound to mean a great deal in human life *somehow* and who therefore insist, in response, that gender meaning exists, has a point, cannot rightly be dismissed out of hand. I agree that even this most basic assumption ought to be challenged; we ought to reexamine and redefine our moral investment in sexual reproduction as such. But a critic who persists in attacking the basic complementarity thesis on the threshold of the conversation about sex is like the wind that tried to get a man to remove his coat by blowing harder and harder. In this case, the harsh edge of the wind is an apparent failure of sense: "Forget 'maternal role' *entirely?* Why are you using the word 'women,' then?"

2. Sex and gender are taken to be "kinds," but this kind of kind is commonly and most defensibly understood as a fabric of resemblance, not as a sharply formulable, rigidly predictive essence. Ordinary sex-gender propositions such as "Boys are naturally more aggressive" are easily interpreted as false or fallacious. But a straightforward logical or empirical critique often fails to touch the nerve of the thinking behind the propositions, which occupies an interesting middle ground between quasi-scientific rigor and subjective whim. The person who asserts that boys are naturally more aggressive may well realize that whether and how a particular boy will fulfill the prediction is not determinable, may even be actively interested in seeing how the boy hypothesis fares in a given case, but at the same time feels solidly in touch with significant patterns in experience in offering this judgment—partly because such patterns are actually perceptible, and partly because the sense and weighing of them seems to give the

thinker a tenable place to stand in the world. We know that this is how belief and reasoning about *anything* works. Gender-critical discussions have led the way, in fact, in fostering lucidity about the role of "standpoint" in belief formation. But critics have also tended, in the heat of battle, to assign all forms of gender typing to a muddled standpoint. If only sexual oppression rested solely on simple confusions![1]

3. Sex and gender are popularly conceived to be "natural," but "natural" has various and flexible meanings. What is "natural" for me might be what functions for me as "the hand I was dealt," my given resources; or it might be what I or others expect to observe in me consistently (as a theater director counts on my flinching at a gunshot); or it might have to do with what seems to be the best use of my resources (as friends might find me "perverse" if I did not use my linguistic ability in a white-collar career); or it might have to do with the requirements for a sustainable system (as excessive pollution threatens the very possibility of our living within a stable "nature"). Each of these senses of the "natural" plays an important role in everyday gender thinking, as, indeed, each of these kinds of constraints must be found somehow in life. Gender criticism too easily shrinks its focus to an easily refuted straw thesis of biological determinism. (Although a certain gambit of modern Western science is to implant a deterministic backbone in the body of gender thinking, the body has plenty of vigor without it.)

4. The concept of gender relates masculinity and femininity to maleness and femaleness, which in turn are defined by reproductive functions, but this does not mean that mothering and fathering are necessarily in the foreground of gender experience. Are women subjected to violence because of their reproductive role? Well, no, a woman's attacker is probably not thinking of the eggs she contains or her lactating capacity, but yes, if we think out the whole structure of the situation, considering why women tend to be vulnerable to male attack in certain ways, why emotions become polarized in certain ways, and so forth.

Similarly, the idea that gender so intimately qualifies a person's identity as to qualify his or her intentions a priori — that it steers choosing, rather than being an object of choice — does not entail that a person feels gendered at every moment or that invoking gender is the most telling way to characterize every intention or action. It does suggest that gender will appear in an adequate overall assessment of a person.

5. Gender critics often admit in theory yet effectively forget that sex

---

[1] I do think, though, that Elizabeth Minnich's examination of fallacies in *Transforming Knowledge* (1990) is a good way to draw people into feminist questioning.

and gender are constituted not simply by perception or conception but by practice. "Woman" is not merely some "mothering type" mirage but always includes in its reference some real individuals who have to deal with the risk or fact of pregnancy. Possibly some advantages, certainly some serious disadvantages for women attend this practical datum in the present order. That is a major reason that the very *meaning* of "woman" (and "sex") is problematic. But "women" do exist, for some of us are in this situation. Now, if we change the situation—if, for example, we realize freedom in conception for females—we will significantly alter the practical basis and thus the meaning of femaleness and femininity.[2] One may reasonably suppose that such a change in practice would result in a reduced saliency and centrality of gender within the larger economy of human character. But we might not get this far in reducing the real force of gender if we are led to think by logical or epistemological arguments that gender lacks real force.

6. Gender is a way of dealing with procreation. But the issue of procreation touches us through other human categories as well. The idea of "races" is an idea of separately procreating communities, and there are weaker but still significant procreation requirements for the maintenance of "classes" and "cultures." Part of what it means to be of an age-type ("child," "adult," "old") is that one occupies a place in the generations, that is, in the larger order of procreation. I urge that we not think oversimply in terms of distinct (perhaps "overlapping") human categories; the relations among them are more intimate than that. Race is very genderish, because an issue of sexual behavior is crucial for it; gender is classish, because the practical importance of procreation makes sexes seem functionally necessary components of a society; class is culturish insofar as it must involve a shared world-interpreting; and more connections of this sort are to be made.

7. A key "confounding" move that gender critics make is to argue that the definitions of the genders are "arbitrary," that they do not tally with any consistent set of underlying biological or psychological or pragmatic facts. This is a liberating thought insofar as it opens doors to other conceivable ways of comporting ourselves in relation to sex. But it does not go far enough to show that a traditional gender scheme falls short of the best way. Should we seek a "less arbitrary" way? No, the real point of the argument is that we should not consider ourselves bound to any supposedly "natural" way. And so, pending careful development of the meanings and applications of the idea of the "natural," it is not at all clear what a desirable rela-

---

[2] With this end in view, I sketched a case in *Gender Thinking* for rendering children reversibly infertile—a reformist alternative to the revolutionary proposal of artificial reproduction.

tion to sex-related facts or logical coherence would be. The arbitrariness argument is only momentarily and weakly empowering, for in moving us away from the constraints of popular gender thinking, it moves us away at the same time from the issues posed by sex's portion of humanity.

More promising, I think, is the way of *performing* gender so much illuminated by Judith Butler. The parodic performance of drag wakes us up to all the other shades and slants of performance that are actual and possible. There has always been a consciousness of performing gender at the sophisticated end of gender consciousness. We have often been fascinated by gender performances in art and literature. (Even before Ugo Tognazzi and Michel Serrault so amazingly "did" John Wayne as gays in *La cage aux folles,* we had a freer sense of what it is to "do" a certain masculinity insofar as we could imitate or refer to the John Wayne screen image.) Socially conformist gender performance is not utterly different from parodic drag performance; that is part of the drag revelation.

Does "performance" boil down to "role-playing"? I still see a difference between the character qualification that gender is thought to be and the behavioral or dispositional add-on that a "sex role" is thought to be; yet I see space even within positive gender thinking for an acknowledgment of conscious free play in the living out of character.

8. Finally, a word about method is needed to extricate my project from deep trouble that appears at the very beginning of Hawkesworth's review of it. Here, especially, I must beg the reader's indulgence for a telegraphic presentation, but I will sin boldly, hoping to provoke more reflection on the roles of different kinds of questions in gender studies.

As a philosopher, I am a student of forms of meaning. But I will not use the word "phenomenological" to characterize my own work (I called *Gender Thinking* "conceptual maneuvering") because it suggests too much factuality or necessity in meaning—as though not only ideal structures but definite performances of meaning were nonnegotiably "given" constraints on life, perhaps as "structures of the life-world." I do not believe in a fixed meaning landscape. But some of the ways in which we freely and changeably perform meaning have impressive cogency because of their power to order thoughts, experiences, and actions. I find that we are always caught up in cogencies of meaning, moving with their motion, even when we undertake to criticize the cogencies themselves. To call oneself "feminist" is to confess the cogency of a sex-related emancipatory project. To be a "philosopher" is to participate consciously in the cogent manifestation of validity in ideas, to learn what can be done in using ideas to judge reality. I do not know if anyone wants to call such projects "structures of the life-world," but I conceive the inescapable concreteness of life primarily in this

way, as a field of rival questions and opportunities. I worry that phenomenologists come at human life thinking they can just *see* it, see *what* it *is;* I
worry even if they are taking extraordinary measures to question ordinary appearance.

Social science, however, has the mission of discovering what people
actually do, as distinct from what they thought they were doing. What
people actually do has to be seen. All theorizing in social science is thinking
for the sake of seeing. (R. W. Connell's *Gender and Power* [1987] is a book
of great philosophical interest, but its main merit is that it is eye-opening.)
Philosophers, in contrast, only open their eyes in order to get clearer on
the forms and relations of ideas, so that they can comment on what our
experience really means, as distinct from what we were saying it meant.
(*Gender Thinking* tries above all to be mind-clarifying.) Hawkesworth
might be marking precisely this boundary between philosophy and social
science when she separates gender-as-explanans, a gender with the binding
power of meaningfulness, from gender-as-analytic-category, a gender that
drops on or lifts off the phenomena at the observer's discretion.

Which way, then, shall we take phenomenology? As a philosophical
effort to adjudicate the ultimate meanings of our experience by reference
to a disciplined seeing, or as a social scientific endeavor to discover what
meanings people actually "do"? There is a problem either way. The flaw in
philosophical phenomenology is that no kind of seeing, however helpful,
can, by itself, adjudicate. The flaw in social scientific phenomenology is
that the "doing" of meaning—what we are really after in using the category "meaning"—*is* always an adjudicating, a positioning, a coming at and
picking up of facts, which can be "seen" only in a meeting of the one positioning by another, that is, in an interpretation. But interpretation means
participation in a conversation in which meaning is up for grabs and not
sitting still, phenomenon-like; so the phenomenological premise of seeing
misleads us here as well.

If I were able to see powerful gender intentions and ideals in the manner
prescribed by philosophical phenomenology, and supposing that philosophical phenomenology is a defensible grounding program, I would indeed vindicate a gender order. Hawkesworth thinks she sees me doing that,
or attempting it, but I think she misinterprets me. My presentations of
gender ideas are consistently *hypothetical.* The point of my appreciative construals is always that there are certain interesting things gender *can* mean,
meanings that can lend their power to everyday gender thinking and comportment. There is an element of vindication in this insofar as my interpretations are carried out in the teeth of objections that gender is inherently
arbitrary and harmful. I want to contribute to a deeper understanding of

gender ideals in feminist and anthropological thought. But that part of my account aims only to show how some gender conceptions are worth taking seriously; it certainly does not prove that gender really makes perfect sense after all, or that it is ultimately benign.

Is it too dangerous even hypothetically to treat gender as meaningful? Is there no way of conceiving gender in all the power it can exert that does not subject us to that power? Is no position available between a rigid acceptance of determinate gender norms and an unrealistically detached "analytic" of gender? Must we either remain in the grip of a despotic gender ethos that has forfeited our trust or take as our ideals of emancipation beings without any emotional or ethical grasp of sex difference—angels of some sort—with only a wispy claim to human trust? Must we confound gender, that is, represent it as lacking any meaningful "function," if we are not to be confounded by incoherently conservative "functionalism"?

I sharpen these dilemmas as a way of advertising for a more reasonable (but not simple) middle way, combining noncomplacent performances of gender with nonpresumptuous performances of its negation.

References

Connell, R. W. 1987. *Gender and Power.* Stanford, Calif.: Stanford University Press.
Minnich, Elizabeth. 1990. *Transforming Knowledge.* Philadelphia: Temple University Press.
Smith, Steven G. 1992. *Gender Thinking.* Philadelphia: Temple University Press. I

Comment on Hawkesworth's "Confounding Gender"

Joan Wallach Scott, *Institute for Advanced Study, Princeton, New Jersey*

hat is the point of Mary Hawkesworth's article (in this volume)? Of this kind of finger-wagging "correction" of the work of people who are presumably her political allies? Let's leave aside for the moment the misrepresentations and distortions she produces to advance her "critique," although these are relevant too. Why go through such contortions as she does, risking the exposure of her own analytic limitations in order to attack—in the name of feminism—some of the most original feminist scholarship we have? If Mary Hawkesworth's article were an isolated piece, it would not be worth asking these questions or, indeed, bothering to address at all. But since it is an example of a genre of academic writing that is increasingly evident in feminist circles, I think its significance needs to be pondered. Why is there now a proliferation of work that tries to patrol the borders of feminist inquiry in the name of "emancipation"? Why these efforts to circumscribe definitions, to prescribe (and proscribe) conclusions in the name of "liberation"? Why this eagerness to impose an ill-conceived form of discipline in a field that takes pride in the rigor of its inter-disciplinarity?

Optimistically, one could say that struggle over terminology, strategy, and theory is but a sign of the growing pains of a maturing field. And that canonical texts become so in part because they are vigorously contested. Pessimistically, one could say that violent polemics are the correlate of po-litical impotence, the last gasps of a movement whose least radical elements are about to be subsumed into the mainstream, while the most radical are lashed back into oblivion. Skeptically, or perhaps materialistically (de-pending on one's perspective), one could say that these "critiques" are nothing more than the signs of an intense careerism. Competition for scarce positions and resources has turned political allies into professional enemies in the area of feminist studies, as elsewhere. In the race for promi-nence, young scholars seek to display their intelligence not by demonstra-ting originality of thought but by finding fault in the work of those whom they want to emulate and displace.

But I do not think any of these possibilities can fully account for the phenomenon of which Hawkesworth's article is only a recent example. Rather, I think these efforts to impose conceptual cleanliness, scrub away ambiguity, and purge contradiction are symptoms of feminism's incurable paradoxical condition (something I have written about at length else-where).[1] The incurable condition is the effect of contradictions in liberal democratic theory that offer universal guarantees of inclusion but hold out a singular standard for inclusion. Difference and multiplicity fit uneasily in this scheme, if at all. That is the source of the dilemma women have repeat-edly confronted since the democratic revolutions of the eighteenth cen-tury: They have needed to prove sameness in order to qualify for equality if they are to meet the singular standard (of masculine individuality) held out for inclusion, but they have had to argue for equality as women, thus raising the issue of their difference. The equality versus difference dilemma does not admit of resolution. It is built into feminism, which at once em-bodies and protests against the contradictions of liberal political theory.

Feminism is not the source of its constitutive problems, and yet many of its adherents act as if that were the case. They make the mistake of blaming

---

[1] See Scott 1996.

feminism for liberalism's contradictions and, like the aspirant saints of the Middle Ages, make self-purification a rationale for existence. They think that by expunging contradiction, complexity, ambiguity, and even disagreement from within the feminist movement, they will also end inequality, hierarchy, injustice, and discrimination in the world. But, since contradiction, complexity, and ambiguity are exactly what need to be addressed, they succeed only in undermining their own cause. They perpetuate the symptoms (and the discursive system that produced them) that they ought to be analyzing.

This is the case with Hawkesworth's article. She rushes from text to text, sweeping away complexity (as so much dirt in the feminist household), and replacing it with seemingly tidier either/or formulations when none have been proposed. Thus she turns Judith Butler's careful attempt to analyze the relationships between the social and subjective aspects of gender into an either/or proposition. "Butler's account makes gender too much a matter of the self," she asserts. It "privatizes gender," disregarding "the economic and political forces that circumscribe women's lives" (150). For Hawkesworth there is a necessary opposition between the symbolic and the material, the abstract and the concrete, the individual and the social, the psychic and the institutional, the subjective and the political. She cannot grasp the fact that Butler refuses these binary divisions. *Gender Trouble* (1990), after all, is meant precisely to confound all these seemingly clear distinctions that are actually not at all clear, but whose false clarity is required to shore up the "natural attitude" that Hawkesworth so passionately wants to refute. Unfortunately, the "natural attitude" cannot be refuted by force of logic or by repudiation. It has to be denaturalized, and that requires understanding how it operates, not only as an abstract logical system, but as the ideology that constitutes subjective experiences of gender. For Hawkesworth, this kind of understanding (because it requires a certain intimate knowledge of "the enemy") is tantamount to betrayal.

Hawkesworth rewrites Steven Smith's (1992) analysis of the operations of the sex/gender distinction as a base/superstructure model when that is not the case. She is so eager to expunge biology as a determinant of gender that she reads his descriptions of how gender ideology works as an endorsement of its assumptions. She makes him an advocate of heterosexual complementarity and reproductive drives, when he is an analyst of these desires. While he understands them to be the *effect* of a certain gender ideology, she takes them to be *causes* of (or explanations for) gender.

It is Hawkesworth who imputes causality, not Smith (or Connell or Butler or Kessler and McKenna). She does this, I think, because she cannot accept the idea that ideologies may have real, material ("palpable" in her terms) effects. ("Is gender after all, a matter of belief more than a structure of social forces?" she asks [96], separating two realms that the authors she reviews insist cannot be separated.) The paradox of language, so eloquently captured by Roland Barthes's discussion of historical discourse ("fact never has any but a linguistic existence . . . , yet everything happens as if this linguistic existence were merely a pure and simple 'copy' of *another* existence, situated in an extra-structural field, the 'real'" [1986, 138]), is intolerable for her. So Hawkesworth replaces paradox (which holds opposites in unresolvable tension) with a set of binary oppositions. Since, in her philosophy, effects must have causes and since "reality" cannot be an effect, she deems it a cause. From this follows her misreading of these five authors as committed to base/superstructure models and to "functionalism." While the authors treat subjective desires, reproductive impulses, heterosexual norms of complementarity, and the like as *effects* of gender ideologies, Hawkesworth reads them the other way around. Since she will not even entertain the idea that ideologies produce biological and psychic realities by claiming to reflect those realities, she not only misses the point of the books she reviews but also fails to grasp their authors' analyses of *how* gender operates.

Hawkesworth's rationalist posture creates the illusion that she has carefully dissected the logic of these books and found their flaws. In fact, she imposes a false logic on them. The distinctions she makes between gender as an analytic category and gender as an explanans do not hold up when applied to these authors. Their work is preeminently analytic; they dissect the problem into its parts and try to understand their interrelationships. It is Hawkesworth who reifies gender, not the five authors, and Hawkesworth who introduces an external measure of adequacy for the work they do. That measure is fundamentally anti-intellectual: the work must serve the liberation of women in the terms she understands it (as a political process that refutes or beats down the "natural attitude") or it is denounced. So if Butler (1990) seeks to understand how gender ideologies produce "women" and enforce normative subjectivities, she is accused of perpetuating "women's invisibility" and "miring them in victimization." And if Kessler and McKenna (1978) want to explore the psychological workings of gender in order to identify its social and political as well as personal effects, they are accused of giving up on the political entirely. "There are dire implications in the displacement of gender from external world to internal, mental terrain," she writes, as if gender could not exist in both realms at once (171). If Smith (1992) shows that gender produces subjectively felt experiences of sexuality that are attributed to biology, he is reviled as a biological determinist since any recognition of biology is, says Hawkesworth, "an impossible ground for feminist accounts of gender" (155). But to recognize the power of biological thinking is not to attribute gender to biology, just as to recognize the power of capitalist ideology is neither to accept the idea that the market is a natural force nor to deny the need for socialism. Poor Robert Connell (1987) is accused of harboring "heterosexist presumptions" because he analyzes the powerful ways in which the impetus to reproduce is made the basis for a gender system that takes heterosexuality and its pleasures as its norm. Somehow, in Hawkesworth's reckoning, even mentioning these things means acceptance of them and this mentioning, therefore, is bad for feminism.

Hawkesworth assumes the stance of the logical reasoner in order to advance propositions that are both outdated and counterproductive. They are outdated because feminists of whatever theoretical persuasion are beyond the point of refusing to take seriously ideas, ideologies, and practices they do not like. It will not work anymore to denounce the false consciousness of antifeminist or nonfeminist women; we need to know how they think as they do, how and in what terms and with what conflicts they experience their femininity. Hawkesworth's propositions are counterproductive because they dismiss as antifeminist theories that might have some use, but that she does not like. Instead of engaging in a serious debate about the very different analyses of gender ideology contained in the four books she reviews, she lumps them all together and refuses their terms in the name of feminism. But who is she to take up that name?

If feminism is to maintain its critical force, if it is to challenge and disrupt the workings of powerful hierarchies designed to keep women "in their place," then it must be allowed to contemplate its paradoxes and the ambiguities of its existence. Such contemplation involves analyzing not only the conditions of existence (psychic as well as social) that produce inequalities of power but also the discursive conditions that produce feminism. The two are obviously interrelated, but not as stimulus and response. Feminism is not an inevitable response to discrimination against women. It is made possible by theories of equality and justice that are also sometimes the source of inequality and injustice. Feminism exists because of these contradictions and as a contradiction in societies that represent themselves as democratic. There is no way to purge contradiction from feminism, nor is it possible to get rid of contradiction in the theorizing of feminists.

We ought to be debating issues, not conducting purity campaigns. And I hope future issues of *Signs* will encourage wide-ranging and serious debate of diverse theoretical points of view: not in the interest of promoting the idea that "anything goes" in feminist theory, but in the interest of impurity, nonconformity, and unruliness—the traits that have made possible feminism's most original contributions and its most important breakthroughs.

References

Barthes, Roland. 1986. "The Discourse of History." In his *The Rustle of Language*, trans. Richard Howard. New York: Hill & Wang.

Butler, Judith. 1990. *Gender Trouble: Feminism and the Subversion of Identity.* New York: Routledge.

Connell, R. W. 1987. *Gender and Power.* Stanford, Calif.: Stanford University Press.

Kessler, Suzanne, and Wendy McKenna. 1978. *Gender: An Ethnomethodological Approach.* New York: Wiley.

Scott, Joan Wallach. 1996. *Only Paradoxes to Offer: French Feminists and the Rights of Man.* Cambridge, Mass.: Harvard University Press.

Smith, Steven G. 1992. *Gender Thinking.* Philadelphia: Temple University Press. I

Comment on Hawkesworth's "Confounding Gender": Re-Structuring Gender

R. W. Connell, *School of Social and Policy Studies in Education, University of Sydney*

Mary Hawkesworth's clear and interesting article (in this volume) centers on the connection between gender politics and gender theory. I share her concern with this connection, and applaud the attempt to grapple with general theories of gender on this terrain. I am pleased to see attention being given to Suzanne Kessler and Wendy McKenna's pioneering, and still highly relevant, work.

Hawkesworth argues, on the basis of a detailed reading of the four texts, that despite their marked differences they share a common problem, a tendency to reductionism and functionalism. This surprising conclusion, if true, is an important critique of gender theory. It is a particularly worrying criticism of *Gender and Power* (Connell 1987), which vigorously rejects functionalism and reductionism and tries to spell out an alternative. Reductionist or functionalist theory, Hawkesworth rightly observes, would lead feminism into pessimism, or into a universalizing stance that would exclude rather than include.

Hawkesworth detects in all these texts a shift in the status of gender from an analytic category to a causal force, a shift that produces bogus explanations. The concern is valid. A universalizing model of gender difference *does* produce bogus explanations. This is a common form of argument, and it is politically important to reject it, for the reasons Hawkesworth gives.

But it is not right to conclude from this that "it is a grave error to attribute explanatory force to gender" (173). If that were the case, it would be impossible to understand the fact that "women experience systematic disadvantages in male-dominated societies" (173), or to make strategic judgments about how to contest and end those disadvantages. Such concepts as the patriarchal state, rape culture, compulsory heterosexuality, the gender division of labor, and the glass ceiling would all be swept away—since all such concepts explain by means of gender and express patterns of causation in gender relations.

The crucial point is what one takes *gender* to be. In her central argument, Hawkesworth takes a strictly categorical view of gender, understanding the term to mean categories of persons. This is common enough, but it is by no means the only way of understanding gender. *Gender and Power* was written to draw together the many strands of thought—in feminism, psychoanalysis, socialism, social science, and political practice—that understand gender as, centrally, a structure of *social relations*. Drawing on this broad tradition, *Gender and Power* identifies three main structures of gender relations—economic relations, power relations, and relations of cathexis—and argues that the categories of everyday life are produced by social practice arising within these structures.

The "causal force," in such an understanding of gender, lies in the historical dynamic of the structure of social relations—for instance, in economic exploitation, political struggle, and emotional contradiction. There are undoubtedly some errors and incoherencies in the way *Gender and Power* works out that argument, but the emphasis on the historical dynamic is, I think, fairly clear and consistent. The historicity of gender is explored at all levels of analysis: from the relation of the body to society (pt. 1), through social structure (pt. 2), personality (pt. 3), and politics (pt. 4).

Without a sense of historicity, an understanding of gender in terms of social relations *could* fall into functionalism. A well-known example is the nonreductionist sex role theory offered in the 1950s by Talcott Parsons. Its conservatism was contested by feminism's recognition of gender politics, the fact that gender relations involved the oppression of women. Unless one assumes that oppression is a timeless universal structure (which a certain kind of cultural feminism did), the recognition of politics disrupts functionalism and requires a move to some other kind of theory.

Gender and Power makes this move, not only by arguing the historicity of gender at all levels of analysis, but also by developing a particular analysis of the politics of gender. This is mainly worked out in the final three chapters of the book and is not much emphasized in Hawkesworth's summary. A summary cannot cover everything, of course. However, this seems to me an important part of the argument. A key advantage of the relational approach to gender is that we can understand gender politics as the clash of *interests* constituted historically within gender relations.

To give a brief, but important, example: in the developing countries as a whole in 1992, women had an average schooling of 3.0 years, men an average of 4.9 years (United Nations Development Programme 1994, 139). This gives the women, broadly speaking, an interest in change, and the men, broadly speaking, a privilege to defend. *Gender and Power* explores the way conflicting interests arise in structures of inequality, how broad social interests are articulated by intellectuals, and how they result in different patterns of political practice, from working-class feminism to gay liberation.

This conception of interests underlies the "sociology of knowledge" approach to sexual ideology. For that reason, I do not agree with Hawkesworth that there is a covert functionalism in the discussion of ideology. It is not functionalist to argue that a particular (sexist) ideology is promoted because it serves a dominant (men's) interest; that is, I would suggest, merely realist. (Of course, such a claim is only a starting point; one must then demonstrate how the job is done, examine countercurrents and contradictions, etc.) The "necessity to shore up gender" (166) is not a universal functional requirement, it is a historically produced strategy in gender practice. *Gender and Power* is clear (and I think unusual in emphasizing) that the scope or reach of gender relations changes historically.

Nevertheless, Hawkesworth is right in sensing a weakness in this part of the analysis. *Gender and Power* subordinates the analysis of cultural practice to the problem of political mobilization and thus underestimates the autonomy of cultural processes, and the specificity of what Nancy Fraser (1995) calls "struggles for recognition" in the politics of justice.

Here, my argument may have been led astray, not by its functionalism, but by the vehemence of its antifunctionalism. In *Gender and Power* I was concerned to show how we could have a strong structural analysis that did not fall into functionalism, by developing an analysis of the *crisis tendencies* in a gender order. The treatment of ideology is framed by this concern. Although the discussion of ideology needs revision, I would still emphasize the issue of crisis tendencies in gender relations. This is, for instance, essential for an understanding of current developments in masculinity politics, an argument worked out in detail in *Masculinities* (Connell 1995).

The center of Hawkesworth's critique is that classic problem in gender analysis, the relation between the body and social practice. *Gender and Power* addresses this issue head-on and attempts an analysis that acknowledges the importance of bodies but refuses to treat them as the "basis" or "foundation" of the social process of gender. Hawkesworth argues (in a nutshell) that the attempt fails, so the analysis ultimately falls back on a naturalized conception of sexual difference.

She offers two lines of argument, about reproduction and about eroticism. First, there is a procreationist premise to the argument. *Gender and Power* does, indeed, have a concern with procreation. I offer no apology for thinking sexual reproduction, mothering and fathering, is a very important part of what gender practice is about. I think "Third World women" would be most surprised to be told that these are matters of "privatized gender." On the contrary, they are major concerns of the "collective struggle," for instance, of black women in South Africa (see, e.g., the concerns of the South African feminist journal *Agenda*). An inclusive feminism, surely, must find ways of thinking about gender that give a prominent place to reproductive issues, for they are prominent concerns of very large numbers of women.

Does *Gender and Power* smuggle a procreationist ideology into the basic categories of gender? I do not think so, although a negative is hard to prove. Hawkesworth is justified in her criticism of my use of the series/group model, borrowed from Sartre; this framework is not as helpful as I thought at the time of writing. Reflecting Sartre's own overdramatized conception of politics, the model rests on too stark a contrast between the inert and the mobilized; my application of it, as Hawkesworth points out, tends to collapse gender into ideology. The problem is not with procreationism, but with a general tendency to skip the mundane and to underplay the institutional level of analysis (families, workplaces, etc.).

Yet the intention behind Sartre's theorizing in the *Critique of Dialectical Reason*, to account for the incorporation of material reality into historical process, was sound. This is an issue a relational theory of gender cannot evade. Here I think the discussion of "practical transformations of the body" in *Gender and Power* should be noted: this is antireductionist and explores the relation between "the body" and "society" as a matter of concrete practices in which bodies, as well as social relations, are changed.

In relation to sexuality, Hawkesworth makes a strong statement (and refers back to it more than once) about the "startling" descent to a complementarity thesis—that *Gender and Power*, in effect, makes a natural-ized heterosexuality the basis of the theory of gender. She quotes from page 113: "Sexual difference is in large part what gives erotic flavor to relationships. It is emphasised as a means of heightening and intensifying pleasure, hence, the systematic exaggeration of gender differences." She goes on to suggest this erotic complementarity is the book's "fundamental explanation of why gender persists" (166).

The critique sounds right, as stated, and leads to some sharp words about heterosexist assumptions. But Hawkesworth has unfortunately done two very problematic things here: misquoted text and taken it out of con-text. What page 113 actually says, in a paragraph specifically about hege-monic heterosexuality, is (differences are italicized): "*More, the* sexual dif-ference is *a large part of what* gives erotic flavour to *the* relationship. Hence it *can be* emphasised as a means of intensifying pleasure. This *goes some way* to explaining the systematic exaggeration of gender differences *discussed in chapters 4 and 8*."

This already sounds a good deal less functionalist. It becomes even more difficult to see the functionalism or reductionism when one notes that this passage occurs in a discussion of cathexis—specified as being only one of three structures of gender—which starts by postulating the social construc-tion of sexuality (111), emphasizes that "sexual attachment has not always been organized in terms of a dichotomy" (112), treats homosexual as well as heterosexual desire, and goes on to discuss inequality within heterosexu-ality, repression as a basis of heterosexuality, ambivalence, and the politics of sexual practice (113–16). What Hawkesworth has done is to take a pas-sage that attempts to analyze the dynamics of a historically specific form of emotional attachment as if it were the ahistorical basis of the whole theory of gender.

I sympathize with Hawkesworth's concern that we should have theories of gender that open up political prospects rather than close them off. And I agree with her about the difficulty of sustaining a fully social analysis of gender. (The difficulty is illustrated in the phrase already quoted from her conclusion, "women experience systematic disadvantage in male-dominated societies" [173]—where Hawkesworth, like many other writ-ers, unconsciously uses the social term *women* alongside the biological term *male*.)

But is the only path forward in the deconstructionist direction proposed by Hawkesworth? That, too, has its problems! In the final analysis, Hawkesworth's argument collapses all alternatives into a single alternative, and in doing so closes off important paths for theory. I think a relational

theory is essential for understanding gender on the large scale, in the world
arena in which we now have to act.

References
Connell, R. W. 1987. *Gender and Power.* Stanford, Calif.: Stanford University Press.
———. 1995. *Masculinities.* Berkeley and Los Angeles: University of California
Press.
Fraser, Nancy. 1995. "From Redistribution to Recognition? Dilemmas of Justice
in a 'Post-Socialist' Age." *New Left Review* 212 (July–August): 68–93.
United Nations Development Programme. 1994. *Human Development Report 1994.*
New York: Oxford University Press. ∎

Reply to McKenna and Kessler, Smith, Scott, and Connell: Interrogating Gender

Mary Hawkesworth, *Department of Political Science,*
University of Louisville

One of the profound insights of feminist scholarship is that claims concerning the "neutrality" of research tools are deeply suspicious. Feminist scholars working in the humanities, social sciences, and natural sciences have provided compelling demonstrations that theories, methodologies, units of analysis, categories, concepts, and genres, as well as substantive arguments, incorporate tacit biases. A commitment to critical interrogation of the analytic categories of traditional academic disciplines might be considered a hallmark of feminist inquiry. Are there reasons to believe that the analytic tools of feminist analysis are insulated from the possibility of bias? Are there reasonable grounds for feminist scholars to exempt our own inquiry from scrutiny?

In "Confounding Gender" (in this volume) I argued that there are good reasons—intellectual and political—for interrogating one of the central analytic categories of feminism, gender. To investigate troubling presuppositions that surface in some feminist accounts of gender in no way denies that gender is enormously complex, that its explication involves diverse terrains (e.g., sexed and raced bodies, sexualities, identities, social relations, social norms, social practices, divisions of labor, distributions of power), or that the concept of gender is deeply in need of theorizing. To argue that feminist use of gender as an analytic category illuminates rich new areas for investigation in no way dismisses the force of traditional gender conceptions in contemporary life and social organization. Nor does it suggest that analysis alone is sufficient to eliminate inequality, hierarchy, injustice, and discrimination. Theoretical analysis may, however, excavate buried assumptions that constrain understandings of social and political problems and impair the formation of political coalitions required to attain democratic solutions to those problems.

When feminist scholars employ gender as an analytic category, they are doing far more than simply describing the world. They are constructing a framework that "points out the problematic nature of the obvious" (Acker 1990, 140). They are making visible relations of hierarchy, differences in power, as well as tensions and contradictions in the relations of men and women and in diverse practices and institutions that structure social life and constitute individual consciousness. Gender as an analytic category frames questions for investigation that are literally inconceivable within traditional disciplines. Identifying a research question, however, is not the same thing as explaining the phenomenon under investigation. Perceiving something as problematic is only the first step in an intellectual process that may be as interminable as it is arduous. To conflate the illumination of an area for inquiry with explanation, then, is to foreclose critical examination of issues prematurely. In cautioning feminists against too hasty a move from gender as analytic category to gender as explanans, I do not mean to "prescribe (and proscribe) conclusions" (Scott, 190) but rather to offer an invitation to further inquiry.

Perhaps the importance of the distinction between gender as analytic category and gender as explanation can be illustrated by considering several of the examples given by Robert Connell in "Re-Structuring Gender." Connell argues that if feminists accept my claim that it is an error to attribute explanatory force to gender, then "it would be impossible to understand the fact that 'women experience systematic disadvantages in male-dominated societies,' or to make strategic judgments about how to contest and end those disadvantages. Such concepts as the patriarchal state, rape culture, compulsory heterosexuality, the gender division of labor, and the glass ceiling would all be swept away—since all such concepts explain by means of gender and express patterns of causation in gender relations" (195). What must be assumed about gender in order to make sense of the claim that gender "explains" the systematic disadvantages women experience in male-dominated societies? If gender is defined as a system of male dominance, then one might say that male dominance itself "explains" disadvantages experienced by women, but then the "explanation" is a matter of stipulative definition and tautology. Circularity supplants inquiry and important questions go unaddressed. In what sense does gender "explain" the concept of the patriarchal state? If gender is defined in terms of a posited male "interest" in domination, linked to men's desire to control women's sexuality for their own gratification and for control of their progeny, then perhaps gender "explains" the patriarchal state. Such an explanation, however, also rests on stipulative definition and imputed interests, subsuming difficult questions about the complex causes of women's oppression under gender's vague rubric. How does gender "explain" compulsory heterosexuality? If gender is defined in terms of the ideology of procreation, then perhaps one has the makings of an explanation for compulsory heterosexuality, but it is a tautological "explanation" bought at the cost of reducing diverse cultural practices to reproductive imperatives. Can these putative reproductive imperatives somehow "explain" a rape culture? If so, then why are not all cultures rape cultures? Can these putative reproductive imperatives "explain" sex segregation in jobs such as computer programming? Can they "explain" the gender symbolism attached to certain occupations, such as the image of a strong, technologically competent manager who is effective in part because "he" keeps "his" emotions under control? If gender is so versatile that it can "explain" so many different things, is it really "explaining" anything?

To answer that question requires examination of the adequacy of stipulative definitions of gender. In "Confounding Gender" I investigated the presuppositions of a number of accounts of gender, suggesting that the ideology of procreation surfaces too frequently for comfort. In his comment on my article, Steven Smith says that he is not "defining" gender, his "presentations of gender ideas are consistently *hypothetical*. The point of [his] appreciative construals is always that there are certain interesting things gender *can* mean, meanings that can lend their power to everyday gender thinking and comportment" (188; emphasis in original). While I do not doubt that gender can be interpreted in terms of sexed bodies that have their own "center of meaning in reproduction: woman as egg producer; man as sperm producer" (Smith 1992, 46), I do not believe that a conception of gender that keeps collapsing into reproductive imperatives will help feminist scholars investigate the range of cultural practices through which gender is constructed, deployed, and re-created at the close of the twentieth century. Nor do I consider it wise feminist practice to "vindicate a gender order" (188) because certain "functions (e.g., childbearing and fighting) are necessary and require that our lives be substantially adapted to them" (Smith 1992, 69). To substantiate my claim that Smith's conception of gender is empirically and normatively inadequate for feminist scholarship, consider the following example.

In a fascinating study of the military's ban on homosexuality, Judith Stiehm (1994) demonstrates that the homophobic fears that fueled this policy initially involved straight men's fears of being sexually objectified and assaulted by gay men, supplemented by management fears that aggression by heterosexuals against gays was growing out of control and undermining discipline within the ranks. Rather than conducting an educational campaign to prove that straight men's fears of sexual assault were unwarranted and rather than prohibiting gay bashing among enlisted personnel, the military chose to ban homosexuals from the armed forces. Although the central issues that gave rise to this policy have grown out of men's fears and men's behavior, Stiehm also shows that the military's ban on homosexuality disproportionately penalizes women. Women have been dismissed from the services for homosexuality at a rate far higher than men. Between 1980 and 1990, women constituted 23 percent of the discharges for homosexuality while they were only 10 percent of military personnel. As a feminist scholar, Stiehm analyzes this disparate impact as a gendered phenomenon, but her understanding of gender has nothing to do with notions of complementarity necessitated by reproduction, much less by putative imperatives pertaining to "fighting." Stiehm's research suggests that the women discharged from the military refused to conform to codes of "feminine" conduct that stipulate that a woman should be flattered by the unwanted attentions of her boss. In a disproportionate number of cases, Stiehm found that the women dismissed on the charge of lesbianism were women who had rebuffed the advances of a male superior officer, who refused to flirt on the job, who rejected the culturally dominant stereotype of woman as sex object. Smith's complementarity model of gender could not capture the power relations operative in this example and Smith's tendency to legitimate "species imperatives" fails to contest such relations of domination and subordination.

In analyzing Connell's *Gender and Power* (1987), my concern was not that he "smuggle[d in] a procreationist ideology" (197) but, rather, that he explicitly conceptualizes gender as an interrelated set of social structures that define men and women in terms of their reproductive role, as an active process that reduces people to, and conceives of social life in terms of, reproductive function. This narrow definition of gender exists in tension with the far richer accounts of gendered phenomena that Connell presents in his discussions of labor, power, and cathexis. Beyond suggesting that his analysis of the complex terrains of gender exceeds the narrowness of the definition he provides, I tried to show that his effort to explicate how gender "works" by invoking Sartre's distinction between series and group fails for a number of theoretical reasons. In addition to the narrowness of his explicit definition of gender and an unsuccessful attempt to explain the mechanics of gender's reduction of people to reproductive roles, I also questioned Connell's attempt to explain why cultures invest so much effort in the production of sexual differences. Connell is quite right to point out that his explanation arises in the context of a discussion of hegemonic heterosexuality. If gender is defined in terms of reducing men and women to their reproductive roles, then there is no where else to turn for an explanation but to heterosexuality. Even in the context of hegemonic heterosexuality, however, I find highly implausible the notion that the "practical transformations of the body" as well as the "hegemonic masculinity and emphasized femininity" that Connell discusses with such sophistication in chapters 4 and 8 of his book stem from efforts to heighten erotic pleasure.

Wendy McKenna and Suzanne Kessler suggest that their project in *Gender: An Ethnomethodological Approach* (1978) "was to describe the interpretive practices that permit us to 'see' and 'do' gender, not to identify the gender-related causes of any particular set of cultural circumstances. Gender is not a mental category (in an ontological sense). Mental schemas (categories) result in seeing gender as an ontological category" (180). Their book is a tour de force. In pressing the implications of their arguments, I did not mean to suggest that their project was not inherently worthwhile or deeply illuminating. It is both. I remain puzzled, however, about the nature of these "mental schemas." Since the eighteenth century, some philosophers have argued that the mind is active, imposing an order upon perception, supplanting ambiguity with psychological certainty, thereby rendering "experience" useful and making survival possible. This form of argument has been highly conservative, validating the "categories of the mind" by linking them to species survival, mastery of the environment, or the very conditions of rationality. In calling attention to the ways in which Kessler and McKenna's discussions of "mental schemas" seem comparable to arguments by Hume and Kant, my point was not to "naturalize 'internal' and 'external', treating them as concrete locations" (181) but, rather, to challenge the displacement of social processes onto mental operations in a way that imputes "necessity" to the categories of the mind. Kessler and McKenna vividly document the social constitution of consciousness, but references to "mental schemas" that produce perceptions of gender as ontology may not be the best way to characterize this process.

I agree completely with McKenna and Kessler that reason has a crucial role to play in denaturalizing gender constructs and I believe their book is an excellent example of feminist scholarship that systematically challenges the natural attitude. In a sense then, I think they accomplish far more than they claim ethnomethodology allows. Their book succeeds precisely because beliefs about gender are not incorrigible, if incorrigible means "not liable or open to correction" or "beyond possibility of amendment" as the *Oxford English Dictionary* suggests. It is futile to try to change incorrigible beliefs, but as Kessler and McKenna so cogently demonstrate in their work, feminist scholarship is not futile. In this sense, then, their feminist methodology breaks with some of the tenets of ethnomethodology, even while borrowing from that approach.

Joan Scott criticizes my attempt to interrogate some of the analytic tools of feminist scholarship, suggesting that contradiction, complexity, and ambiguity are the conditions of feminism's existence. Setting aside Scott's uncharitable ruminations about personal motivations, I have no quarrel with feminist efforts to "contemplate its paradoxes and the ambiguities of its existence" (193). I would note, however, that all contradictions are not of the same order. Some contradictions are existential; others are the product of errors in reasoning. Women athletes barred from competition in the Southeast Asian Games after failing "gender tests," that is, chromosomal tests to determine whether they possess the XX chromosomal configuration deemed to constitute "scientific proof of the feminine gender," are the embodiment of a gender contradiction (Condit 1993). They are women with female bodies who have a clear conception of themselves as women, yet they are publicly pronounced to be "a sex which is not one"[1] — neither female nor male as a consequence of the conflation of gender with biological sex — a sex determined not by genitals but by genes. If feminist scholars assert that gender is an enormously complex phenomenon that is historically variable and culturally constituted across the terrains of psyche, self, social relations, and symbolic systems, while simultaneously holding that gender is invariably a system of concord rooted in sexual reproduction, they are producing a contradiction of a different sort, an error in reasoning. Feminists gain nothing by attributing such a contradiction to liberalism. Liberalism is riddled with functionalist commitments that legitimate a hierarchical gender order as an antidote to the centrifugal forces of rugged individualism, but an unwitting replication of such assumptions does not help feminist scholars to contest liberalism's many defects. Nor is it accurate to say that all the problems I address in "Confounding Gender" are simply manifestations of a pervasive "gender ideology" that these authors are seeking to explicate. Butler, Connell, and Kessler and McKenna do present insightful critiques of gender ideology, but their works also advance substantive claims about how gender "works," that is, about the role

---

[1] This phrase is borrowed from Luce Irigaray (1985), although I am giving it a markedly different meaning than in Irigaray's text of the same name.

gender plays in society and the functions it serves. It is that aspect of their rich and various accounts that I have sought to probe and contest.

Feminists need analytic tools that advance our intellectual and political objectives. If tacit values incorporated in feminist methods of inquiry are incompatible with feminist transformative projects, then subjecting those values to critical scrutiny can be beneficial. Systematic attention to gender as an analytic category can enable feminists to preserve the creative insights of new and diverse modes of intellectual inquiry without falling into untenable claims concerning gender's explanatory force or reproductive roots.

References

Acker, Joan. 1990. "Hierarchies, Jobs, Bodies: A Theory of Gendered Organizations." *Gender and Society* 4(2):139–58.

Condit, Deirdre. 1993. "Unmasking the Sex/Gender Myth and Rethinking the Rhetoric of Political Bodies." Paper presented at the Foundations of Political Theory Workshop on Political Myth, Rhetoric, and Symbolism held in conjunction with the annual meeting of the American Political Science Association, Washington, D.C., September 2–5.

Connell, Robert W. 1987. *Gender and Power.* Stanford, Calif.: Stanford University Press.

Irigaray, Luce. 1985. *This Sex Which Is Not One,* trans. Catherine Porter. Ithaca, N.Y.: Cornell University Press.

Kessler, Suzanne, and Wendy McKenna. 1978. *Gender: An Ethnomethodological Approach.* New York: Wiley.

Smith, Steven G. 1992. *Gender Thinking.* Philadelphia: Temple University Press.

Stiehm, Judith Hicks. 1994. "Difference Is Not Opposite." Paper presented at the annual meeting of the Western Political Science Association, Albuquerque, N. Mex., March 10–13.

De-confounding Gender: Feminist Theorizing and Western Culture, a Comment on Hawkesworth's "Confounding Gender"

Oyeronke Oyewumi, *Department of Black Studies, University of California, Santa Barbara*

In her article, "Confounding Gender," published in this volume, Mary Hawkesworth undertakes an inventory of the state of gender theorizing through a close reading of four major texts in the field:[1] Steven G. Smith's *Gender Thinking* (1992), a fundamentalist account of gender for species survival; Judith Butler's *Gender Trouble* (1990), a dazzling analysis of gender as performance; Robert Connell's *Gender and Power* (1987), an elucidation of gender as multilayered social practice; and Suzanne Kessler and Wendy McKenna's *Gender: An Ethnomethodological Approach* (1978), an insightful definition of gender as a way of thinking. Hawkesworth concludes that, despite varied approaches to the conceptualization of gender, an unsettling common thread of biologism is discernible in these works, which, she argues, "construct a narrative that implicates gender in 'the ideology of procreation'" (146). In other words, after all is said and done, the specter of biological determinism stalks even feminist accounts of gender. For Hawkesworth, what accounts for this disturbing state of affairs is the conflation of what she calls "gender as analytic category" and "gender as explanans," both in the aforementioned texts and indeed in many other feminist accounts of gender (146).

Hawkesworth's intervention, although a necessary stocktaking, does not move far from this biologism. I would argue that the distinction she makes between "gender as analytic category" and "gender as explanans" is false. I therefore find unfounded her claim that the "natural attitude" that haunts many feminist statements about gender would disappear if scholars used gender only as an analytic category and not as an explanatory

---

[1] Hawkesworth's choice of these books seems logical because they appear to be the most extended accounts in gender theory. However, that much of the discussion of gender in these works is based on Western culture makes it difficult to "confront the reality of other possibilities" (Kessler and McKenna 1978, 164) in other cultures that is absolutely necessary for understanding gender as social construction. Attention to the work of feminist anthropologists may provide another perspective through which gender questions can be posed. Ortner 1996 and Atkinson and Errington 1990 are two good examples of works that discuss gender in other cultures.

[*Signs: Journal of Women in Culture and Society* 1998, vol. 23, no. 4]

cause.[2] What is missing in many feminist theories of gender, including Hawkesworth's, is a notion of culture(s). That is, "the idea that people have their own historically sedimented frames of reference, and come at events [the social world] with their own ways of thinking and feeling which means that people of different cultures organize their world in distinct ways" (Ortner 1996, 183).[3] Gender is first, and foremost, a cultural construct. As such, it is intelligible only in a cultural frame; any theory of gender, therefore, must be attentive to the fact that there are many cultures in the world and Western culture is only one of them. Thus any claims made on the basis of studies in one culture cannot necessarily hold true for other cultures and should not be universalized. Many Western theorists of gender seem to be impervious to the existence of other cultures; they make their case for gender from the narrow confines of the West. It is clear that the biological determinism that rears its head in much feminist scholarship is very much tied to Westocentrism — the treatment of Western culture as Culture (with a capital *C*), suggesting that it is the only one. This in turn leads many Western theorists to universalize Western biologism as if all societies engage in such thinking.[4]

There is a widespread fixation among feminists on Western culture. Many scholarly tomes on gender draw their evidence exclusively from within Western culture, and sometimes from within even narrower slices of American culture, to make universalist claims. Surely, if gender is indeed socially constructed and "woman" is a heterogeneous, culture-bound category, as many feminists have come to assert, making grand claims about gender or women after having examined only one culture should be unthinkable. To sharpen my point, I highlight a recent book that is unremarkable because it is typical. In *Gender Trials: Emotional Lives in Contemporary Law Firms* (1995), sociologist Jennifer Pierce conducts a study of gender in American law firms and draws some general conclusions about gender and emotional labor in the workplace. The book is based on the United States, yet nowhere in her conclusions does she introduce that qualifica-

---

[2] See Hawkesworth, in this volume, 141, for elucidation of the term *natural attitude*.

[3] Sandra Harding makes a similar point: "Cultures have different locations in the heterogeneous natural world. . . . They bring different interests even to the 'same' natural or social environment. . . . They draw on, and are positioned in different ways with respect to, culturally distinctive discursive resources — metaphors, models, narratives, conceptual frameworks — with which to think about themselves and the world around them. Moreover, they have culturally distinctive ways of organizing . . . knowledge, usually highly related to how they produce everything else" (1997, 386).

[4] If, indeed, the claim is that all societies engage in this ideology, proof will have to be offered; it cannot be taken for granted. Ortner 1996 offers some interesting counterarguments to this unbridled universalism.

tion. Arlie Hochschild's endorsement of the book on the dust jacket is even more startling: "This is an exciting contribution to our understanding of gender and emotion in workplaces *everywhere*" (my emphasis). This is a book that cannot provide an understanding of the emotional labor involved in working in U.S. law firms without acknowledging that both attorneys and paralegals are not only gendered beings but also racialized beings, a fact that Pierce alludes to but fails to incorporate into her analysis. The only subjects with racial identities in her account are African Americans and other so-called minorities. Tom is "Tom, a young student" (59), and Patricia is "Patricia, a young woman attorney" (58); but Yolanda is a "black woman" (120), and Kimberly is the African American secretary (203). "Naturally," white men are "men" and white women are "women," and all this from a self-aware, politically conscious author who gives us an extended account of how her whiteness may have influenced her research (200–207). Pierce offers the usual caveat about how other social identities such as race and ethnicity are important (180), but, in fact, she focuses exclusively on gender and neglects race and ethnicity.

In a review of *Gender Trials,* Jennifer Russell sums up nicely the import of Pierce's analytic segregation: "Pierce misses an essential connection. . . . Doing gender, simultaneously and in ways that are inseparable, does race. . . . [Her] isolation of gender from race and ethnicity obscures the ways in which some — white women — although victimized, are in a position to contribute to the exclusion of others. . . . The bottom line: Jennifer Pierce loses an exciting opportunity to expose how institutionalized sexism operates in race-specific ways" (Russell 1996, 15). The exclusion of women and men of other cultural groups within the United States in this account that uses *women* and *men* as generic terms continues to promote the idea of the transparent white woman as Woman, an old but continuing problem in feminist discourse. If such an account fails to take into consideration different cultural groups within the United States, is it then surprising that it discounts the fact that there are law firms and workplaces in Jamaica or India for which the arguments may not apply? As a starting point, the book should not claim the title *Gender Trials: Emotional Lives in Contemporary Law Firms,* but should qualify its focus on contemporary law firms *in the United States.* Those of us who write on other cultures and societies are routinely asked to qualify our claims, and the titles of our books display the specific societies or countries from which we draw our evidence. Why should (white) American accounts be different? I single out the United States because, increasingly, the titles of European publications specify the national and societal contexts of their research.

Culture(s): The missing base

The explanatory power of each of the theories considered in Hawkes-worth's "Confounding Gender" is directly proportionate to the author's attention to the West as but one local theater for gender construction. It is no accident then that, despite having been written twenty years ago, Suzanne Kessler and Wendy McKenna's *Gender: An Ethnomethodological Approach* offers the most profound statement on gender written to date.[5] The strength of Kessler and McKenna's analysis is that even as they analyze Western culture, they understand that it offers only one way of con-structing gender, that other cultures have different ways of organizing the world (1978, 164). Their work is unique in that it does not display any form of overt biodeterminism or Eurodeterminism. But for some reason, which remains unclear, Kessler and McKenna's work has not received the attention it deserves, and they themselves seem to underestimate the im-portance of their contribution to the field (this volume).

Consequently, my comments will revisit some of their insightful state-ments, which illuminate a number of critical issues. The objective is to move the debate forward by drawing attention to their writing and to what has been left out of the debate and to elucidate those aspects of Kessler and McKenna's thinking in need of further theorizing. In the process, it will become clear why Hawkesworth's distinction between "gender as analytic category" and "gender as explanans" cannot be sustained. My comments encompass four propositions that came out of Kessler and McKenna's book and examine their implications for gender studies. The four asser-tions are as follows: (1) Gender is socially constructed. (2) Every culture has incorrigible propositions. (3) Gender construction involves a process of attribution. (4) Gender is implicated in a cognitive schema; therefore, it is a way of thinking.

The idea that gender is socially constructed has become trite. In 1978, however, when Kessler and McKenna put forward this proposition, it was considered radical in a society in which the "natural attitude" was en-trenched and seemed unequivocal. Social construction implies that differ-ences between males and females are to be located in social practices and not in biological facts. Not surprisingly, feminists found the concept partic-ularly attractive, because it was interpreted to mean that gender differences are not ordained by nature, that they are mutable. This in turn led to the opposition in feminist scholarship between social constructionism and bio-

---

[5] That the most profound statement in the field was written twenty years ago says some-thing about the state of the gender theorizing art.

logical determinism, as if they were mutually exclusive. It soon became apparent that the dichotomy between social construction and the essentialism of the natural attitude was unwarranted, because even feminist social constructionist accounts were informed by notions of inherent differences between males and females. Robert Connell (1987), Holly Devor (1989), Linda Nicholson (1994), and now Hawkesworth, among others, have articulated this problem of biological "foundationalism" (to borrow Nicholson's term) in feminist scholarship. But what accounts for this biologism?

This was one of the questions I set out to answer in my book *The Invention of Women: Making an African Sense of Western Gender Discourses* (Oyewumi 1997). The goal was to account for the biological determinism that remains very much at the heart of Western theories (including those of self-described feminists) about society. Through a detailed comparative study of Western culture and Yoruba culture of southwestern Nigeria, I show that not all cultures necessarily organize their social world through a perception of human bodies. I argue that the cultural logic of the West is actually a "biologic" encapsulated in an ideology of biological determinism, that is, the idea that biology provides the rationale for the organization of the social world. Thus, in this biologic, those with certain kinds of bodies are superior to others by virtue of having certain favored body parts; men are superior to women and whites to blacks. This way of organizing the social world is not inherent in nature; it is produced by a specific conception, a cognitive schema, a way of seeing the world. In the words of McKenna and Kessler, the Western "mental schemas (categories) result in seeing gender as an ontological category" (180).

In contrast, in the conceptual framework on Yoruba, there are neither concepts/words connoting son, daughter, brother, or sister, nor are there any corresponding social roles. As a cue to discerning the fact that gender is absent, the Yoruba language does not "do" gender; instead, it does seniority defined by relative age. Thus, pronouns and kinship categories do not indicate sex but rather rest on who is older than the speaker in any social situation. Siblings are siblings; whether they are older or younger than the speaker is the crucial point in any interaction. Concepts of power and authority are not gendered, and no exclusive male or female social roles or identities exist. The only thing exclusive to female bodies is pregnancy. With regard to the institution of marriage, wives are defined as females marrying into a family; in relation to the wives, all family members by birth, regardless of sex, are defined as their conjugal partners and must play the social role that this entails. In my book, I demonstrate that the Yoruba cognitive schema has no place for gender categories; thus, gender was not constructed in the society. Hence, there were no social categories "man" or "woman."[6] What are the implications of my findings for gender theory?

Gender attribution on a global scale

Despite the idea that gender is socially constructed, many feminists continue to insist that all cultures across time and space *do* and *must* construct gender. In their discussion of gender, Kessler and McKenna "suggest that these categorizing schemas arise from the incorrigible propositions of specific cultures, bracketing questions concerning the origins of the incorrigible propositions themselves" (Hawkesworth, in this volume a, 170). The notion that all cultures across time and space *do* and *must* construct gender introduces an incorrigible proposition in feminist thought. In spite of contrary evidence from other cultures,[7] scholars continue to seek gender and male dominance in other cultures without first establishing whether gender as a social category is transcultural. This question has been bracketed off. If gender is indeed a social construction, as a dominant group of feminists unequivocally and correctly affirm, then logically it cannot be transcultural. The universality attributed to gender asymmetry suggests a biological rather than a cultural basis, given that the human anatomy is universal whereas cultures speak in myriad voices.

> If gender is truly socially constructed, then gender cannot behave in the same way across time and space. If gender is a social construction, then we must examine the various cultural/architectural sites where it was constructed and we must acknowledge that variously located actors (aggregates, groups, interested parties) were part of the construction. We must further acknowledge that if gender is a social construction, there was a specific time (in different cultural/architectural sites) when it was constructed and therefore a time before which, it was not. Thus, gender, being a social construction is also an historical and a cultural phenomenon. Consequently, it is also logical to assume that in some societies, gender construction need not have existed at all. (Oyewumi 1997, 10)

---

[6] I use the past tense here, not because Yoruba ways of organizing the world have disappeared, but because through sustained contact with the West in a colonial relationship there now exist increasingly in Yorubaland Western gender categories, coexisting and comingling with the indigenous. Gender construction is an ongoing process.

[7] See, e.g., Herskovitz 1937; Amadiume 1987; Atkinson and Errington 1990; and Nanda 1990.

What underscores the indebtedness of many gender theorists to the enduring idea of biological determinism in Western thought is precisely their failure to recognize that not all societies through time and space have constructed gender. If gender construction is transcultural, as countless feminist accounts have argued, then gender must be a natural, biological imperative. There is nothing covert about this biologic in feminist thought.

Hawkesworth states that "whatever the cause of th[e] tendency toward biological determinism, it is an impossible ground for feminist accounts of gender" (in this volume, 155). I disagree, in that this has been the very ground on which feminism as a universal(izing) discourse and movement has been constituted. From a cross-cultural standpoint, the very ground on which the feminist claim about the universal subordination of the category "woman" was founded is biologically deterministic. In fact, the categorization of "women" in feminist discourses as a homogeneous, bio-anatomically determined group that is always already constituted as powerless and victimized does not take into account that gender relations are social relations and, therefore, historically grounded and culturally bound. To assume that the social category "women" exists historically and geographically in every human society is to naturalize it.

Hawkesworth, quoting Donna Haraway, suggests that the goal of feminist discourse is "to contest the naturalization of sex differences" (147).[8] It is clear that many feminists assume that the natural attitude is universal and not an attitude specific to Western culture. After all, the existence of the *berdache* in some Native American cultures cited by Kessler and Mc-Kenna challenges the view that the natural attitude is present in all cultures. It is not accidental that the "natural attitude" shows up in feminist accounts of gender; feminism itself promotes the natural attitude worldwide by a process of gender attribution even in cultures that originally eschewed gender in their conceptual framework. Connell writes that the "naturalization [of gender] is not a naive mistake about what biology can explain or not explain. At a collective level, it is a highly motivated ideological practice which constantly overrides biological facts" (1987, 246; quoted in Hawkesworth, in this volume, 163) and, I would add, *other cultures' social facts.*

Kessler and McKenna provide a comprehensive account of gender attribution, the instantaneous process by which one person classifies the other as man or woman. They point out a number of factors concomitant to gender attribution: the urgency that governs gender attribution, the conviction that every individual can be categorized as a man or a woman, and

---

[8] From Haraway 1991, 131.

the need to classify people by gender (1978, 126–28). Although Kessler and McKenna are concerned with gender attribution within one culture in particular, the process they describe and the factors they identify as governing it are no less true of what Western scholars do when they study other cultures. Many scholars make gender attributions, assuming that genitalia determines a person's social location. In Western thought and social practice — and feminism is not an exception — genital attribution constitutes gender attribution. But again, since genitals are not always in view (even in the land of the "primitives"), the primary basis for gender attribution becomes "cultural genitals," a term Kessler and McKenna coined to encapsulate the culturally specific markers that maintain notions of gender (153–54).

In a cross-cultural situation in which a Western researcher has attributed gender even before arriving at the research site, it is clear that the culture underpinning the conceptualization of "cultural genitals" is Western culture. Hence, the presence of such a construction in the culture being studied becomes questionable. The following will illustrate my point. In a study of the Ga people of Ghana, West Africa, American historian Claire Robertson begins her account: "Improving our [Western] analysis of *women* and class formation is necessary. . . . This study of a long-settled urban population, the Ga of Central Accra, Ghana, will explore change in *women*'s access" (Robertson 1984, 23; my emphasis). Which women? Nowhere in this book does Robertson explain how she identified the category "woman" in Ga society; she assumes it. On what basis? one should ask. Since gender is not a natural category, the answers to these questions should not be self-evident. Even if one concedes that all cultures construct their own cultural genitals, it would still be necessary to rely on specific cultural cues detectable within the culture to be able to identify gender and the categories attached to it.

If gender is not self-evident, why is gender attribution so easy for Western scholars even in culturally unfamiliar societies? I have yet to find a cross-cultural gender study in which a Western researcher first systematically establishes the cultural cues necessary to identify the social categories "man" and "woman" in a particular cultural location. This is no idle charge, since in many cultures social categories do not derive from anatomy. How does one, for example, identify a female husband in a woman marriage in Igboland in southeastern Nigeria, particularly because she does not dress differently from her "wife"? Do genitals help us to locate this female husband?

Some Native American cultures have categories such as the *berdache*. Indian culture includes the *hijra* (Nanda 1990); in institutions such as the woman marriage of the Igbo (Amadiume 1987), and many other African cultures (Herskovitz 1937), a woman marries another woman and plays the social role of her husband and father to her children. And in cultures such as the Yoruba, all members of the family (regardless of sex) are universally conceived of as, and play the role of, conjugal partners toward the females marrying into the family. It is clear that if these cultures have come up with constructions that are different and confounding to the Western mind, then such cultures are not based on the natural attitude, or even on the notion that the body is the key to social location. The natural attitude according to Hawkesworth includes a number of unquestionable axioms: "there are two and only two genders; gender is invariant; genitals are the essential signs of gender" (in this volume, 141). One cannot but question the ethnocentrism that structures Western gender attribution and the imputation of the natural attitude on a global scale.

Enframement: The problem in the gender debate

The questions we can ask about the world are enabled, and other questions disabled, by the frame that orders the questioning. When we are busy arguing about the questions that appear within a certain frame, the frame itself becomes invisible; we become enframed in it. (Ferguson 1993, 8)

The gender debate suffers from the problem of enframement articulated above by Kathy Ferguson. Too many feminist accounts of gender are trapped in Western culture; findings from other cultures do not seem to be taken into account in the grand narratives of gender construction. It is also obvious that cross-cultural findings have not been taken seriously despite the understanding that gender is a cultural construct. Hawkesworth's article illustrates the problem very well.

In the body of her article, Hawkesworth fails to incorporate any research or findings from other cultures to dispute or validate a claim being made by any of the theorists she interrogates. By the end of her article, however, she suddenly "discovers" Third World women by citing Chandra Mohanty, in the second to last paragraph: "Feminist strategies that privilege privatized gender fail to engage Third World women who locate their politics in a collective struggle against racism, sexism, colonialism, imperialism, and monopoly capital" (104).[9] If, indeed, she had taken the existence of Third World women into account in the first place, then her cri-

---

[9] See Mohanty, Russo, and Torres 1991, 2–38.

tique of the works of Butler and Smith would have been structured differently and need not have been narrowly argued on the basis of Western culture. It is difficult to sustain Butler's notion that gender emanates from an imposition of compulsory heterosexuality if one looks at the category of the *hijra* in Indian culture or the female husband of the Igbo. From the Igbo standpoint, Butler, in order to sustain her narrative of "compulsory heterosexuality," obviously and mistakenly takes for granted the notion that sexual desire can be expressed only within the marriage institution. Many African societies organize marriage for reproduction but not necessarily to promote or support sexual desire between conjugal partners. In other words, there *are* institutionalized conjugal partnerships like the woman marriage that do not involve sexual intercourse. Believe me, "gender trouble" is not universal.

According to Smith, "human genders also work as systems of concord insofar as distinctive ways of speaking and acting are assigned to persons of different sexes" (1992, 43; quoted in Hawkesworth, in this volume, 151). Despite Hawkesworth's having pointed out in her earlier discussion of language and gender that not all languages "do" gender, she does not apply this critique to Smith's claim that human societies have gender-specific linguistic styles. The Yoruba language is one of many languages that do not mark sex distinctions. The statements that Hawkesworth makes as she tries to analyze these theorists are telling enough about her notion or lack of a notion of culture: "Yet culture's mission in inducing complementarity makes sense only . . ." (153); "But why does culture insist upon heterosexuality?" (159) or "If gender is construed as a category of the mind, then no thinking subject can escape its grip" (171). These statements make sense only if the words *culture, mind,* and *subject* are all qualified with *Western.* There is no indication that the culture being referred to, despite the lowercase *c,* alludes to anything but a generic Culture — an oxymoron — an obviously impossible notion.

Rhetorically speaking, what then is the meaning of Hawkesworth's gesture to Third World women (173–74)? What gives Third World women their particularity? It is remarkable that in the two instances in which she specifically identifies other factors apart from gender that should be considered in analyzing society, all she recognizes are race, class, and ethnicity (172, 173). Hawkesworth writes of the five theorists whose work she reviews: "Race, class, and ethnicity disappear from these accounts as the cunning of culture produces species survival, compulsory heterosexuality, heightened sexual pleasure, or categories of the mind" (172). But like Butler and Smith, who treat culture as generic, Hawkesworth ignores culture in her own account. Are the so-called Third World women different only because of their race, class, or ethnicity? Are they situated within cultures? At no point in Hawkesworth's article does she raise any questions about the idea of culture as it is understood in the books she reviews.

Finally, I would like to consider Hawkesworth's own assertions about gender. First, she advocates using gender as an analytic category because it "illuminates a range of questions for feminist investigation and provides a framework for those investigations," which are impossible in traditional academic disciplines (172). She explains that as a heuristic device, gender has a positive and negative function. As a positive device, "gender as analytic tool *identifies* puzzles or problems" (147; my emphasis). My contention is that an analytic tool does not merely identify already existing puzzles; it actually *constitutes* them. Hawkesworth echoes the recurrent feminist charge to make gender visible,[10] as if gender is always already there, and, therefore, all that researchers need do is to unveil it. Her thinking is yet another example of the problem with gender discourses: the assumption of gender as present everywhere, both historically and geographically, can be sustained only in a biologically deterministic framework.

Hawkesworth goes on to argue that using gender as an analytic category is bound up with challenging the natural attitude toward "sex differences." Using gender as an analytic tool, then, assumes that gender is always present in the social structure of any society. Hence, it would constitute, at the very least, part of the explanation for whatever social phenomenon is under investigation. Consequently, there is no fundamental distinction between gender as analytic category and gender as explanans. I have argued that the incorrigible proposition that gender is inherent in human society derives from a tradition of biological determinism and shows the limit of Western thinking on gender. As Connell puts it, in Western culture, "the notion of natural sex difference forms a limit beyond which thought will not go" (1987, 66).

Moreover, Hawkesworth's distinction between gender as analytic category and gender as explanans, or causal factor, is false. To assume gender as an analytic category in any society is to assume that it constitutes the society's social structure and as such, it explains something about the society. It is to assume gender as a causal factor in interpreting social phenomena. To use gender as an analytic category is to impute that the social categories "man" and "woman," dichotomized categories with differing social access, are present in a society. Even if one finds that access is also structured by other factors, gender remains an integral element affecting access or lack of it.

[10] See, e.g., Lorber 1994.

There is a distinction to be made between a refined and a less refined analysis, but it is a difference in degree, not kind. Using gender as an analytic category represents a gender attribution process in which the social structure is perceived to be characterized by gender constructs. The interest in invoking gender as an analytic category stems from an understanding that gender *causes* some aspect of the social structure. Therefore, unless gender is invoked as an analytic category, this causal factor cannot be understood. Consequently, applying gender categories is the first and primary move in building gender as explanans. It is entirely possible that many more moves will have to be made in order to make a better (more nuanced, more sophisticated) argument, but there is still no fundamental difference between invoking gender as analytic category and gender as explanation.

Using gender as a starting point is the first step in both cases. As Serge Tcherkezoff points out, "an analysis that starts from male/female pairing simply produces further dichotomies" (Tcherkezoff 1993, 55). The starting point of research is crucial because it frames the outcome, or even determines the result of the study. When gender is invoked as an analytic category, gender difference will inevitably be found in social relations. It could be more gender or less gender than was supposed from the outset of the research, but there is no question that gender will constitute part of the explanation. Consequently, gender functions not merely as an analytic tool; it is also implicated as cause, inherent in the use of the tool.

Hawkesworth correctly points out that "one of the profound insights of feminist scholarship is that claims concerning the 'neutrality' of research tools are deeply suspicious" (in this volume, 199). To claim that gender can be used as an analytic category without at the same time using it as cause is to hold that it is a neutral research tool. This is obviously not the case. Hawkesworth explains: "When feminist scholars employ gender as an analytic category, they are doing far more than simply *describing the world*. They are constructing a framework that 'points out the *problematic nature of the obvious*'" (200, quoting Acker 1990, 140; emphasis added). This is precisely my point. Feminist use of gender category does not merely describe the world, it *inscribes* it. Feminist scholars make visible "the problematic nature of the obvious" — problematic to whom? And obvious to whom? Recall the old feminist debate over the absence of race as a category in much white American women's research in the seventies and eighties; clearly, race as a social category was not obvious to them at the time, for whatever reason.

Ultimately, the choice of research questions and research tools is a political one.[11] In choosing an analytic category one privileges certain kinds of

---

[11] Compare the argument in Nicholson 1994.

explanations and promotes certain causes over others. Therein lies the reason the distinction between gender as analytic category and gender as explanans is not sustainable. Hawkesworth herself states that "feminists need analytic tools that advance our intellectual and political objectives" (205). There is nothing wrong with pursuing one's political objectives; it becomes problematic, however, when the basis for such an objective is assumed for other peoples and cultures that may privilege other kinds of categories. There is no reason to believe that present scholarship has exhausted social categories that could be invoked in research programs, many of which are politico-culturally determined. I, for one, have argued that if scholarship on Yorubaland had been determined by Yoruba intellectuals in the first place, then seniority would have been privileged over gender as a research tool for interpreting the society.

Globally, gender has become the analytic category of "choice" in many research programs not because it is inherent in social organization but because of the international politics of Western feminism that has promoted and continues to promote it transculturally. Gender as an analytic tool is imbricated in gender as causal explanation. The two are inseparable. Similarly, feminist entanglement with biological determinism is a function of feminist Westocentrism. The two are inseparable.

References
Acker, Joan. 1990. "Hierarchies, Jobs, Bodies: A Theory of Gendered Organizations." *Gender and Society* 4(2):139–58.
Amadiume, Ifi. 1987. *Male Daughters, Female Husbands: Gender and Sex in an African Society*. London: Zed.
Atkinson, Jane, and Shelly Errington, eds. 1990. *Power and Difference: Gender in Island Southeast Asia*. Stanford, Calif.: Stanford University Press.
Butler, Judith. 1990. *Gender Trouble: Feminism and the Subversion of Identity*. New York and London: Routledge.
Connell, R. W. 1987. *Gender and Power: Society, the Person, and Sexual Politics*. Stanford, Calif.: Stanford University Press.
Devor, Holly. 1989. *Gender Blending: Confronting the Limits of Duality*. Bloomington: Indiana University Press.
Ferguson, Kathy. 1993. *The Man Question: Visions of Subjectivity in Feminist Theory*. Berkeley and Los Angeles: University of California Press.
Haraway, Donna. 1991. "'Gender' for a Marxist Dictionary: The Sexual Politics of a Word." In her *Simians, Cyborgs and Women*, 127–48. New York: Routledge.
Harding, Sandra. 1997. "Comment on Hekman's 'Truth and Method: Feminist Standpoint Theory Revisited': Whose Standpoint Needs the Regimes of Truth and Reality?" *Signs: Journal of Women in Culture and Society* 22(2):382–91.
Hawkesworth, Mary. In this volume. "Confounding Gender."

―――. In this volume. "Reply to McKenna and Kessler, Smith, Scott, and Connell: Interrogating Gender."

Herskovitz, Melville J. 1937. "A Note on Woman Marriage in Dahomey." *Africa* 10:335–41.

Kessler, Suzanne, and Wendy McKenna. 1978. *Gender: An Ethnomethodological Approach.* New York: Wiley.

Lorber, Judith. 1994. *Paradoxes of Gender.* New Haven, Conn.: Yale University Press.

Mohanty, Chandra, Ann Russo, and Lourdes Torres, eds. 1991. *Third World Women and the Politics of Feminism.* Bloomington: Indiana University Press.

Nanda, Serena. 1990. *Neither Man nor Woman: The Hijras of India.* Belmont, Calif.: Wadsworth.

Nicholson, Linda. 1994. "Interpreting *Gender.*" *Signs* 20(1):79–105.

Ortner, Sherry. 1996. *Making Gender: The Politics and Erotics of Culture.* Boston: Beacon.

Oyewumi, Oyeronke. 1997. *The Invention of Women: Making an African Sense of Western Gender Discourses.* Minneapolis: University of Minnesota Press.

Pierce, Jennifer. 1995. *Gender Trials: Emotional Lives in Contemporary Law Firms.* Berkeley and Los Angeles: University of California Press.

Robertson, Claire. 1984. *Sharing the Same Bowl: A Socioeconomic History of Women and Class in Accra, Ghana.* Bloomington: Indiana University Press.

Russell, Jennifer. 1996. Review of *Gender Trials: Emotional Lives in Contemporary Law Firms,* by Jennifer Pierce. *Women's Review of Books* 14(1):14–15.

Smith, Steven G. 1992. *Gender Thinking.* Philadelphia: Temple University Press.

Tcherkezoff, Serge. 1993. "The Illusion of Dualism in Samoa: 'Brothers-and-Sisters' Are Not 'Men-and-Women.'" In *Gendered Anthropology,* ed. Teresa del Valle, 54–87. New York: Routledge.

Privacy, Privation, Perversity: Toward New Representations of the Personal

When is the personal *not* political?

There can be little doubt that feminist and postmodernist critiques (Elshtain 1981; Pateman 1989; Connolly 1991), as well as the "discursive" turn in democratic theory (Habermas 1996), have revitalized critical inquiry and democratic political struggle. Yet these movements may have succeeded too well, in the sense of rendering every appeal to the "private" suspect. I argue that privacy should be reconstructed rather than abandoned, for otherwise it is impossible to think critically about central problems in democratic theory—among them the very possibility of citizens' representing, or translating into a common language, what is most singular, secret, ineffable, internal, that is, private, about themselves.

What is needed, then, is a positive political theory of privacy. With few exceptions, modern social and political critics have defined privacy negatively, with the private serving precisely to mark the limits of collective action, the gentle abeyance of power—or whatever opposes politics and the political. Contemporary views are uniformly critical: privacy is judged an incoherent and confused value, a poisonous public philosophy, a perverse and infantile demand, a masculinist prerogative that only enhances the vulnerability and powerlessness of women, and, once enshrined as a "right," a positive hindrance to any more expansive notion of social good or more lasting kind of social peace.[1] This repudiation of privacy coincides,

Carolyn Allen, Judith Howard, and two anonymous readers offered that rare advice and support, namely, how to make the argument I wanted to make, *better.* I thank Michael Uebel for reading countless drafts and for enriching beyond measure my private life and my public work. Sharon Hays and Rita Felski, colleagues at the University of Virginia, held me to the high standards of feminist scholarship and political criticism.

[1] On privacy as confused value, see Barber 1984; as public philosophy, Sandel 1996; as infantile demand, Benjamin 1988; as masculinist prerogative, Elshtain 1981, MacKinnon 1987, and Okin 1989; and as self-serving right, Young 1990. Rorty 1989 is an important exception, although as many have pointed out already, his understanding of the private realm, with its promise of intensive self-reflection and self-creation, is not yet a political theory of it.

[*Signs: Journal of Women in Culture and Society* 2000, vol. 25 no. 2]

however, with genuine distress over its present state. We are advised that privacy—real privacy, that is—has been irreparably damaged: commodified, colonized, dissolved, infiltrated.[2] There is nothing authentic, and very little that is respectable, in the type of private self-regard that has survived, indeed thrived, as public philosophy and public culture.[3]

But I suspect that there is a more complex story to be told and that critics of privacy, most notably feminists and postmodernists, will benefit from the retelling. I agree with Jean Cohen that, given the basic feminist claim that private and public evolve together, what feminists require is an alternative conception of the private every bit as cogent as their account of public space and public culture, that is, a fully "adequate complement" to it (1997, 135). Democratic theorists also have much to gain. Although I support their efforts to reconceive democracy as a broadly ethical way of life and not simply a system of government, I also worry that this encourages us to exalt the public self, at some expense to our care and concern for the private; to evade tensions between the universalizable claims of the public self and the singular needs of the private; and to deny the propensity for spirited public discourse to elicit, feed upon, even to degenerate into dispiriting confession. Yet these projects—feminist, postmodernist, democratic—set crucial parameters for any reclamation of privacy. I draw upon their penetrating analyses of liberal individualism in order to show why viewing privacy as a certain kind of reprieve from power does not require thinking of it as the very opposite of power.[4]

[2] See Habermas on the colonization of what may be termed, not unreasonably, the private lifeworld (1975, 79–80). Also see Bogard 1996 for a terrifying account of "telematic" or perfectly simulated societies, including the perfectly simulated "interiority" by which they subsist. Of the privacy possible in such societies, Bogard remarks that it is a kind of "transfixion, . . . of not moving as a means of invisibility and interiority. . . . What is unseen does not move, what is unseen is private, secret" (139).

[3] See Barber 1984 and Sandel 1996. For a fascinating account that credits Ralph Waldo Emerson with this "hybridized" political subjectivity in which the private and public are confused to the enormous advantage of corporate forms of social control, see Newfield 1996. This particular brand of "liberal imagination" is most prominent in the professional class, occupying as it does a "psychic and social middle zone . . . especially susceptible to mixed Emersonian modes like individualization without self-determination and democracy without group sovereignty" (13). See Berlant 1997 for a similar account of the "intimate public sphere"; according to Berlant, this intermingling of sex and citizenship hardly improves upon the older division between public and private but rather impoverishes both.

[4] My understanding of privacy is akin to Drucilla Cornell's. Both of us emphasize privacy's value as psychic space rather than well-defined place. This is the significance of Cornell's appeal to the "imaginary domain," which she claims "illuminates more profoundly what traditional legal theory has dubbed sexual privacy. The notion of the imaginary domain recognizes that literal space cannot be conflated with psychic space and reveals that our sense of freedom

I open the first section of the essay with Hanna Pitkin's classic medita-
tions on justice and its central role in relating private and public (1981).
Pitkin shifts our understanding from a spheres-based view to one focused
on the contingent and changing connections between private and public.
Even more important for my argument is the reworking of this basic point
by object-relations theorists such as Jane Flax (1993) and Axel Honneth
(1995), who stress the affective dimensions of justice and its dependence
on complex dynamics of reciprocal recognition. However, rather than
complicate our sense of the private, object-relations theory has encouraged
a new consensus in which the aim is to rationally transform the private *into*
the public in such a way as to remove all ambiguity, all intractability, from
the former. I want to unsettle this consensus, in turn, and suggest that
numerous resources accrue to individual identity — not to mention our understanding of it — from a theory emphasizing privacy's intractable, incongruous, and singular aspects.

The second section of this essay takes up a familiar criticism of contemporary identity politics and identity movements, namely, that in politicizing
the personal, they destroy the private. I argue, rather, that such movements
actually vindicate the private through resignifying it as a "higher-order
norm," the purpose of which is to attenuate normalizing pressures more
generally (Kelvin 1973, 257). What privacy signifies, then, is a "limitation
or nullification of the perceived power of others" (254). My point is that
the radical criticism characteristic of identity movements does not preclude
understanding the private as incommensurate or singular experience, that
is, as a special kind of reprieve from social control. This is the basis for my
claim that identity movements serve, as well, to vindicate the messy and
oppositional parts of politics against a particular class of normalizing pressures and normalizing judgments, namely, those issuing from social
science.

The notion of reprieve figures importantly in the work of Patricia Williams (1991), which is analyzed in the third section of this essay. My hunch
is that a radical analysis of power, like Williams's, establishes most forcefully the need for some relief from power — the need, that is, for the time,
space, and opportunity to come into one's own, to emerge as a singular
presence in the world. Others, most notably Wendy Brown (1995), see in
Williams's work, particularly in her highly personalized language of pain
and injury, a costly contradiction — a radical analysis of power vying with

---

is intimately tied to the renewal of the imagination" (1995, 8–9). Compare object-relations
theory for another such idealization of private psychic space: a "productive solitude" differs
from a pathological one in terms of the "quality of attention" induced (Phillips 1993, 40–41).

a defense of private, even profoundly mysterious, space and experience. I believe, on the contrary, that such discourse is capable of revolutionizing our understanding of the private. Williams's work undermines, among other things, the expectation that privacy should have clearly beneficent or clearly troubling repercussions *for* the public. That is to say, privacy, once reconstructed through the singular experience of pain and injury, challenges the very idea of determinate effects. It thus points the way toward innovative solutions to political problems of power, powerlessness, and vulnerability, solutions in which individuality returns invigorated and radicalized. Does privacy signify, in fact, the intractability of personality? I suggest that there is considerable reprieve possible through resignifying individuality in this way—in other words, perversely, as that which resists systematic analysis and perfect representation.

Just relations and transitional spaces:
Privacy in the political imaginary

Throughout this essay, I draw on studies of privacy from a variety of disciplines other than political science in order to emphasize the sorts of relations—including relations with oneself—that privacy promotes. This relational understanding of privacy would seem a necessary first step toward any genuinely political theory of it. Just such an understanding is implied in John Chapman's pointed remark of 1960s radicals that "lack[ing] the capacity to enjoy and sustain privacy," their relations, sadly, "can be neither personal nor political; they must rather be said to be politicized" (1971, 240). Chapman's assumption then, and an increasingly common one today, is that "politicization"—whatever that turns out to mean—is a feeble substitute for a particularly vital relation between the personal and the political. Hanna Pitkin, the first to designate this relation with a name, called it "justice."

Relations are the very material of justice, according to Pitkin. The "linkage" necessary between private and public consists, she says, not only in "relating 'I' to 'you' . . . but . . . 'I' to 'we,' in a context where many other selves also have claims on that 'we.' " What this means is that the justice we seek is not an ideal or, more precisely, it is not a set of "hypothetical general maxims." It consists in actual practical and political relations. Justice concerns, moreover, "conditions of . . . membership," and we "learn these in a context of responsibility," according to Pitkin, "not in abstract thought, but in action that will have broad and tangible consequences" (1981, 345). Justice requires, just as it did for the Greeks, a separation between the private and the public, a separation providing the very possibility for deft transitions between them, transitions of the sort distinguishing men and women from gods and beasts.

Following Hannah Arendt in this, as in other crucial respects, Pitkin stresses the intermediary role of justice, its purpose in bridging such things as "profit and right, utility and meaning, private claim and public policy" (343). Thus she characterizes our central theoretical task as "finding a way to conceptualize the public that recognizes its roots in human need and its consequences for power, privilege, and suffering, without incurring the dangers Arendt fears [i.e., making the public merely instrumental to private need]. . . . The concept of justice . . . would be central to such a theoretical task, for justice is precisely about . . . connections" (343). What I contest is the sort of connection privileged here. The radical potential of Pitkin's intervention into the public-private debate is sacrificed if the connections between private and public are domesticated, understood as largely conceptual ones. Pitkin is clear that private and public belong to the same experiential field, where power permeates all spaces, not only the public ones. Justice may connect private need and public policy, but both exist in the same political space, arising between "human need," on the one hand, and its consequences for "power, privilege, and suffering," on the other. The significance of this point is lost, however, if we continue, with Pitkin, to stress the necessity — that is, the *rational necessity* — of connecting private and public. Even if it is not enough simply to link the private and public — rather we must *transform* the former into the latter — Pitkin's seems a tendentious reading of what should be deeply contestable terms. The private, for instance, is whatever must be transformed — causality, profit, utility; in short, it is a mere "claim" as opposed to a "policy." "It is the connection that matters," according to Pitkin, "the transformation of social conditions into political issues, of need and interest into principle and justice" (346). Consider Patricia Boling's recent attempt to derive an entire "politics of intimate life" from this central claim: "Political engagement depends," she insists, "on our discovering how our private lives are connected to politics; the task is to learn to translate private need into political claim" (1996, 160).

We are talking, in other words, of a central and indispensable type of judgment, political judgment and "not merely mutuality" (Pitkin 1981, 345). It is not enough simply to share a common space, a common past. In addition, citizens must be able to "translate private need into political claim" because what is "at stake," according to Boling, "are the norms of discourse of a truly political community" (1996, 36). At the very moment theorists such as Pitkin and Boling contest the older spheres-based view, they risk installing a new rationalist logic. Consider, for instance, Pitkin's criticism of the public sphere envisioned by Arendt: it seems strangely expressivist, she says, with exhibition and distinction counting for everything. Pitkin assures us, however, that Arendt ultimately favors mature "self-development," not "vain self-display" (341). Yet the only thing distinguishing these two modes of self-assertion is the latter's effects for the public: egotistic posturing would undermine the "revelatory" power that Arendt attributes to speech, ravaging the trust sustaining the social world and impairing our ability to make the right sorts of judgments, the just and proper "connections" (341; see esp. 336–38).

It is difficult to say, however, whether an active and engaged individual would immediately intuit, or greatly appreciate, the difference between "development" and "display." The practice of "coming out" as gay or lesbian is apropos of this point: it may seem an archetypal instance of self-display, but for those who must undertake it, again and again, coming out is "explicitly correlated with the process of individuation: the progressive retreat from living a lie" (Peter Davies, as quoted in Boling 1996, 134). I suggest that it makes perfect sense to view coming out, and individuation more generally, as a matter of achieving a better, even more just, relationship to oneself. But I also hold that because this relationship would require little (if any) of the "translation" emphasized by Pitkin and Boling, individuation can tip us off to the limits of justice, at least justice conceived as essentially a matter of rational transformation, the conversion of a singular need into a publicly sanctioned claim.

Contemporary psychoanalytic accounts of politics support the kind of rethinking I have in mind. If, as Pitkin insists, justice "is precisely about connections," theorists such as Jane Flax (1993), James Glass (1995), and Axel Honneth (1995) show why these connections must be understood as object-relations as well. A diffuse social system of reciprocal recognition equips us, or not, for rational political judgment—for the elevation of "need," for instance, to "principle." Against Pitkin's preoccupation with transformative concepts, then, Flax and Honneth stress the dynamics of mutual recognition, drawing on D. W. Winnicott's classic account of transitional phenomena. Transitional objects are a familiar enough aspect of childhood; most of us know of the fierce attachment that a thumb or blanket can provoke. Winnicott's genius consists, however, in recognizing the huge significance of transitional phenomena for adults. The "reality-testing" function of transitional objects persists in the manifold form of "intersubjectively accepted illusions," or what he calls, more generally, "culture." In fact, "it is assumed here," writes Winnicott, "that the task of reality-acceptance is never completed, that no human being is free from the strain of relating inner and outer reality." It is simply that adults accomplish this through increasingly sophisticated means: for Winnicott, by the "arts, religion, etc." (1971, 13–14); and crucially enough, for Flax and Honneth, by way of experiments in justice.

Justice, say Flax and Honneth, is a special kind of transitional "space." Its very possibility circumscribes "a neutral area of experience which will not be challenged" (Winnicott 1971, 12) but will be, rather, exploited in order to cope with challenge, the specific challenge of relating inner and outer reality. Flax details a number of purposes served by this "intermediate area of experience," among them the containment of aggression, the impetus given to symbolization, and the opportunity for "pleasure and creativity" as well as for creative and responsible action. Most important, "transitional spaces serve as defenses against the fear of multiplicity, ambivalence, and uncertainty that leads us to try to collapse all our worlds into one" (Flax 1993, 340). It is in its capacity as transitional space that justice directly supports and sustains ethical relations, defusing the defensiveness, paranoia, and solipsism that corrupt rational judgment, the very translation that preoccupies Pitkin and Boling.

Yet "transition" sounds very much like "translation." Why should we suppose that the former is any less vulnerable to rationalist misappropriation, to a misplaced emphasis on correct judgment and the presumably more elevated and responsible state we attain by way of transitional phenomena? I suggest that there is, in Winnicott's work at least, a powerful resistance to domesticating cultural and phantasmatic phenomena in this way. As long as the strain of relating "inner" and "outer" remains acute, such things as public culture and private fantasy serve, at least in part, to deny the demand for enunciation, the need for clear and univocal meaning. Winnicott's understanding of culture as a vast transitional space—neither subjective nor objective, both imagined and real—is indispensable, I suggest, for theorizing the limits of positivist theory, for thinking outside its bounds. Only a perspective sensitive, for instance, to the myriad means by which we assert a "right *not* to communicate"—by which we deliberately and stubbornly resist "being found," as Winnicott says (1965, 179)—is capable of pressing the analysis of privacy to a critical new level.[5]

[5] Consider Winnicott's claim that within the transitional space of culture, there exist two fundamental imperatives, which, significantly enough for political theory, he calls "rights." These are "the urgent need to communicate and the still more urgent need not to be found" (1965, 185). The artist may experience these competing imperatives more acutely than the ordinary person, but Winnicott insists that we all feel the strain. "At the centre of each person," he claims, "is an incommunicado element, and this is sacred and most worthy of preservation" (187). And this is why culture provides, for everyone and not only the artist, an "intermediate . . . area, . . . a mode of communication which is [itself] a most valuable

To see this more clearly we must reckon with the vital role of transitional phenomena in rendering certain things ambiguous, unseen, and unspoken. I believe this to be the significance of one of Winnicott's more curious (and curiously insistent) claims. Regarding transitional phenomena—the beloved blanket, certainly, but also the accoutrements of culture—he insists that certain questions, certain inquiries, are simply forbidden to us. Among these, he says, *"it is a matter of agreement between us . . . that we will never ask the question: 'Did you conceive of this or was it presented to you from without?' . . . The question is not to be formulated"* (1971, 12). Issued to a child, such a question would only confuse and silence. But Winnicott makes plain why it is no less cruel when posed to an adult, someone who presumably could muster a response. In either case, the question is "demoralizing" in calling into question what must not be questioned but simply accepted, admitting as it does no direct or decisive verification.[6] This is the realm of fantasy, or what Winnicott calls "play," to which the entire cultural domain bears a direct lineage (1965, 184–87). The payoff for rethinking privacy lies here, in Winnicott's strangely unequivocal counsel: recall that certain questions are *"not to be formulated."* What this bespeaks is a powerful regard for the private, conceived as that which is consolidated, if at all, precisely through being unquestioned. The private designates that part of experience properly (if only contingently) secure from judgment.[7]

I suggest following Winnicott wholeheartedly and thinking of the private in terms of the intractable, the incongruous, the incommensurate. This privacy signifies the necessity for a reprieve from scrutiny and public judgment, a dispensation no less real and valuable for being contingent— and no less a matter of privacy, I contend, for being claimed, possessed, and asserted in manifestly public ways. I now return to the issue of identity politics and suggest several respects in which the more complex, indeed

---

compromise" between communicating and not communicating (192). According to Adam Phillips, the intermediate area of culture serves, more precisely, to defuse "that most primitive, that most essentially perplexing form of power," that is to say, "misrecognition—misrecognition as appropriation" (1993, 45).

[6] "Demoralizing" is John Turner's characterization in an essay on the literary uses of Winnicott's "potential space" (1993, 177).

[7] This is not to imply a private language or a private realm of fantasy wholly untroubled by claims or judgments from without. Phillips clarifies the sense in which object-relations theory understands private experience: the secrets we tell in and through our dreams, he says, testify to the "impenetrable privacy of the Self. . . . Clearly, there cannot be a private language; but here can be a sense, . . . conveyed in language, of a person's irreducible privacy. The dreaming experience comes to signify that which is beyond description in the total *vecu* of the patient" (1993, 65).

ambivalent, conception of privacy urged here bears directly upon our assessment of identity, its significance, and its frequently noisy manifestations in the public sphere.

Identity politics is often portrayed as an incursion of disorderly "presence" into representative systems—as a perversion of private and public alike.[8] Not only do we lack the tools, without some understanding of affective as opposed to merely cognitive connections, to explain why many choose to act politically by asserting themselves rather than bargaining over scarce resources (compare Honneth 1995, 117–30), neither can we address the genuine anxiety attending identity politics in order to distinguish real from imagined dangers. But, as Pitkin says, "it is no use banishing the body, economic concerns, or the social question from public life; we do not rid ourselves of their power in that way, but only impoverish public life" (1981, 346). Likewise, however, it is not enough simply to translate bodily and other plainly private concerns into "principles," for this sidesteps every respect in which identity politics is meant to be disruptive, a challenge to "the norms of discourse of a truly political community" (Boling 1996, 36).

Viewing privacy as a special kind of reprieve opens up a consideration of identity as a form of resistance, of recalcitrance. This view politicizes both terms—private and public—simultaneously, situating them on a more directly political terrain, that of contestation and struggle. Perhaps this is why the space opened up by actual controversies over identity admits of a more nuanced *adjustment* of private to public, and public to private, than does an abstract and overly rationalist understanding of this famous divide.[9] Similarly, an understanding of privacy emphasizing its significance as a reprieve advances the study of power in ways surpassing even the contributions made by theorists such as Pitkin and Boling. It confirms the radical thesis—the insistence that there is no place where power does not operate—yet the notion of reprieve also clarifies why not every genuinely progressive political act must occur "in the open," as it were. That is

[8] For arguments showing the contemporary distinction between a "politics of ideas" and a "politics of presence" to be untenable, because insufficiently complex, see Gould 1996 and Phillips 1996 (in Benhabib 1996). It is interesting, however, that both theorists virtually conflate identity politics with the "politics of presence."

[9] For a novel argument on this point, see Stark 1997. Disputes over the "sincerity" and "consistency" of politicians' policy commitments are really discussions about the boundaries of the self—about the proper bases of political judgment, according to Stark. "But what is noteworthy," he says, ". . . is that disagreement in any given case—as to whether a personal feature is best understood as constitutive of, or an encumbrance on, the subject's capacity for political judgment—is so polar and fundamental" (495), unlikely, that is, to be resolved in theory.

to say, against the dangers of an aggressive politics of authenticity, privacy does just what many of its critics claim: it privatizes, pulling inward the anxious reflection on the self, its urgent needs, depth, and unspeakable mystery — enlivening even as it complicates our sense of self.[10] Yet it is precisely this privatization that is said to compromise radical thought, or the determination to understand power in terms of its systematic effects for, and compulsive origins in, social processes of identity-formation. This tension is the subject of the next section.

Acting up: Politics against science

I contend that the radical criticism associated with many (though not all) identity movements does not preclude thinking of the private as incommensurate or singular experience, that is, as a special kind of reprieve from social control. But this is to argue against the grain, against a deeply felt (though unreflective) suspicion that radical critique must deny or discredit the singular and ungeneralizable. In one of the first contemporary inquiries into privacy, two features of '60s radicalism, the student movement and the encounter group, are singled out as especially pernicious threats (see Chapman 1971; Silber 1971). What interests me is the supposed locus of this privacy threat: it issues from the crude "scientism" of such groups. The encounter group, for instance, substitutes a wan if well-meaning "transaction" for an anguished and uncertain confrontation with one's god. But because "complete openness and honesty are wholly beneficial only in relation with a wholly benevolent Other," according to John Silber,

---

[10] For a more cynical appraisal, however, one that is greatly indebted to Foucault's classic studies of the bourgeois origins of "interiority," that is, "the privatization of . . . bodies and their passions [as] instances of a new ensemble of what can only be described as power relations," see Barker 1984, 10–11. Barker proposes, however, a "radical counter-narration," a transvaluation of values in which the peculiar pain of interiority would seem to figure prominently: " 'Is there anything,' Descartes asks, somewhat querulously, 'more intimate or internal than pain?'" "It is precisely the intimacy of that pain, the mark of a violence which is structural to the modern subject and no doubt largely unconscious," to which Barker's counternarration appeals (109, 116). Compare Foucault's own fascination with "solitude," indeed his decision to theorize sexuality under its aegis (1997, 182–83). When I say that the concept of privacy functions to pull anxiety regarding the self inward and that this may have progressive political effects — or at least not the dangerous ones associated with philosophies of authenticity — I have in mind something like Stanley Cavell's Emersonian reconstruction of individualism, his effort to "thin[k] about individuality (or the loss of it) under the spell of revenge, of getting even for oddness" (1988, 106). He continues: "Emerson's . . . is a fantasy of finding your own voice, so that others, among them mothers and fathers, may shun you" (114). This suggests the considerable risk, but also the necessity, of learning to live privately.

privacy laws must function to restore and to sustain our communion with god, largely through securing us against the judgments of "limited men" (1971, 234–35). For Silber, the most objectionable judgments are those made out of dispassionate motives, that is to say, on the authority of science.

What I hope to establish in this section is that a delicate and even dangerous sort of privacy emerges once a right to resist the normalizing powers of science and society, the illegitimate incursion of limits and limited men, is acknowledged. For, in delineating a space of nonjudgment, privacy opens up a space of transgression: any reprieve from judgment is a tacit invitation to behave differently, perhaps deviantly. Certainly this jibes with our sense that behaving well derives much of its significance and value from the real (if largely unrealized) opportunity to behave badly. Moreover, a certain sanction inheres in this very opportunity, in the fact that our society provides it, even if that sanction consists precisely in our refusing to speak of the private.[11] This is why I say that a perverse kind of privacy emerges, one that consigns a nontrivial part of behavior — perhaps even the core of personality — to a time and space beyond public judgment. The law, as Silber insists, "preserve[s] as much pretense and hypocrisy as virtue and redemption require" (1971, 235).

This sanctioning of a time and place beyond social sanction constitutes one of privacy's more important, if little appreciated, social and cultural functions, namely, protecting behavior from public judgment in order to create thereby the necessary "illusion that one is the author of one's acts" (Flax 1993, 344).[12] The behavior in question may be "experimental" and daring, or perfectly trivial, but, by necessity, it includes perverse behavior. If the encounter group, in contrast, has any hope of managing the life crises and psychic systems of its members, according to Silber, it is only because — and only to the extent that — it conceives itself scientifically. It is

[11] See Kelvin 1973; Laufer and Wolfe 1977; and Gavison 1984, 364–70 on the "conscious and unconscious fears of undisclosed knowledge . . . generic to personality and social structure" (Laufer and Wolfe 1977, 23) that make privacy an inherently "anxious" issue. Kelvin posits, in fact, a "complex but fundamentally inverse relationship between privacy and permissiveness" (1973, 256): the more permissive a society, the less urgent the need for privacy and thus the less value it comes to have.

[12] Some theorists praise privacy for instilling a crucial sense of dignity (Benn 1984; Bloustein 1984), in the very least, an "autonomous self-concept" (Kupfer 1987). Others emphasize its importance for the acquisition of skills necessary to relationships ranging from intimacy (Fried 1984) to citizenship (Regan 1995). Compare with Gerstein (1984), however, who insists that privacy's entire significance lies in suspending evaluation of this kind and the tendency, more generally, to conceive privacy in terms of its beneficent effects. A person "submerged in an intimate relationship," Gerstein explains, does "not intend to be observed at all, even by himself" (267–68).

science, after all, that has banished the perverse: the genuinely perverse, in the shape of the surprising and untoward.[13] The encounter group is an essential part of science, a science that has exploded its traditional borders and now functions, culturally and socially, "as *scientism,* a quasi-religion . . . that . . . will deliver us from evil and provide solutions to life's greatest perplexities" (Silber 1971, 229).

Like the encounter group, the student movement substitutes a surefire theory (in this case Marxism) for a judicious and fluid practice, or the kind of sensibility and political know-how that John Chapman calls "Hegelianism." There is simply no room, in theory, for an intractable private space and personal experience — for a depth immeasurably good and bad, defying the abstraction and instrumentalism of politics. "A Hegel would say" of the student radicals, according to Chapman, that "these are selves unable to sustain a form of ethical life in which the claims of abstract right and morality are synchronized" (1971, 239). Synchronization requires "rationally structured sentiments," indeed a "romantic rationalism" best exemplified by Hegelians; the opposite of this is a crude "Sorellian contempt for the corrupt and the inauthentic" (239; see, as well, 245–48). As bizarrely cantankerous as these statements may sound today, they were hardly unusual; many faulted student activists for being power-mad, solipsistic, infantile — or, the same thing, perverse.

What I want to highlight is the presumed significance of radical theory, the great travail over the degenerate "scientism" of people barely old enough to vote. For one hears roughly the same complaint against contemporary identity movements and the radical theory thought to inspire them: these show, say their critics, the same clumsy contempt for the ambiguous, ambivalent, and impenetrable. Recall Chapman's charge against the student radicals, those who had forgotten how to live privately and whose relations, therefore, must be judged diminished — "neither personal nor

[13] There are reasons I say "perverse" rather than, e.g., "unobservable." This is not only because recent philosophy of science denies that unobservability is a positive bar to scientific explanation. (See, e.g., Will 1986 and Ruben 1988 on the scientific status of psychoanalysis.) For I do mean by "private" and "subjective" something more than the "uniqueness of occurrence" that Ruben stipulates; I wish to retain the specific transgression involved in events or occurrences of this kind, namely, unique ones. This is in order to clarify one of privacy's more potent functions, which Harper 1994 explicates by way of the "open secret," such as that contained in a public kiss: "The necessity for this concealment . . . derives from a subject's desire to disavow the degree to which he or she has been absorbed and accounted for. . . . That is to say that secrecy serves as a sort of 'defense mechanism' by which . . . 'the subject is allowed to conceive of himself as a resistance: a friction in the smooth functioning of the social order' " (119–20).

political" but merely politicized (1971, 240). Jean Elshtain's assessment of present-day movements dedicated to self-assertion rather than the acquisition of rights and resources is nearly identical: this "ugly phenomenon, this eruption of *publicity* and the substitution of publicity for that which is authentically either private or public, is now America's leading growth industry" (1995, 40). Elshtain, like Chapman, ties this particular brand of political radicalism to, if not science exactly, then the pretensions of theory, the desire to grasp with certainty and exactitude those things most resistant to prediction, categorization, generalization. Presumably the "authentically private" is one such mystery, defying the judgment necessary to justice, the very justice that radical movements would have us do. Of one "radical feminist" proposal for submitting family life to community review and instilling in women a "sense of entitlement to a violence-free life" (48, quoting Schechter), Elshtain warns: "In the society of scrutiny, total accountability, and instant justice, the social space for difference, dissent, refusal, and indifference is squeezed out. This is where matters stand unless or until advocates who share this theoretical orientation tell us how the future community of scrutiny will preserve any freedom worthy of the name" (49). Apparently this "theoretical orientation" is incapable of subtle judgments: it cannot distinguish fruitful difference, or mere indifference, from the truly villainous. As such, it is unfit to theorize the private domain, a domain defined by mixed blessings — the allure and risk of something new, the solace and disquiet of things familiar. Still more serious, this way of thinking actively menaces private life. Although the precise connection between "theory" and "life" remains unspecified, we are assured that the danger runs in one direction only: "The total collapse of public and private . . . followed, at least in theory. The private sphere fell under a thoroughgoing politicized definition. . . . [T]here was nowhere to hide. This situation got nasty fast" (Elshtain 1995, 43).

Once again, radical movements — feminism, in this case — have succeeded too well, obliterating a private space in which one could seek refuge, safe from angry judgments and "instant justice." It is interesting to compare Michael Sandel's (1996) diagnosis of American political culture, since he shares Elshtain's concerns regarding the demise of genuinely democratic forms of civility and community yet charts a very different radical victory with respect to the private. What has triumphed unconditionally, in Sandel's view, is voluntarism, a view of the individual as radically undetermined, liberated (at least in principle) from even the most elemental social constraints. Thus U.S. Supreme Court justices affirm what is perhaps the ultimate trump, a fundamental right to "define one's own concept of

existence, of meaning, of the universe, and of the mystery of human life"
(Sandel 1996, 99).[14] Sandel's complaint would seem to be the mirror image of Elshtain's. Rather than privacy offering no refuge, it offers the most
exclusive kind, with every last person claiming an arena of unfettered
choice and conduct, even outright fantasy, commensurate with his or her
"inviolate personality."[15] Elshtain claims that privacy has fallen, "at least
in theory, . . . under a thoroughgoing politicized definition"; but perhaps
because of this, it has resurfaced with a vengeance in the democratic imagination, signifying everything precious, pure, authentic: a realm of one's
own. Sandel makes clear, in fact, that a certain kind of privacy is far from
endangered. Indeed, as private decision, it represents the autonomous personality's sublime refuge from the ordinary world, from the claims and
needs of others.[16]

Of course, Elshtain also deplores this obsessive self-regard: what a "politicized ontology" does, after all, is elevate "who we *are*" over "what [we]
do or say" (1995, 53–55). She simply doubts that it provides anything in
the way of privacy, meaning some measure of protection against judgment
and denunciation. Of its other huge costs, she appears fully in agreement
with Sandel: once injustice is privatized as injury, the complex lexicon of
self-government wastes away and with it, all understanding of such things
as obligation, conscience, civility, shared purpose, accountability. The latter
are concepts that cannot be recast—at least not easily—as acts of "self-
expression." But I want to push a bit the specifically political connection
assumed here between the "authentically public" and the "authentically
private." In the "politics of displacement" traced by Elshtain, what is lost
or displaced is politics, at least politics understood as a specific set of concepts for making rational judgments and just "connections." Here Elshtain
follows Arendt and Pitkin exactly: the political is fundamentally intermediary, that is to say, all about reconciliation or regulating rather than "collaps-
[ing] . . . a distinction between public and private" (38). Once that distinc-

[14] Sandel is citing the opinion of Justices O'Connor, Kennedy, and Souter in the 1992
case *Planned Parenthood v Casey* (505 U.S. 833), which reaffirms a woman's right to choose.

[15] Samuel Warren and Louis Brandeis placed "inviolate personality" at the core of the
privacy interest in their classic piece "The Right to Privacy" ([1890] 1984). Much of their
discussion deals with impermissible or inappropriate use of the "products and processes of
the mind," photographs and gossip. That is, "inviolate personality" refers mainly to control
over personal information, though some "interaction control" is conceded as well. See Dandekar 1993 on this important distinction.

[16] See Rosenblum 1987 on the romantic sublime, esp. for the kind of sanctuary it is
thought to provide. Rosenblum establishes the political dangers attending romanticism and
its apotheosis of genius and singularity, yet she insists, too, that romantic "impulses" enliven
and sustain liberal democratic societies.

tion is collapsed, anything may be "defined as 'political' and watered down to the lowest common denominator" (41), which means, among other things, that there is then no precise or principled way to discuss such things as power, powerlessness, cooperation, refusal, obligation, choice, difference, indifference. It appears, too, that persons who wither in their capacity for this sort of discrimination also lose their ability to convey what is distinctive about themselves, what deserves notice and respect of a special kind as their "personal secret, as something valuable, inviolable, the basis of . . . originality" (46, quoting Milan Kundera).

But notice the huge stress placed on communication — not only on connecting private and public but on articulating the full and authentic meaning of our experience, wherever it may arise. I am not denying that such communication is necessary and good, but I would suggest that in the context of public-private debates, especially, it bespeaks an excessive regard for what Ferdinand Schoeman (1992) calls "articulated rationality." This he defines as "a public standard of evaluation of all aspects of a person's life and being . . . with the expectation that adequate arguments can be offered for all aspects of one's outlook. Philosophy has not been engaged in an inquisition. . . . Nevertheless, it has assigned to the agent's own conscience the responsibility for revealing and examining all that matters, in light of public standards . . . as if these were things a person should be competent to defend before an objective public" (23). The notion of articulated rationality is symptomatic, according to Schoeman, of a diffuse and largely unexamined skepticism toward the cultural and the contingent, common among theorists, who tend to believe that sound deliberation and evaluation must swing free of felt attachments, cultural norms, preferences, indeed of any "social pressure" whatsoever. (Of course, Sandel and Elshtain are rather famous for invoking such pressure; the problem is that they assume it to be more benign than not.) Schoeman insists that we acknowledge the inevitability of such pressure, and grapple with its decidedly complex effects, for freedom as well as for restraint and social control.

My hunch is that privacy allows us to represent — without rationalizing away — those desires, needs, and experiences that implicitly challenge the demand for articulated rationality. Only such a view, which concedes the need for a space and time whose sole purpose is *recalcitrance,* is capable of dispelling several central confusions regarding privacy. Consider, for instance, Schoeman's suggestion that we view something like socialization indifferently, that is to say, as a force with many consequences, some favoring individual freedom and others social control. Such a view envisions a role for privacy "in modulating this force" (Schoeman 1992, 38); privacy is considered a counterforce, in other words, having equally indeterminate effects. This should combat the tendency, still common in the privacy debates, simply to conflate privacy with autonomy or, worse still, to view the former as a means to the latter. For any suggestion that autonomy is the value toward which privacy naturally inclines, or that it represents a more responsible or more reasonable version of privacy, evades precisely what is controversial in the latter, by reneging on the decision to view it as a counterforce neither wholly good nor wholly bad.[17]

We have now come full circle: this ambivalent view of privacy is very close to Chapman's and Silber's own. I suggest that we reclaim it, for in the intervening twenty-five years an important insight has been lost. Critics such as Chapman and Silber seem to have understood why some ways of politicizing the personal are undesirable with respect to the private: ultimately they may only buttress the power of science against the contingent achievements of contestation and struggle, subsuming politics to rationalist dictates more generally. This has the effect—precisely the one Arendt, Pitkin, and now Elshtain, fear—of obliterating the distinction between public and private, since in science nothing is "private" in the sense of inexplicable or radically resistant to systematic analysis. Given a sense that everything is open, at least in principle, to generalizability and thus to manipulation, I can see the expressly political and even progressive purposes served by something like Chapman's and Silber's understanding.

We need such an understanding of the private, and we need the rigorous and systematic analysis with which it seems, at first, to conflict: both redeem politics against science. Otherwise, this particular contest is loaded from the beginning. For it is only once we have lost all sense of the private as radical singularity, the vast exception to the rule, that critics of radical analyses of power can blame the analyses themselves—that is, scientism rather than any consequent politics—for the demise of private space and private experience. Although eccentric, Chapman's and Silber's remarks testify to an important fact, the political implications of which are little appreciated. It has to do with privacy's necessary, if necessarily equivocal, connection to deviation, transgression, even taboo. Recall that privacy law "preserve[s] as much pretense and hypocrisy as virtue and redemption require" (Silber 1971, 235). This sort of multivalent view, with respect to

---

[17] Boling also cautions against the conflation of privacy and autonomy; she credits Schoeman (1992) as well as Rubenfeld (1989) with detaching privacy from an idealized conception of the person and analyzing it, instead, as a defense against the normalizing pressures of state and society (Boling 1996, 22–24). Compare with Cohen (1997), who argues that privacy rights *confer* "decisional autonomy," understood as a legal status, without, however, presupposing "an atomist or voluntarist conception of the individual" (149–50).

privacy not the least, should also complicate our understanding of the science proper to politics.

The issue of privacy raises the "science question" in a particularly urgent way; reconstructing the former thus requires engaging the latter. It is not hard to imagine Chapman and Silber remarking of the militant "politics of presence" associated with contemporary identity movements that this is just what we might expect from overweening scientists: here, political assertiveness derives from the pretensions of systematic theory. Against this we hear invoked the ideal of subtle transformations between the private and the public, the personal and the political, transformations that depend on rationally structured sentiments and a mature political sense. Contemporary theorists such as Sandel and Elshtain ultimately prefer the latter, gentler method of discussion and deliberation—while professing, however, the need for an understanding of power as ambitious and systematic as the much maligned radical alternative. It is only because Sandel and Elshtain believe that public and private operate systematically, distributing power along certain specifiable axes, that the apotheosis of privacy concerns them. As Sandel writes, "it is as if the triumph of autonomy in matters of religion, speech, and sexual morality were a kind of consolation for the loss of agency in an economic and political order increasingly governed by vast structures of power" (1996, 118). But it is cold consolation, incapable of restoring that lost agency, since it substitutes pure and unworkable affect for an objective command over power and power relations. There can be nothing more misguided, then, than the declaration of an American Civil Liberties Union (ACLU) official that "free speech exists in the most extreme cases or it doesn't exist at all" (quoted in Sandel 1996, 85). This is an enormously seductive stance, to be sure, mainly for reinforcing a view of the self as willful, self-sovereign, constituted in and through its singular and "non-negotiable demands" (Elshtain 1995, 61). But, like all seductive self-concepts, it abandons the difficult business of specifying how precisely the private and public, the singular and the general, are interrelated—or, as Elshtain puts it, "analogous to each other along certain axes of power and privilege" (43).

This is, of course, the business of social scientists. What I hope to have established is the insufficiency of two alternatives—both a science encompassing, in order to judge, everything and the gentleman's science proffered against it, which seems little more than an elusive sixth sense. Neither is capable of explaining, for instance, why conceptualizing privacy as a crucial reprieve from power does not require thinking of it as the very opposite of power. Contrast the notion of transitional space, which supplies invaluable resources for appraisals of this kind: neither subjective nor objective, transitional space serves precisely to bridge the two dimensions of experience, thus proving as indispensable, and real, as it is beyond our deliberate grasp and manipulation. I agree with Michael Rustin (1991) that there is likely to be tremendous resistance to any analysis — any science, such as his own psychoanalysis — that deliberately foregrounds the indeterminate and ungovernable. For the same reasons, there will be resistance to the "diffuse conception of social justice" necessitated by such a science. "It must be a very delicate and complicated social mechanism," Rustin concedes, "which both asserts a common principle — the right to care and development for all in a good society — yet can actualize it only by allowing discretion, autonomy and variation in each instance" (1991, 51).

In the next section I take up the work of Patricia Williams (1991) in order to determine whether she compromises her own penetrating insights into power by appealing to the radically singular and unspeakably private. Wendy Brown (1995) contends that this is more than a tension in Williams's analysis, indeed, that it borders on delusion, an unfortunate if understandable seduction to liberal fantasies of radical freedom. I insist, on the contrary, that Williams's work provides a crucial opportunity for rethinking privacy, including its complex relationship to fantasy, not to mention fantasy's place in the democratic imagination. Williams points the way toward innovative new solutions to political problems of power, powerlessness, and vulnerability, solutions predicated on the "discretion . . . and variation in each instance" that Rustin places at the very heart of democracy. I believe this "discretion" to be the key to advancing feminist, postmodernist, and radical-democratic projects, to pushing their critique of liberal individualism one decisive step further.

"The specifics of my pain": Transgression in theory and practice

Postmodernist critics, like the communitarian (Sandel 1996) and democratic (Barber 1984; also Elshtain 1995), stress the social, interactive, and contingent parts of personhood. Yet their rejection of the liberal ideal of solitary self-possession is more radical still, extending even to properties, such as gender, by which other theorists routinely distinguish self from other, inside from outside. According to Judith Butler (1990), for instance, gender eludes — slips over and through — somatic barriers, not to mention flimsy theoretical ones like the public-private distinction. It is "a norm that can never be fully internalized" but only continuously performed, Butler insists; " 'the internal' is a surface signification, and gender norms are finally phantasmatic, impossible to embody" (1990, 141). It is doubtful, on such a view, that the characterization of a sphere, experience, or state as "authentically either private or public" (Elshtain 1995, 40) — that is to say, residing outside contingent performative possibilities — would make much sense. Indeed, it would certainly be rejected, for "blind-[ing] us to the political role that the idea of an inner world plays" (Digeser 1994, 658).[18]

I believe that the notion of interiority can be turned to progressive purposes. Nevertheless, the postmodernist critique — represented here by Brown's (1995) reflections on the discourse of pain and injury pervading identity politics — is a formidable one and deserves special notice. My sense is that if anything marks the authentically private and can be used to chart further the axes of power and privilege that constitute us, it is felt pain and suffering. Brown is extremely wary of such discourse — conceived as one of the central contemporary "modalities of . . . opposition" (3) — for its tendency to enmesh injured parties in systems of power and privilege while also concealing the ways in which those systems disfigure, dispossess, and disgrace. The vindication of felt pain and suffering — whether through rights-claims or that particular kind of activism known as identity politics — rarely ends there, according to Brown, but rather inscribes in law what should be viewed as contingent, that is, the relation of identity to its "current constitutive injuries" (134). The discourse of pain and suffering thus "renaturalizes" as identity, and privatizes as a "status," what a rigorous analysis of domination would reveal: relations of power and the causal forces and effects arising from them (10).

Brown skillfully interweaves a Marxist concern for the causal processes working through social relations of domination with a Foucauldian appreciation for what I would call interiority, or the range of ways in which we are conditioned to respond to, attune ourselves to, even embrace those relations. Indeed, this is the hallmark of disciplinary power, in which empowerment — or a platitudinous "power *to*" — is hardly distinguishable from "power *over*" (1995, 22–23; emphasis added). Vulnerability, the vulnerability of some to the power and predations of others, is transformed into a more diffuse susceptibility, a good word for the mosaic of incitement, excitement, and interdiction sustaining the liberal-individualist order. "Those highly individuated, self-interested subjects produced by liberal cultures and capitalist political economies," writes Brown, "turn out

---

[18] See Digeser 1994, esp. 662–67, on why Butler's notion of performativity also throws into question "interiority," that is to say, private mental space. Ultimately, however, Digeser and I agree: the sensation of privacy — which Butler includes among "fabricated notions about the ineffable interiority of . . . sex or . . . true identity" (1990, 136) — is one of those "constative" phenomena on which performative acts actually depend for their success.

to be the subjects quintessentially susceptible to disciplinary power: their individuation and false autonomy is also their vulnerability" (19).

Leading feminist thinkers prove surprisingly vulnerable to this kind of power, according to Brown; two of them, Catharine MacKinnon and Patricia Williams, are singled out for especially pointed criticism. Their work (MacKinnon 1987; Williams 1991) testifies powerfully to liberal fantasies of individuation and radical choice, fantasies that intricately structure desire, including its disavowal as desire and its reconfiguration as rational self-interest. Williams's tendency, for instance, to tie every last tangible good and personal need to the possession of "rights"—as well as the manifest good sense of all such demands, "where rights are currency"—traces exactly this path, so typical of liberal fantasy, from intense desire, through disavowal, to a more temperate self-interest (Brown 1995, 122–28). None of this, however, begins to dodge a familiar "conundrum," says Brown, namely, the likelihood that a "deeply enmeshed symbol operates not only in but against that psyche, working as self-reproach, depoliticized suffering, and dissimulation of extralegal forms of power" (122). The vulnerability in evidence here is so interior, so inescapable, and so continuous that the privatization, individuation, and false autonomy that rights regimes inevitably foster would seem the cruelest remedy—and the most hopeless passion—of all.

Brown's critique is a forceful one—to my mind, the most challenging with respect to any contemporary reclamation of privacy. First, then, we must grapple with the obvious paradox in Williams's defense of privacy, including individual rights thereto. Brown is correct. Williams's veneration of rights, her passion for the "luminous golden spirit" that dawns in those finally possessed of rights, is greatly at odds with her own sober assessment of them, her denunciation of the mechanical "privatization" and eviscerated public conscience that they invariably foster (Williams 1991, 165). But this is not simply a tension in Williams's analysis; Brown suspects it is closer to delusion. After all, what could be more private, in the special sense of incommensurate, than passionate desire? Or, conversely, what could be more passionately fantasized than being alone, thus omnipotent, "never being told of difference, . . . [nor] rent apart by the singularity of others"? "It is a feeling," Williams herself concedes, that many of us "equate with the quintessence of freedom; this powerful fancy, the unconditionality of self-will alone" (102). No doubt Williams would agree with Elshtain and Sandel that this "fancy" is insidious and perversely effective: it has made it nearly impossible to speak of such things as "social evil, communal wrong, states of affairs that implicate us whether we will it or not" (102). All three would insist, moreover, that the discourse of rights has fueled this powerful fantasy of self-sufficiency and unconditional will. Yet Williams demands a redoubling of our efforts, an intensification of our commitment to rights: "Give to all of society's objects and untouchables," she says, "the rights of privacy, integrity, and self-assertion; give them distance and respect" (165).

My point is not that Williams, Elshtain, and Sandel agree in principle, their differences being empirical ones only, disputes over who does and does not have rights or whose right of privacy trumps whose right to equal protection. For Williams is one of those determined to make a politics of her identity, pace Elshtain and Sandel and pace Brown, to make law out of life: "My personal concern is with identifying the specifics of my pain." To inventory "real sources of misery in even the most powerful institutions" — to chart, that is, the complete and complex interpenetration of pain and power, not their antithesis — is, in addition to being a theory, an *endeavor:* the very opposite of powerlessness. Indeed, says Williams, to resist in this way is to "participate in a meaningful and great-souled manner" *in* power (1991, 94).

Still, insofar as we understand Williams's work to be a study in power, it is a meticulous one in which power has, so to speak, both head and heart — and contains all the paradox that follows from that.[19] This is why the most clear-headed calculations alternate, in Williams's writing, with the fiercest confessions of need and desire. This is why a black female contracts professor, whose great-great-grandmother was chattel to a wealthy white lawyer and whose knowledge of the law — acquired in those "most powerful institutions" — assures that she really does *know* better, believes even rights of contract to be a "magic wand." This is why she speaks of magic, alchemy, sorcery, and not only formal equal opportunity. This is why, and how, the rights she conjures work their magic indifferently, the magic "of visibility and invisibility, of inclusion and exclusion, of power and no power" (1991, 163–64). On this theory of power — my hope being to have established that it is a theory and not simply a litany of private sensations — rights have, if not an altogether different meaning, then a different

[19] See Digeser 1992 on the "fourth face" of power and, more generally, on the power debate in political science. My point here is that there are not only different types of power but also different ways of analyzing it. Perhaps the most penetrating account of all would generate less a bottom line — "A causes B to do something" — than a manifold perceptual field. This is how Williams describes her own work: "It is this perspective, the ambivalent, multivalent way of seeing, that is at the core of what is called critical theory, feminist theory, and much of the minority critique of law. It has to do with a fluid positioning that sees back and forth across boundary, which acknowledges that I can be black and good and black and bad, and that I can also be black and white, . . . love and hate" (1991, 130).

function and effect.[20] They secure both visibility and invisibility, after all. Thus, when Williams invokes the "rights of privacy, integrity, and self-assertion" (165), it cannot be the case, as her critics claim, that she means to privatize rights or merely to politicize herself. And she must mean something very particular with regard to privacy.

Of the clues she scatters throughout her work, none seem more significant than the references, literally dozens of them, to "the taboo"—meaning, variously, the secret, forbidden, or sacred. This association of privacy with taboo is not itself surprising: the forbidden is precisely what we demand be kept private, if it cannot be eliminated altogether; what is private is often secret as well; what is private and secret is also frequently sacred (one's relationship to God, for example). What is new and provocative is Williams's insistent return to such associations, not to mention that the taboo is also transformed by her alchemy: its great danger always exists in close proximity to the most intense desire and most urgent hope, and the possibilities it reveals are precious, often unspeakably so.

I will conclude with a parable; it is unclear, of course, whether it is Williams's or my own. Drawn from her speculations on the Baby M case, it concerns the very definition of taboo, that is to say, "boundary crossing, . . . this willing transgression of a line" (129). Yet Williams's point seems to be that we have, in the act of crossing, and perhaps there alone, the material and opportunity for real transformation, reconciliation, even a complex "renewal" of self. There is manifest risk in this parable: "When [Judge] Sorkow declared that it was only to be expected that parents would want to breed children 'like' themselves, he simultaneously created a legal right to the same, . . . encas[ing] the children conforming to likeliness in protective custody, far from whole ranges of taboo. Taboo about touch and smell and intimacy and boundary. Taboo about ardor, possession, license, equivocation, equanimity, indifference, intolerance, rancor, dispossession, innocence, exile, and candor" (227). And yet, precisely because there is this risk, there is the potential for the most miraculous transformations. Listen, too, to Williams's interpolation, her reweaving of Judge Sorkow's own "complex magic," his insinuating into life and law the presumption that we naturally desire those "like" ourselves:

> These questions turn, perhaps, on not-so-subtle images of which mothers should be bearing which children. Is there not something unseemly . . . about the spectacle of a white woman mothering a

---

[20] As Brown also notes, Williams does not insist upon new words but, rather, demands that we expand the "constricted referential universe" in which rights-discourse functions (Williams 1991, 159).

black child? A white woman giving totally to a black child; a black child totally and demandingly dependent for everything, sustenance itself, from a white woman. The image of a white woman suckling a black child, . . . the utter interdependence of such an image; the merging it implies; the giving up of boundary; the encompassing of other within self; the unbounded generosity and interconnectedness of such an image. Such a picture says there is no difference; it places the hope of continuous generation, of immortality of the white self, in a little black face. (226–27)

I trust that Williams intends to leave this parable vague and unsettling: to suggest both that a white mother will always see the "black" in that face and that she will see past it, indeed, that she will see her own future there, too. Certainly both ways of seeing are necessary for doing justice — and for working magic — in such a situation. When Williams invokes, then, a right to privacy, I believe she means to lay claim to an entire range of experience, to include "visibility and invisibility, . . . power and no power" (163–64) — a range of experience that resolves itself, if at all, in the space of a face, a gaze, and the "great-souled" hope that integrates them.

We associate privacy with many things — secrecy, intimacy, isolation, solitude. The taboo is one of the more lasting of these associations, besides being the one thing we have managed to confine, more or less completely, to the private realm. Could it be that privacy itself constitutes a taboo, though of a surprising new kind, since in rendering certain things unspeakable, it also makes them less vulnerable to a voracious critical gaze? Perhaps the especially close connection between the private and the taboo in Williams's work is meant to suggest that there is also some privacy to be had from taboo, from small and solitary — in the precise sense of individuating — transgressions. This is a mark of transitional space, as well, if we are to believe Winnicott: "An essential feature of transitional phenomena and objects," he notes, "is a quality in our attitude when we observe them" (1993, 4). That is to say, a vital part of transitional phenomena comes from without, in the forbearance they require from third parties — the parent, the analyst, the social and political critic. Transitional space consists in — it is constituted by — our willingness to suspend judgment, to decline to parse subjective and objective, mine and yours, the authentically private and the authentically public. But this is precisely the kind of judgment that is reinscribed in theories emphasizing the transformation of private into public, the representation of our most urgent needs and interests to one another, a representation that can also seem a renunciation. Isn't this the significance of Williams's very last allusion to privacy, where she assimilates it to the secret, the sacred, the finally and truly "inviolate"? Admonishing her more critical colleagues not to "discard rights but to see . . . past them," she yearns for a "larger definition of privacy and property: so that privacy is turned from exclusion based on self-regard into regard for another's fragile, mysterious autonomy" (1991, 164).[21]

Conclusion

It is not possible to specify this autonomy fully and precisely; what Williams does, instead, is to reclaim the private as its potent signifier. Of course, this conditions how privacy is reclaimed and reworked. The first step is to attend to what Winnicott calls a "protest" from within, a protest issuing from the depths of the "non-communicating central self" and imparted, most urgently and directly, in testimonies of pain and injury. With regard to this central self, whose essential needs or contours cannot be delineated in advance, in the abstract, our attitude must be reverence, silent witness to another's "right *not* to communicate" (Winnicott 1965, 179). I am interested in the possibilities that reside in such acts of forbearance.

Thus my aim, in emphasizing the taboo in privacy, is not to encourage transgressive acts. By necessity it is a more limited theoretical intervention meant to change the significance of privacy, especially with respect to things public. We should not expect privacy to designate a sphere ontologically, socially, or otherwise distinct from the public; but neither is it a transitional space or time with only beneficent, or only troubling, repercussions for the public. Its implications for autonomy, finally, are as elusive as they are profound. A key distinction between the two is that privacy serves, as autonomy does not, to hold judgment in abeyance. For privacy signifies the sacred and incomparable experience of relating to oneself; perhaps this is why Winnicott insists that for all its "futility" to observers, such "cul-de-sac communication (communication with subjective objects) carries all the sense of real" (1965, 184). There is a reason autonomy does not contribute to the same intense self-realization: autonomy norms are not about self-relating at all.

I suggest that recovering privacy, and reconceiving it as the perverse singularity residing in the political, has progressive and even distinctly dem-

---

[21] Since the "mysterious" is what resists complete understanding, the hope is that it would resist complete assimilation as well. Baudrillard has no such hope, although he does hazard a guess as to what the private would be were it still possible: "The secret, were there such, would be such that it could not be betrayed" (quoted in Bogard 1996, 125). I believe this to be Williams's point as well: another's secret may be known—known well enough, as her *autonomy*—and yet remain mysterious, thus unforsaken.

ocratic effects. We enlist privacy on the side of the political against the positivistic, the possible against the predictable, the strange and singular against the timeless, gaining, thereby, a range of denotations unavailable on conventional rationalist models of politics. But this is not because privacy reinstates a naive essentialism, or "presencing," against positivist science. Rather, to borrow from Joan Scott's famous formulation of "the evidence of experience," the private sustains a "vision beyond the visible, a vision that contains the fantastic projections . . . that are the basis for political identification" (1991, 794). This *in*sight, I suggest, can slacken pressures to convert the personal into the general, to transform—without remainder—desire into policy and difference into legitimate public claim, to wring from public discourse a demoralizing kind of confession and exposure of self. We enlist a powerful counterforce, privacy, against the normalizing forces of contemporary public culture, but we do so in such a way as to see clearly the diverse *uses* of privacy. That is to say, such a view would still permit us to detect when privacy operates as a mere cover for other, less savory, fantastic projections—solipsism, an infantile fear of others, intolerance, hierarchy and privilege, simple self-seeking behavior.

In place of the older private-public dichotomy, we gain a transitional space, a vital resource for navigating between the personal and the public, the singular and the general. Because this privacy lies squarely within the flow of power, it can be used to participate in power in that great-souled manner of which Williams speaks. In this way, we are pushed past dichotomies and dichotomizing thought onto an explicitly political terrain. Perhaps surprisingly, then, reclaiming privacy enriches social and political analysis. A certain forbearance makes thought more penetrating, more sensitive to the complexities of power, powerlessness, and vulnerability. Retrieving privacy as potent signifier—as a solemn nod to singular and incommensurate experience—is already to theorize differently, to have our thinking invigorated as well as deepened through confrontation with what is never fully articulate, never fully theorizable.

I claim for ambivalent, multivalent readings of central political concepts, such as privacy, what Larry Preston claims for literature. In fact, the former function more directly and more deliberately to "reterritorialize" the language of theory, to change "the ways in which theory is written, the range of experience that informs theoretical writing, and the conceptions of important political ideas that are the heart of theoretical visions" (Preston 1995, 949). This is, I suggest, the considerable appeal of Williams's work, of a "fluid positioning that sees back and forth across boundary" (1991, 130), a positioning by which we come to know more precisely through slackening our drive to categorize, to translate, and to judge. In addition, then, to the impetus given to a less pathological politics, one less bent on normalizing judgments, a perverse reading of privacy points the way to a different kind of theory. This is a type of thought and thinking with especially important implications for my own discipline of political science.

Claims such as these may only perplex those who believe that responsible social analysis consists in specifying determinate relations among clearly delineated social spheres, of parsing "mine" and "yours," "mine" and "ours." But the ambivalent view of privacy defended here should prove perfectly familiar to those accustomed to thinking from the margins, those who take a slightly irregular perspective on society's laws and norms. This is true of feminists, I would argue, whose legacy is a long one of misbehaving: by speaking radical truths to power, by speaking the unspeakable, and by theorizing such things as sex and sexuality. Now, perhaps feminists should be quite *obscene*, embracing those "dimension[s] of culture that allo[w] us to cross boundaries, exceed limits . . . , and experience the dialectic between life and death," taking for granted that without such transgressions, "there would be no sense of the beyond" (Caputi 1994, 7). Likewise, without a conception of private and, by necessity, perverse will, it is impossible to appreciate the suspension of that will in public space.

Woodrow Wilson Department of Government and Foreign Affairs
University of Virginia

References

Barber, Benjamin. 1984. *Strong Democracy: Participatory Politics for a New Age.* Berkeley and Los Angeles: University of California Press.

Barker, Francis. 1984. *The Tremulous Private Body: Essays on Subjection.* London: Methuen.

Benhabib, Seyla, ed. 1996. *Democracy and Difference: Contesting the Boundaries of the Political.* Princeton, N.J.: Princeton University Press.

Benjamin, Jessica. 1988. *The Bonds of Love: Psychoanalysis, Feminism, and the Problem of Domination.* New York: Pantheon.

Benn, Stanley I. 1984. "Privacy, Freedom, and Respect for Persons." In Schoeman 1984, 223–44.

Berlant, Lauren. 1997. *The Queen of America Goes to Washington City: Essays on Sex and Citizenship.* Durham, N.C.: Duke University Press.

Bloustein, Edward J. 1984. "Privacy as an Aspect of Human Dignity: An Answer to Dean Prosser." In Schoeman 1984, 156–202.

Bogard, William. 1996. *The Simulation of Surveillance: Hypercontrol in Telematic Societies.* Cambridge: Cambridge University Press.

Boling, Patricia. 1996. *Privacy and the Politics of Intimate Life*. Ithaca, N.Y.: Cornell University Press.

Brown, Wendy. 1995. *States of Injury: Power and Freedom in Late Modernity*. Princeton, N.J.: Princeton University Press.

Butler, Judith. 1990. *Gender Trouble: Feminism and the Subversion of Identity*. New York: Routledge.

Caputi, Mary. 1994. *Voluptuous Yearnings: A Feminist Theory of the Obscene*. Lanham, Md.: Rowman & Littlefield.

Cavell, Stanley. 1988. *In Quest of the Ordinary: Lines of Skepticism and Romanticism*. Chicago: University of Chicago Press.

Chapman, John W. 1971. "Personality and Privacy." In *NOMOS XIII: Privacy*, ed. J. Roland Pennock and John W. Chapman, 236–55. New York: Atherton.

Cohen, Jean L. 1997. "Rethinking Privacy: Autonomy, Identity, and the Abortion Controversy." In *Public and Private in Thought and Practice: Perspectives on a Grand Dichotomy*, ed. Jeff Weintraub and Krishan Kumar, 133–65. Chicago: University of Chicago Press.

Connolly, William. 1991. *Identity/Difference: Democratic Negotiations of Political Paradox*. Ithaca, N.Y.: Cornell University Press.

Cornell, Drucilla. 1995. *The Imaginary Domain: Abortion, Pornography, and Sexual Harassment*. New York: Routledge.

Dandekar, Natalie. 1993. "Privacy: An Understanding for Embodied Persons." *The Philosophical Forum* 24(4):331–48.

Digeser, Peter. 1992. "The Fourth Face of Power." *Journal of Politics* 54(4): 977–1007.

———. 1994. "Performativity Trouble: Postmodern Feminism and Essential Subjects." *Political Research Quarterly* 47(3):655–73.

Elshtain, Jean Bethke. 1981. *Public Man, Private Woman: Women in Social and Political Thought*. Princeton, N.J.: Princeton University Press.

———. 1995. *Democracy on Trial*. New York: Basic.

Flax, Jane. 1993. "The Play of Justice: Justice as a Transitional Space." *Political Psychology* 14(2):331–46.

Foucault, Michel. 1997. *Ethics: Subjectivity and Truth*. Ed. Paul Rabinow, trans. Robert Hurley et al. Vol. 1 of *The Essential Works of Michel Foucault, 1954–1984*. New York: New Press.

Fried, Charles. 1984. "Privacy (a Moral Analysis)." In Schoeman 1984, 203–22.

Gavison, Ruth. 1984. "Privacy and the Limits of Law." In Schoeman 1984, 346–402.

Gerstein, Robert S. 1984. "Intimacy and Privacy." In Schoeman 1984, 265–71.

Glass, James M. 1995. *Psychosis and Power: Threats to Democracy in the Self and the Group*. Ithaca, N.Y.: Cornell University Press.

Gould, Carol C. 1996. "Diversity and Democracy: Representing Differences." In Benhabib 1996, 171–86.

Habermas, Jürgen. 1975. *Legitimation Crisis*. Trans. Thomas McCarthy. Boston: Beacon.

———. 1996. *Between Facts and Norms: Contributions to a Discourse Theory of Law and Democracy*. Trans. William Rehg. Cambridge, Mass.: MIT Press.

Harper, Phillip Brian. 1994. "Private Affairs: Race, Sex, Property, and Persons." *GLQ: A Journal of Lesbian and Gay Studies* 1(2):111–33.

Honneth, Axel. 1995. *The Struggle for Recognition: The Moral Grammar of Social Conflicts*. Trans. Joel Anderson. Cambridge: Polity.

Kelvin, Peter. 1973. "A Social-Psychological Examination of Privacy." *British Journal of Social and Clinical Psychology* 12:248–61.

Kupfer, Joseph. 1987. "Privacy, Autonomy, and Self-Concept." *American Philosophical Quarterly* 24(1):81–89.

Laufer, Robert S., and Maxine Wolfe. 1977. "Privacy as a Concept and a Social Issue: A Multi-Dimensional Developmental Theory." *Journal of Social Issues* 33: 22–42.

MacKinnon, Catharine. 1987. *Feminism Unmodified: Discourses on Life and Law*. Cambridge, Mass.: Harvard University Press.

Newfield, Christopher. 1996. *The Emerson Effect: Individualism and Submission in America*. Chicago: University of Chicago Press.

Okin, Susan Moller. 1989. *Justice, Gender, and the Family*. New York: Basic.

Pateman, Carole. 1989. "Feminist Critiques of the Public/Private Dichotomy." In *The Disorder of Women: Democracy, Feminism, and Political Theory*. Stanford, Calif.: Stanford University Press.

Phillips, Adam. 1993. *On Kissing, Tickling, and Being Bored: Psychoanalytic Essays on the Unexamined Life*. Cambridge, Mass.: Harvard University Press.

Phillips, Anne. 1996. "Dealing with Difference: A Politics of Ideas, or a Politics of Presence?" In Benhabib 1996, 139–52.

Pitkin, Hanna. 1981. "Justice: On Relating Private and Public." *Political Theory* 9(3):327–52.

Preston, Larry M. 1995. "Theorizing Difference: Voices from the Margins." *American Political Science Review* 89(4):941–53.

Regan, Priscilla. 1995. *Legislating Privacy: Technology, Social Values, and Public Policy*. Chapel Hill: University of North Carolina Press.

Rorty, Richard. 1989. *Contingency, Irony, and Solidarity*. Cambridge: Cambridge University Press.

Rosenblum, Nancy L. 1987. *Another Liberalism: Romanticism and the Reconstruction of Liberal Thought*. Cambridge, Mass.: Harvard University Press.

Ruben, Douglas. 1988. "Private Events Revisited: Does Unobservable Mean Private?" *Journal of Contemporary Psychotherapy* 18(1):16–27.

Rubenfeld, Jed. 1989. "The Right of Privacy." *Harvard Law Review* 102(4): 737–807.

Rudnytsky, Peter L., ed. 1993. *Transitional Objects and Potential Spaces: Literary Uses of D. W. Winnicott*. New York: Columbia University Press.

Rustin, Michael. 1991. *The Good Society and the Inner World: Psychoanalysis, Politics, and Culture*. London: Verso.

Sandel, Michael. 1996. *Democracy's Discontent: America in Search of a Public Philosophy*. Cambridge, Mass.: Harvard University Press.

Schoeman, Ferdinand David, ed. 1984. *Philosophical Dimensions of Privacy: An Anthology.* Cambridge: Cambridge University Press.

———. 1992. *Privacy and Social Freedom.* Cambridge: Cambridge University Press.

Scott, Joan W. 1991. "The Evidence of Experience." *Critical Inquiry* 17:773–97.

Silber, John R. 1971. "Masks and Fig Leaves." In *NOMOS XIII: Privacy,* ed. J. Roland Pennock and John W. Chapman, 226–35. New York: Atherton.

Stark, Andrew. 1997. "Limousine Liberals, Welfare Conservatives: On Belief, Interest, and Inconsistency in Democratic Discourse." *Political Theory* 25(4): 475–501.

Turner, John. 1993. "Wordsworth and Winnicott in the Area of Play." In Rudnytsky 1993, 161–88.

Warren, Samuel D., and Louis D. Brandeis. (1890) 1984. "The Right to Privacy." In Schoeman 1984, 75–103.

Will, David. 1986. "Psychoanalysis and the New Philosophy of Science." *International Review of Psycho-Analysis* 13:163–73.

Williams, Patricia. 1991. *The Alchemy of Race and Rights.* Cambridge, Mass.: Harvard University Press.

Winnicott, D. W. 1965. *The Maturational Processes and the Facilitating Environment: Studies in the Theory of Emotional Development.* New York: International Universities Press, Inc.

———. 1971. *Playing and Reality.* London: Tavistock/Routledge.

———. 1993. "The Location of Cultural Experience." In Rudnytsky 1993, 3–12.

Young, Iris Marion. 1990. *Justice and the Politics of Difference.* Princeton, N.J.: Princeton University Press.

Comments and Reply

Comment on Morris's "Privacy, Privation, Perversity: Toward New Representations of the Personal"

Patricia Boling, *Department of Political Science and Women's Studies Program, Purdue University*

Drawing on Patricia Williams's highly personalized language of pain and injury (1991) and D. W. Winnicott's notion of transitional spaces (1965), Debra Morris develops a theory of privacy that she claims will help us think critically about central problems in democratic theory, including power and powerlessness, vulnerability, and preserving "what is most singular, secret, ineffable, internal, that is, private, about [individuals]" (221). I agree with her claim that we need to tell a more complex story about privacy than much contemporary theorizing provides, and I learned a lot from her argument for understanding privacy as a transitional space and a reprieve from power. Taking Morris's essay as a point of departure, I shall address these questions: Why do we need a political theory of privacy? What are some of the contributions that have already been made to thinking about privacy? What should a theory of privacy look like or do?

Like Morris, I think understanding privacy is central to revitalizing democratic theory and politics. Many theorists dismiss the concept of privacy because it functions in an ideological way to keep us from examining oppressive relationships. This approach is frequently rooted in an understanding of privacy protections or private life as inextricable from the constellation of power and political values associated with liberalism, such as private property, market capitalism, or the patriarchal family.[1] Yet concern with public and private was central to thinking about politics long before the advent of liberalism, and privacy does not always or only reinforce lines of power and privilege. Sometimes "private" demarcates decisions, places, or experiences that we want to protect from the intrusion or intervention

---

[1] See, e.g., Catharine MacKinnon (1987); Carole Pateman (1988); and Wendy Brown (1995).

[*Signs: Journal of Women in Culture and Society* 2000, vol. 25 no. 2]

of the state, our fellow citizens, or social pressure. Private life is home to many important experiences, values, practices, and relationships that exist nowhere else and that would be destroyed if exposed to public scrutiny.[2]

Morris's concerns with revitalizing privacy run in similar directions. She worries about the tendency "to exalt the public self, at some expense to our care and concern for the private" (222); the move to understand private life as merely the substratum of politics, a ground out of which problems arise that must then be translated into political claims that can produce public action; and the progressive articulation and rationalization of the self. But while Morris is attentive to the dangers of subsuming private life and experience to politics, she doesn't worry about the dangers privacy may pose to public life: that privacy may blind us to oppressive arrangements that seem natural or simply "off limits" or that taking privacy seriously as an overarching public value may lead to a public life that is little more than the orderly pursuit of private interest. Morris postulates that a discerning understanding of privacy would permit us to distinguish between more or less "savory" ways of enlisting privacy, which simply begs the question.[3] Morris simply is not much interested in how private, public, and political connect as ways of being in the world or in locating tensions or problems in privacy as a value or concept. I agree that thinking about privacy is important in part because we are in danger of losing sight of why privacy and the experiences of private life are valuable, but I am drawn to think about privacy for other reasons as well: because too much or the wrong kind of respect for privacy can undermine aspirations for justice or lead people to slight the common concerns of public life that are central to democratic politics.

Not only does Morris neglect the danger that an overly privatistic society may undermine the ideal of politics as active citizen engagement in communal self-determination and turn a blind eye to oppressive relationships that take place in private or by means of privacy rights (to property, or to read pornography, for example), but she also tends to read other theorists as less attentive to the value of privacy and individuality than I

---

[2] Many have articulated this idea of privacy as the existential home to central human modes of being, including Hannah Arendt (1958); Hanna Pitkin (1981); Robert Post (1989); Ferdinand Schoeman (1992); and me (Boling 1996).

[3] She mentions these concerns in passing near the end of her essay: "We enlist a powerful counterforce, privacy, against the normalizing forces of contemporary public culture, but we do so in such a way as to see clearly the diverse *uses* of privacy. That is to say, such a view would still permit us to detect when privacy operates as a mere cover for other, less savory, fantastic projections—solipsism, an infantile fear of others, intolerance, hierarchy and privilege, simple self-seeking behavior" (245).

think they are. For example, she begins her essay by discussing Hanna Pitkin's (1981) influential essay on connecting public and private through the principle of justice. Morris reads Pitkin as arguing that an injury or grievance that arises from private life must be translated into claims that are intelligible to one's fellow citizens, thus connecting " 'I' to 'we,' in a context where many other selves also have claims on that 'we' " (224). Morris continues: "What I contest is the sort of connection privileged here. The radical potential of Pitkin's intervention into the public-private debate is sacrificed if the connections between private and public are domesticated, understood as largely conceptual ones" (225). She sees Pitkin as arguing that private need and public policy exist "in the same political space, arising between 'human need,' on the one hand, and its consequences for 'power, privilege, and suffering,' on the other" (225). Morris believes the significance of such a connection is lost "if we continue, with Pitkin, to stress the necessity—that is, the *rational necessity*—of connecting private and public" (225). This reading, which carries through Morris's interpretation of my work as well, is not well founded. First of all, Pitkin does, in fact, appreciate the experiential gulf between the private sufferer and the citizen; it is central to her attempt to work out how to make needs rooted in the private realm—the hunger of the poor, the misery of the bored, isolated housewife—understood as legitimate political claims so that others who are situated differently can hear them and understand their force. "Translation" is not simply about finding fodder for public policy in people's private lives; it is about transforming the private sufferer into a citizen who has a stake in the process, who knows that deliberations and decisions are about not just arid conceptual matters but issues of real and lasting importance to her life.

Second, Morris writes as though Pitkin only saw private life as the ground out of which political matters arose, as though what she really wanted to do was deracinate and transform those private problems so that they become mutually intelligible claims and issues governed by the requisites of political discourse. But such a reading is unfounded since for Pitkin (and for me and Hannah Arendt, to whom both Pitkin and I are indebted), private life is a crucial ground for aspects of human life that are possible only when they are hidden from view, protected from public scrutiny and official standards of conduct. *When* problems arise in private life that ought to be addressed as political issues, because we citizens see them as matters of widespread importance, because we recognize them as connected to notions of fairness, and perhaps because we think they can be remedied through public action, then Pitkin and I would argue that we should translate them into political issues. That doesn't mean that every problem that resides in private life ought to be translated into a political issue, nor does it mean that purely private matters are trivial. I argue at length that privacy nurtures intimacy, relationships with varied degrees of social distance, experimentation, individuality, and unconventionality, a point that Robert Post (1989) and Ferdinand Schoeman (1992) have also made.[4]

Third, Morris seems particularly bothered by the notion of translating problems whose existential home is in private experience into political language. She fears that translating private-life grievances into political claims "install[s] a new rationalist logic" that flattens out the uniqueness and ineffability, even the wordlessness, of private experience (225). This seems to be connected to political judgment, which is "central and indispensable" to a democratic polity and its citizens (225). Again, the criticism would carry more weight if one read Pitkin or me as arguing that *all* private matters ought to be transformed into political claims; then such a logic would seem unduly intrusive and destructive of a variety of experiences and relationships. But I think Morris's claim is more far-reaching, that she is objecting to the idea of translating private experience into political claim under *any* circumstance. For Morris, the "rationality" that would be imposed by making claims that are understandable to a broad group of one's fellow citizens, the "rationality" suggested by learning to engage in public discourse, to "dress" one's private-life self or troubles so they are ready to go out in public, is antithetical to privacy. When writing about privacy, Morris repeatedly evokes images of reprieve and respite, including the ideas of privacy as a counterforce to the "normalizing forces of public culture," as a "resource for navigating between the personal and the political," and as a "transitional space" that permits us manifold ways to resist "being found," to assert the "right *not* to communicate," to recognize that there are certain questions that are *"not to be formulated"* (quoting Winnicott). Morris writes: "I suggest . . . thinking of the private in terms of the intractable, the incongruous, the incommensurate. This privacy signifies the necessity for a reprieve from scrutiny and public judgment" (228). Thus, for Morris, translating private matters into claims that can be held up to political standards or having the private sufferer develop political judgment undercuts the core of what privacy *is:* a reprieve from public scrutiny and judgment.

While I respect that Morris wants to emphasize privacy as a resource for protecting a realm of experience she does not want to spell out too minutely—what she alludes to as the intractable, the incongruous, the per-

---

[4] See also Jeffrey Reiman (1976); James Rachels (1984); Frank Michelman (1988); Morris Kaplan (1991, 1994); and Ruth Gavison (1992a, 1992b).

verse—I find her approach troubling. If we understand the private as a hedge against scrutiny and public judgment, what does that imply about how we think about judging? I think there are important differences between expressions like "passing judgment on someone" or "being judgmental" and "using one's judgment" or "exercising good judgment." The first pair implies a violation of the reprieve from public judgment with which Morris is concerned, while the second pair evokes capacities we value and cultivate. Apparently "political judgment," which I think of as including discernment, weighing a variety of factors accurately and sensitively, and caring about the broader political context and consequences of an argument, claim, strategy, or decision evokes, for Morris, only the sense of judgment as a normalizing pressure that constrains the unpredictable, incongruous, and intractable. Morris's evocation of privacy as a liminal, evocative resource for avoiding public judgment, like her failure to see an overly privatized society as a threat to our common life as citizens, suggests that she is inattentive to an important debate about public and private and that she is disquietingly unpolitical.

When I think about the question, "What does it mean to think well about privacy?" I have in mind a particular model of theoretical discourse. For example, while I suppose there are many who admire John Rawls's effort to construct a theory of justice, most people who want to understand justice would read widely, acquainting themselves with a variety of approaches and perspectives (including perhaps Rawls's) and engaging debates and disagreements that seem especially fruitful or troubling. The point is, a particular contribution to current work on privacy does not need to work out a comprehensive theory or model of privacy; it needs to push discourse along in constructive ways, to show us how perspectives that have not heretofore "spoken" to each other can raise new questions or make efforts to speak to problems that have been kicking around for a while.

I am attracted to theoretical work, such as Morris's, that encourages us to consider divergent approaches and perspectives to thinking about privacy, treats contradiction and ambiguity as a source of insight rather than as a defect to be explained away, and articulates problems and engages significant debates. Morris makes a powerful case for privacy as a metaphoric, psychic space or barrier connected to the taboo, the perverse or incongruent, which helps individuals preserve such sources of our selves from the normalizing power of collective life. She crafts from various sources—Winnicott, Honneth, Flax, Williams—a protective and empowering notion of privacy based not on exclusion and self-regard but on " 'regard for another's fragile, mysterious autonomy' " (quoting Williams), a notion that suggests new understandings of selfhood and new connections and discontinuities between individual and collective life (244). She locates her thinking in terms of several enduring debates — about the promise and peril of identity politics, the best way to connect private life and politics, and the ways privacy is connected to power.

Although I appreciate Morris's effort to provide an "ambivalent, multivalent" reading of privacy (245), I found some frustrations in reading her work. Not only was I troubled by the partial and inappreciative readings she gave to Arendtian approaches to thinking about public and private; it also seemed to me that several times Morris asserted that her theory would address an issue or solve a problem but then never articulated how it did so. For example, Morris claims her notion of privacy would "allo[w] . . . us to represent — without rationalizing away — those desires, needs, and experiences that implicitly challenge the demand for articulated rationality," and that "only such a view . . . is capable of dispelling several central confusions regarding privacy" (235). But Morris never explains what those central confusions regarding privacy are. Or again, she claims that because her notion of "privacy lies squarely within the flow of power, it can be used to participate in power in that great-souled manner of which Williams speaks" (245). She obviously means to offer a formulation of privacy that will get us beyond dichotomies onto an explicitly political terrain and thus help to enrich social and political analysis. But what is it about this notion of privacy that puts it squarely within the flow of power? She seems simply to assert what needs to be demonstrated and explained, especially since she claims she wants to think about privacy in ways that will be attentive to power and powerlessness, vulnerability, and the position of those who are accustomed to thinking from the margins. This brings me to my final frustration, which is with Morris's response to Wendy Brown's (1995) critique of Patricia Williams (1991). I thought Morris fairly presented Brown's criticisms, but instead of responding to them, Morris simply set them to the side and proceeded to explain how Williams addresses power. But Brown's arguments about the way rights and privacy "draw a circle around the individual" and turn all responsibility back on her "for her failures . . . privatiz[ing] her situation and mystify[ing] the powers that construct . . . her" are powerful and need to be engaged, not simply identified and then ignored (1995, 128).

In sum, Morris wrestles with important questions, treats ambiguity and ambivalence as resources rather than problems, and develops a powerful and original defense of privacy. Her work makes an important contribution to dialogue about privacy among contemporary theorists, and as she engages others' arguments more fully and pushes herself to answer hard questions about power and politics, Morris's position will become even more interesting.

References

Arendt, Hannah. 1958. *The Human Condition.* Chicago: University of Chicago Press.

Boling, Patricia. 1996. *Privacy and the Politics of Intimate Life.* Ithaca, N.Y.: Cornell University Press.

Brown, Wendy. 1995. *States of Injury.* Princeton, N.J.: Princeton University Press.

Gavison, Ruth. 1992a. "Feminism and the Public/Private Distinction." *Stanford Law Review* 45 (November): 1–45.

———. 1992b. "Too Early for a Requiem: Warren and Brandeis Were Right on Privacy vs. Free Speech." *South Carolina Law Review* 43(3):437–71.

Kaplan, Morris. 1991. "Autonomy, Equality, Community: The Question of Lesbian and Gay Rights." *Praxis International* 11(2):195–213.

———. 1994. "Intimacy and Equality: The Question of Lesbian and Gay Marriage." *Philosophical Forum* 25(4):333–60.

MacKinnon, Catharine. 1987. *Feminism Unmodified.* Cambridge, Mass.: Harvard University Press.

Michelman, Frank. 1988. "Law's Republic." *Yale Law Journal* 97(8):1493–1533.

Pateman, Carole. 1988. *The Sexual Contract.* Stanford, Calif.: Stanford University Press.

Pitkin, Hanna. 1981. "Justice: On Relating Private and Public." *Political Theory* 9(3):327–52.

Post, Robert. 1989. "The Social Foundations of Privacy: Community and Self in the Common Law Tort." *California Law Review* 77 (October): 957–1010.

Rachels, James. 1984. "Why Privacy Is Important." In *Philosophical Dimensions of Privacy,* ed. Ferdinand Schoeman, 290–99. Cambridge: Cambridge University Press.

Reiman, Jeffrey. 1976. "Privacy, Intimacy, and Personhood." *Philosophy & Public Affairs* 6(1):26–44.

Schoeman, Ferdinand. 1992. *Privacy and Social Freedom.* Cambridge: Cambridge University Press.

Williams, Patricia. 1991. *The Alchemy of Race and Rights.* Cambridge, Mass.: Harvard University Press.

Winnicott, D. W. 1965. *The Maturational Processes and the Facilitating Environment.* New York: International Universities Press, Inc. ∎

Comment on Morris's "Privacy, Privation, Perversity: Toward New Representations of the Personal"

Jean Bethke Elshtain, *Divinity School, University of Chicago*

Debra Morris has written a challenging, nuanced, lively piece that helps us to understand and to situate many of the most keenly contested points in political, legal, and feminist theory over the past decades (in this volume). One piece cannot do everything, of course, including fleshing out fully some of the author's most passionately held points: there is so much to say and so few pages in which to say it. So what I propose to do with my precious pages is to elaborate, briefly, on four points or themes, not so much to criticize Morris (though there will, inevitably, be some of that) but to continue a dialogue with her.

First, it strikes me that Morris takes on board many of the problems she associates, not without reason, with thinkers whose work revolves around the categories of public and private. That is, she, too, embraces those terms as her most singular and important marker of theoretical and analytic demarcation—and, finally, political value. As one who has been centrally involved in debates about the range and rightful purview of private and public as essentially contested but nonetheless inescapable terms (perhaps precisely because of their always ambiguous status), I thought some years ago that I should have said in my own early work much more about the social dimensions of democratic political life and private life. Neither public nor private is ever asocial, in any of its aspects, manifestations, meanings, and forms of representation—including when we are alone. Our being alone, whether bad loneliness or good solitude, signifies that we are part of a social world, and that is why we hold some notions of what constitute solitude or loneliness and isolation. Any talk of reconstructing public and private must, then, pay explicit attention to our sociality. We are intrinsically social—human beings could not survive outside a network of sociality—even as we are trouble as well as succor to one another. In Saint Augustine's terms, we are both "social" and "quarrelsome."

The category of the social I have in mind is very different from what political philosopher Hannah Arendt condemned in the term. For Arendt, the social, or what she called civic housekeeping, is to be lamented because the social, in modernity, swamps the political, making it less likely that we will see ourselves as *citizens* and more likely that we will see ourselves as *clients* or *consumers.* As the social triumphs, the state becomes a giant instrumentality devoted to providing certain sorts of goods or responding to certain sorts of interest claims, and a more robust and invigorating notion of politics and of the *res publica* is lost. As with nearly every Arendtian formulation, this one is simultaneously challenging and vexing. For democracy, certainly in America, makes no sense if you don't see it as a form of social democracy, a civic world in which citizens enter public life because they care about big matters at hand *some of the time* but what is happening with their lives, schools, neighborhoods, jobs, overall well-being *all of the time*. So, in sum, let us put the social back in explicitly. That way no mistake will arise that one is somehow offering a radically stripped down, and therefore wholly inadequate, account of the complexities of social and political life. This social dimension seems to fall out of much of Morris's discussion.

Second, Morris's discussion of private and privacy as a "kind of reprieve from power" is keenly expressed. I see no problem with it so long as one does not push a monistic view of power as the basis for such a claim. With private and public held aloft as the operative categories, let me turn to Morris's discussion of identity movements. For those of us who have criticized the totalizing nature of such movements — as competition between epistemologically incommensurate "movements" and claims erupts — Morris's criticisms seem somewhat misplaced. My criticism of the tendency of identity politics to politicize an ontological category, or a category that has been given the status of such (as has race, gender, etc., in many cases), is that it often leads to a politics in which we are invited, not so much to evaluate the arguments people bring to the public square but to assess their claims to authenticity. For example, is this really the "black voice," as if there were any such thing? Or the "true female" voice by contrast to some ostensibly counterfeit discourse? My point throughout has been that we should not overpoliticize all areas of life — here Morris agrees — and, as well, that contemporary identity movements too often wind up quashing politics rather than generating politics. If I lay down a set of absolute claims and you either buy them or you "just don't get it," the invitation is to shut up and acquiesce silently or to walk away. It would be rather strained to see such "conversation stoppers," as they are sometimes called, as capacious openings to democratic discourse! So any transformation of private into public, on my argument, must effect a kind of civic translation. At the same time, no such translation of private into public is obligatory in all instances or desirable in many. There are characteristic ways of being associated with privacy and the private that are precious to human persons and that, while social, are not necessarily civic.

Related closely to my second point above, the third point I want to amplify about public into private is the way Morris evokes images of "an incursion of disorderly 'presence' " and the like (229). Let me be clear that the problem with those forms of identity movement politics I criticized above is not that they are disorderly per se but that they are so often disorderly to no discernable civic purpose, so far as I can tell. In fact, they may well be not "disorderly" enough, given the tremendous pressure to conform within the group. Identity politics cannot tolerate dissent, difference, ambiguity within. As a result, one winds up with a sort of cookie-cutter form of what is trumpeted as a voice speaking from the edge or the margin, and the political behavior of certain groups becomes almost entirely predictable. The upshot is that such groups can be taken more or less for granted: we know how they will vote on everything, we know whom they will endorse for everything, and so on. I am thinking here, to speak directly, of the way the African-American caucus functions in Congress. Given the block voting — and of course many others do this but that isn't my point; my point is that the potentially transformative dimension of what some groups claim to be up to is blunted if they are dependable shock troops for this side or that — the black vote can be taken for granted or written off. An analogue, at present, is the so-called religious vote in Congress, if we mean by that those whose base is the "Christian right." This predictable pattern is what is called "settling" in the African-American community, and one can, of course, understand the historic reasons for it. But it is problematic nonetheless, just as the "feminist" presence in the public square, through its most visible talking heads, is similarly predictable — hence, troubling. We know that there will never really be anything transgressive or shocking, in a good sense, that will be said. The "agenda" has become an "ideology" and can, therefore, be taken entirely for granted. Hardening of the categories set in long ago. What was once fresh is now stale. How would Morris respond to this civic problem?

Finally, I couldn't concur more heartily with Morris that there are real problems in setting the bar for what is to count as public reason or deliberation so high that only the small number of Habermasians clustered in our institutions of higher learning qualify for the task. Thinking more humbly, we understand that people have lives to live and that the living of a life is mostly not about doing something big and decisive at every turn. Rather, it is about doing one's best in the place in which one finds oneself. We don't seem to have a way to talk about the complexity and dignity of the quotidian. The West's two great religious traditions — Christianity and Judaism — do have such ways, of course, but there has been such an ardent push to marginalize the "religious voice" and to associate any form of religion in the public sphere with that all-purpose bogeyman, the "Christian right," that we are left with an ethically sanitized way of talking about many of the most important things. Putting in such considerations helps us to build in criteria that distinguish "bad" from "good" instances of civil society. Here I don't think Morris is quite fair in saddling Michael Sandel and me with the view that we think all norms, preferences, and attachments are "wholly benign." To the best of my knowledge, and racking my brain for possible examples, I have stated no such thing. What I have been up to, along with many others, is to thematize our "felt attachments" so they can enter discussion rather than persist in a kind of prepolitical and even presocial haze entirely outside the world of civic claims and counterclaims.

A quick comment on the way Morris concludes, and it relates to my third point above. I refer to her suggestion that "perhaps feminists should be quite *obscene*" and participate in embracing dimensions of the culture that allow us to cross boundaries, and so forth (246). Perhaps I'm missing something, but I see nothing inherently transformative about such a move at all. In a culture, our own, in which every barrier to the appearance of nearly anything in public has collapsed, obscenity has become a commodity: it is up for sale daily. Big deal. Just the other evening I saw on television a group that hangs out at night in cavelike places, features very pale people with pieces of metal dangling from all visible body parts, and practices "vampirism." The "vampirists" were sucking one another's blood as the cameras rolled. They were being ever so "obscene." What was amazing was just how dull it was. All a "vampire" can do is suck blood. Citizens have a few more arrows in the quiver. Am I missing something here? I

Reply to Boling and Elshtain

Debra Morris, *Woodrow Wilson Department of Government and Foreign Affairs, University of Virginia*

I thank Patricia Boling and Jean Elshtain for their exceptionally thoughtful criticisms (in this volume); engaging them has allowed me to see more clearly the essay's aim. Since I haven't the space to respond to all of their points, I will attempt to address their chief concerns through the single issue that preoccupies even as it ultimately divides us, namely, what it means today to rethink privacy. We agree that any attempt to do so must engage debates having to do with the nature of public reason, the cause of social justice, the demands of democratic civil society.

If I claim as my starting point the feminist insight that public-private is a central axis for the organization and consolidation of power but neglect to make that argument here, it is not to evade or deny the dangers inhering in "too much or the wrong kind of respect for privacy" (Boling, 252). I simply believe that other theorists — Elshtain, Okin, Pateman, MacKinnon, and Boling, to name but a few — have articulated those dangers very well already. Indeed, it is precisely because others have established so convincingly the deficiencies of *privatism* that I feel able to raise certain questions and possibilities regarding *privacy*. Further, if I take issue with Boling's and Elshtain's stress on the rational translation of private into public, it is not because I believe them (or Pitkin and Arendt, for that matter) guilty of an imperious "rationalist logic." Indeed, I applaud their efforts to understand such translation experientially, as a matter of *transforming* the "private sufferer into a citizen" (Boling, 253). This is why their work proves so invaluable for engaging the problem of privacy's relation to public reason and political judgment: Boling's nuanced account of the language of public and private, for instance, and Elshtain's insistence that we view problems and problem-solving on a human (or quotidian) scale help us to transcend arid Kantian conceptions of judgment. But I do insist that there are costs, for any further theorization of private, public, and the relationship between the two, of work like Boling's and Elshtain's. Feminist criticism has succeeded spectacularly in undermining the quaint image of privacy as the space of intimacy, family, and the interdependence of mutual care — in other words, as the absence of competitive and zero-sum struggle over power. Yet many feminist theorists espouse a conception of the public realm that proves perfectly analogous. It is a conception of public space in which power relations are legitimated — that is to say, transformed from competitive and zero-sum struggle into something else, something different and better, whether that is "strong," deliberative, or "discursive" democracy. That this is a conception of public space with which it would be foolish to disagree is a sign not of its falsity but of its limits in exploding the parameters of the privacy debate. For instance, such a conception does not encourage a deep engagement with postmodernist inquiries into the forms of power contained in otherwise benign democratic practices, inquiries that do open up the possibility of theorizing private and public *together.*

Such theorization is necessary, I contend, for apprehending privacy's essential ambivalence today: its significance as lost ideal and its ascendancy as privatism. I am interested in connecting, as well as interpreting, these two things — a task for which the notion of privacy as indifferent force, open to multiple uses, may prove useful. Boling insists that this is a tautological formulation, though I would deny that it is especially so — at least when compared to dominant views that simply define the private in opposition to the public, it mattering little whether the aim is to criticize privacy (as mere "private interest") or to commend it (as the essential human ground for intimacy, unconventionality, etc.). A particularly seductive example of the latter (i.e., privacy's definition through its affirmation) is Rochelle Gurstein's understanding of the private as a timeless feature of "human topography," an essential "protective container for vulnerable experiences" (1996, 9, 13), a view with which Boling and Elshtain clearly sympathize. It is not that I do not; clearly the "protective container" view is relevant to my own understanding of privacy as a reprieve from power. But there is a crucial difference between privacy containing vulnerable experiences and privacy constituting, if only retrospectively or reflexively, a critical perspective on experiences, vulnerability being just one. We might put it this way: the former stresses the essential human form of privacy, the latter its contingent content over time. And, for this very reason, the "container" conception implies that something of unspeakable human importance is lost, is always at risk, in translating private into public, but as I suggest below of political protest, there may be some things of private significance — some things of significance to privacy — that are only constituted thereby.

My aim in "Privacy, Privation, Perversity" is not only to rethink privacy, but also to think otherwise about it, that is, to enlist new and different resources and theoretical perspectives, ones capable of eliciting new valuations. All three of us agree that the public-private debate is in need of just this sort of radical repair. Significantly, Boling places at the heart of the privacy struggle "a particular model of theoretical discourse," and it is here that she commends my use of "divergent approaches" and my attempt to "trea[t] contradiction and ambiguity as a source of insight rather than as a defect to be explained away" (255). Likewise with Elshtain's call to "put the social back in" (259) and, more particularly, to affirm and to foreground the quotidian: this is a struggle over the *discourse* of public and private, and it too insists that we understand them in terms of their immediate, interanimating effects in individual lives rather than as abstract valuations. But it is strange, then, that certain valuations appear so persistent.

So, this is where I begin to diverge from Boling and Elshtain: I wish to move theorization past especially tenacious terms, to use those terms by putting them at risk, to push to the hilt the disturbances within the concept (and experience) of privacy. Lest my point here seem too enigmatic, let me say a few things about my use of Wendy Brown's (1995) work in the third section of the essay. Boling complains that I do not engage Brown's criticisms of the highly personalized language of pain and injury favored by Patricia Williams (1991), that, rather, I "simply identif[y] and then ignor[e]" those criticisms (256). But my intention in a deliberately specula-tive reading of Williams's work—and my point in highlighting certain odd and evocative turns in that work—is to show that Williams is hardly vul-nerable in the ways Brown suggests, that is, "mystif[ied by] the powers that construct . . . her" (1995, 128), though to be sure Williams appre-hends and contends with those powers in novel ways (many of them predi-cated on her own "mysterious autonomy"). The exigencies of contempo-rary politics—in particular, the degree to which an insidious control confounds the logic of rights, of political personhood, or precisely the problem analyzed so deftly by Brown—require that we cultivate as varied and imaginative a repertoire of responses, of strategies for redeploying the powers that construct us, as possible.

Thus my objective in each of the essay's three sections is to highlight one perspective on privacy, at least one dimension of it, that seems to elude dominant conceptions—that allows us, more crucially, to connect such things as personal, public, and political in new and untried ways. I should have said as much: my entire aim is to use privacy as a gateway to unantici-pated "connections and discontinuities between individual and collective life" (Boling, 256–57) and to employ these, in turn, to articulate more precisely privacy's complex status and function today. Hence the impor-tance of terms like "transitional space"—a highly suggestive concept for articulating the way in which central political and social norms are crucially dependent upon an ambivalent fantasy (itself neither private nor public, of course) *of* privacy, of interiority and self-containment.

To connect in this way is to complicate the private and the public simul-taneously. Let me elaborate this with respect to identity politics. In the section "Acting Up," I contest the specific connection among private, per-sonal, and political so often assumed in assessments of identity move-ments, namely, that in politicizing the personal, such movements destroy the private (this is essentially the point of Gurstein's influential *The Repeal of Reticence* [1996]). I have since explored this criticism in more detail with regard to sexual-identity politics. My argument, very briefly, is that if iden-tity movements do make a claim to "authenticity," as Elshtain worries, then this claim has as much to do with individual as with group identity, and the former builds into political protest a necessarily equivocal mo-ment. The political payoff is this: the possibility that if our private lives are lived more equivocally—that is to say, with a greater respect for our capac-ity to deviate, to demur—then our public lives, our public personae, will show a greater capacity for freedom (a political ideal surprisingly resurgent in theoretical reflections on sexual-identity politics; see, e.g., Cornell 1998). The third section of my essay is predicated on a similar gamble, namely, that the special kind of insight and self-understanding generated in singular and exquisitely individuating events—a particular look, a particular longing or desire—sensitizes rather than blinds citizens to "the powers that construct . . . [them]" (Brown 1995, 128). These are ways, finally, of integrating feminist with postmodernist critique, an exercise for which I feel more enthusiasm, perhaps, than do Boling and Elshtain!

As for my call to the "obscene," I appreciate Elshtain's concerns: politically speaking, there is nothing more banal than vampirism (as becomes plain once vampirism is understood as just one more manifestation of "Gen-X" cool, a sensibility more disastrous in its political implications than any rhetoric of authenticity). But it is against the banal that the genuinely obscene promises some corrective. I suggest that the essential question regarding privacy is whether it can function critically, that is to say, against a political culture characterized by (in)difference more than diversity, privatism more than privacy? Is there a part of what we habitually think of as "inner reality" that, if not utterly beyond interpellation or the "taboos . . . operat[ing] in the ritualized repetition of norms," as Judith Butler puts it (1993, 21), nevertheless consistently "exceeds" them? And is this stubborn and excessive subjectivity, finally, a more viable basis for political agency than the radical autonomy promised in liberal theory? Whatever the answer, it is no longer enough simply to posit, against subjectivity, a pleasing political symmetry, objectivity, community. Rethinking the private person requires that we rethink, as well, the democratic citizen she is to become.

References

Brown, Wendy. 1995. *States of Injury: Power and Freedom in Late Modernity.* Princeton, N.J.: Princeton University Press.

Butler, Judith. 1993. "Critically Queer." *GLQ: A Journal of Lesbian and Gay Studies.* 1(1):17–32.

Cornell, Drucilla. 1998. *At the Heart of Freedom: Feminism, Sex, and Equality.* Princeton, N.J.: Princeton University Press.

Gurstein, Rochelle. 1996. *The Repeal of Reticence: America's Cultural and Legal Struggles over Free Speech, Obscenity, Sexual Liberation, and Modern Art.* New York: Hill & Wang.

Williams, Patricia. 1991. *The Alchemy of Race and Rights.* Cambridge, Mass.: Harvard University Press. I

About the Contributors

Carolyn Allen is professor of English and adjunct professor of women studies at the University of Washington. She is author of *Following Djuna: Women Lovers and the Erotics of Loss* (Indianapolis: Indiana University Press, 1996) and articles on a variety of topics in twentieth-century studies and in feminist theory. Her most recent project is on cultural power and theories of emotion. She is coeditor of *Signs: Journal of Women in Culture and Society.*

Ien Ang is professor of cultural studies and director of the Research Centre in Intercommunal Studies at the University of Western Sydney in Australia. She has published widely on a range of issues in media and cultural studies, feminism and the politics of difference, and the cultural politics of the Chinese diaspora. Her forthcoming book is *Together in Difference: Living between Asia and the West* (London: Routledge, 2001).

Patricia Boling is associate professor of political science and women's studies at Purdue University. She has written widely on connections between private and public life in *Privacy and the Politics of Intimate Life* (Ithaca, N.Y.: Cornell University Press, 1996), "Private Interest and the Public Good in Japan," *Pacific Review* 3, no. 2 (1990): 138–50, and "The Democratic Potential of Mothering," *Political Theory* 19, no. 4 (November 1991): 606–25. Her current work examines the intersections between public and private in family support policies in Japan, the United States, Germany, and France. She was a Fulbright research fellow in Tokyo in the fall of 1999 and is currently working on a book that takes a feminist and political approach to comparative family policy.

Rosi Braidotti is professor of women's studies on the arts faculty at Utrecht University and scientific director of the Netherlands Research School of Women's Studies. She coordinates ATHENA, the European Thematic Network of women's studies for the SOCRATES program of the commission for the European Union. She has published extensively in feminist philosophy, epistemology, poststructuralism, and psychoanalysis. Her most recent book is *Nomadic Subjects: Embodiment and Sexual Difference* (New York: Columbia University Press, 1994), and a new one, titled *Metamorphoses,* is forthcoming from Polity in 2000.

Patricia Hill Collins is professor and chair of African American studies at the University of Cincinnati. She is author of *Fighting Words: Black Women and the Search* *for Justice* (Minneapolis: University of Minnesota Press, 1998) and *Black Feminist Thought: Knowledge, Consciousness, and the Politics of Empowerment* (1990; rev. ed., New York: Routledge, 2000), and coeditor, with Margaret Anderson, of *Race, Class, and Gender: An Anthology,* 4th ed. (Belmont, Calif.: Wadsworth, 2000).

R. W. Connell is professor of education at the University of Sydney. He has taught at the University of California, Santa Cruz, and at other institutions in the United States and Australia. He has been active in movements for peace and social justice and has done research on questions of social theory, gender relations, education, class, and politics. His recent publications include *Masculinities* (Berkeley: University of California Press, 1995), *Schools and Social Justice* (Philadelphia: Temple University Press, 1993), and *Rethinking Sex* (Philadelphia: Temple University Press, 1992). His new book, *The Men and the Boys, Bringing Together the Results of International Research on Gender Issues about Men,* will be published in 2001 by Polity.

Drucilla Cornell is professor of political science and women's studies at Rutgers University. She is author of *Beyond Accommodation: Ethical Feminism, Deconstruction, and the Law* (New York: Routledge, 1991), *The Philosophy of the Limit* (New York: Routledge, 1992), *Transformations: Recollective Imagination and Sexual Difference* (New York: Routledge, 1993), *The Imaginary Domain: Abortion, Pornography, and Sexual Harassment* (New York: Routledge, 1995), and *At the Heart of Freedom* (Princeton, N.J.: Princeton University Press, 1998). She is also editor of a recently released collection of essays on pornography. Two of her plays, *The Dream Cure* and *Background Interference,* have been performed in New York and Los Angeles.

Jean Bethke Elshtain is Laura Spelman Rockefeller Professor of Social and Political Ethics at the University of Chicago. Her many books include *Public Man, Private Woman: Women in Social and Political Thought,* 2d ed. (Princeton, N.J.: Princeton University Press, 1993), *Women and War,* 2d ed. (Chicago: University of Chicago Press, 1995), *Democracy on Trial* (New York: Basic, 1995), and *Real Politics: At the Center of Everyday Life* (Baltimore: Johns Hopkins University Press, 1997).

Rita Felski is professor of English at the University of Virginia. Her publications include *Beyond Feminist Aesthetics: Feminist Literature and Social Change* (Cambridge, Mass.: Harvard University Press, 1989), *The Gender of Modernity* (Cambridge, Mass.: Harvard University Press, 1995), and *Doing Time: Feminist Theory and Postmodern Culture* (New York: New York University Press, 2000). She is also coeditor of a special issue of *Cultural Studies* on Australian feminisms (vol. 10, no. 3 [1996]).

Sandra Harding is a philosopher in the Graduate School of Education and Information Studies and director of the Center for the Study of Women at the University of California, Los Angeles. Her most recent books are *Is Science Multicultural? Post-*

colonialisms, Feminisms, and Epistemologies (Indianapolis: Indiana University Press, 1998) and, with Uma Narayan, an edited collection titled *Decentering the Center: Philosophy for a Multicultural, Postcolonial, and Feminist World* (Indianapolis: Indiana University Press, 2000). Effective July 2000 she will be coeditor, with Kathryn Norberg, of *Signs: Journal of Women in Culture and Society.*

Nancy C. M. Hartsock is professor of political science and women studies at the University of Washington. She is author of *Money, Sex, and Power: Toward a Feminist Historical Materialism* (New York: Longman, 1983), *The Feminist Standpoint Revisited and Other Essays* (Boulder, Colo.: Westview, 1998), and many other works in feminist theory. She is currently working on a project tentatively titled "Feminizing Marx," which reexamines Marxist methods and categories from a contemporary feminist perspective.

Mary Hawkesworth is professor of political science and director of the Center for American Women and Politics at Rutgers University. Her research interests include contemporary political philosophy, feminist theory, and social policy. She is author of *Beyond Oppression: Feminist Theory and Political Strategy* (New York: Continuum, 1990) and *Theoretical Issues in Policy Analysis* (Albany: State University of New York Press, 1998) and editor of *The Encyclopedia of Government and Politics* (London: Routledge, 1992) and "Feminism and Public Policy," a special issue of *Policy Sciences,* vol. 27, nos. 2–3 (1994).

Susan Hekman is professor of political science at the University of Texas at Arlington. She is author of *Gender and Knowledge: Elements of a Postmodern Feminism* (Boston: Northeastern University Press, 1990), *Moral Voices, Moral Selves: Carol Gilligan and Feminist Moral Theory* (University Park: Pennsylvania State University Press, 1995), and *The Future of Differences: Truth and Method in Feminist Theory* (Malden, Mass.: Blackwell, 1999).

Judith A. Howard is professor of sociology and adjunct professor of women studies at the University of Washington. She studies gender dynamics and their intersections with race, class, and sexuality, emphasizing microlevel cognitions and interpersonal interactions. She is coauthor, with Jocelyn A. Hollander, of *Gendered Situations, Gendered Selves: A Gender Lens on Social Psychology* (Thousand Oaks, Calif.: Sage, 1997) and coeditor, with Jodi O'Brien, of *Everyday Inequalities: Critical Inquiries* (Malden, Mass.: Blackwell, 1998). She is coeditor of *Signs: Journal of Women in Culture and Society* and of Sage Publications' Gender Lens book series, which promotes scholarship and pedagogies that contribute to analyses of social inequalities based on race, class, gender, and sexuality.

Suzanne Kessler is professor of psychology at Purchase College, State University of New York. She is author of *Lessons from the Intersexed* (New Brunswick, N.J.: Rutgers University Press, 1998) and coauthor, with Wendy McKenna, of *Gender:*

An Ethnomethodological Approach (1978; reprint, Chicago: University of Chicago Press, 1985).

Wendy McKenna is adjunct associate professor of psychology at Barnard College and adjunct associate professor of sociology at Purchase College, State University of New York. She is coauthor, with Suzanne Kessler, of *Gender: An Ethnomethodological Approach* (1978; reprint, Chicago: University of Chicago Press, 1985). She teaches courses in psychology, human sexuality, and women's studies and is a licensed psychologist and certified sex educator.

Debra Morris (dam6m@virginia.edu) has taught political theory and gender politics at the University of Virginia since 1993. She also writes on pragmatist and postmodernist philosophies of science, which, like the view of privacy defended here, embrace more fully the singular event, the perverse detail, the individual and unrepeatable parts of experience. Morris now resides in Lexington, Kentucky, where she is writing a book that plots the decline over three decades of political literacy or the ability to read political and social events critically.

Oyeronke Oyewumi is assistant professor of black studies at the University of California, Santa Barbara. Her research interests include critical social theory, Western culture, and African societies and cultures in their local and global dimensions. She is author of *The Invention of Women: Making an African Sense of Western Gender Discourses* (Minneapolis: University of Minnesota Press, 1997), which won a 1998 distinguished book award from the American Sociological Association and was also a 1998 finalist for the Herskovitts Prize of the African Studies Association. She is also editor of *African Women and Feminism: Reflecting on the Politics of Sisterhood* (Trenton, N.J.: Africa World Press, 2000), in press.

Joan Wallach Scott is professor of social science at the Institute for Advanced Study in Princeton, New Jersey. She is author of *Only Paradoxes to Offer: French Feminists and the Rights of Man* (Cambridge, Mass.: Harvard University Press, 1996) and *Gender and the Politics of History* (New York: Columbia University Press, 1988); editor of *Feminism and History* (Oxford: Oxford University Press, 1996); and co-editor, with Judith Butler, of *Feminists Theorize the Political* (New York: Routledge, 1992).

Dorothy E. Smith is professor emerita of sociology and equity studies at the University of Toronto. She is author of *The Everyday World as Problematic: A Feminist Sociology* (Boston: Northeastern University Press, 1987), *The Conceptual Practices of Power: A Feminist Sociology of Knowledge* (Boston: Northeastern University Press, 1990), *Texts, Facts, and Femininity: Exploring the Relations of Ruling* (1990; reprint, New York: Routledge, 1993), and *Writing the Social: Critique, Theory, and Investigations* (Toronto: University of Toronto Press, 1999).

Steven G. Smith is professor of philosophy and religious studies at Millsaps College. He is author of *Gender Thinking* (Philadelphia: Temple University Press, 1992), *The Concept of the Spiritual: An Essay in First Philosophy* (Philadelphia: Temple University Press, 1992), and articles in philosophical anthropology, aesthetics, and philosophy of religion.

Index

class, and gender, 82; and power, 78; and sexual difference, 75, 77
coalition, politics of, 98
code, cultural, 105; symbolic, 104
Code, Lorraine, 10, 26
codes of Womanhood, 105
coexistence, and incommensurability, 133
cognitive purification, 163
Cohen, Jean, 222
collaboration, in feminist studies, 8
collective subjects, 40–41; and standpoint theory, 45; and voice, 47–48
Collins, Patricia Hill, 2, 9, 20–21, 56–57, 60, 66–67
colonialism, European, 99; and see imperialism
coming out, and individualism, 226
communication, music as, 130–31; and negotiation, 129; and politics, 235; and privacy, 244, 254
community, moral, 111, 115–17
competition, academic, 190; within the private, 262
complementarity, 4, 149, 152, 154, 156, 166, 183–84, 191, 198; and sociobiological accounts of gender, 170
concepts, opposed to reality, 14–16; in sociology, 15; and see reality
condensation, principle of, 120
Connell, R. W., 3, 146, 154, 161, 163–66, 188, 191, 193, 200, 202–4, 207, 211, 213, 217
Connor, Steven, 87
consciousness, bifurcated, 15; oppositional, 40; and subjectivity, 102
Corbett, Greville J., 149
Cornell, Drucilla, 3, 74, 75–78, 85, 95, 134, 136
Coward, Rosalind, 13
creolization, 82
cross-culturalism, see hybridity
cultural genitals, 169, 179, 214
culture, defined, 227; homogenization of, 136; and sexual difference, 75; and transitional objects, 226–27
cultures, and gender theories, 208–19
cunning of culture, 160, 167, 172, 174

D

deconstruction, and difference, 99; misunderstanding of, 87–88; and power politics, 100
degradation prohibition, 116
Deleuze, Gilles, 94, 100
dematerializing of women, 75
democratic politics and privacy, 244–45, 251, 258
Derrida, Jacques, 37, 40, 71, 74, 94, 100, 123
development vs. display, 226
deviance, and norms, 115
Devor, Holly, 154, 211
dichotomies, see binarism
différance, 73
difference, and categories, 61–62; definitions of, 73; and dissension, 78–85; and doxa, 3; and equality, 3, 6; and European philosophy, 99, 100; and feminist politics, 18; and feminist standpoint theory, 20–21; across/within genders, 166–67; and identity, 71, 87–88; and identity politics, 260; and liberal democratic theory, 190; making a, 105; multiplicity, and mimesis, 107; and negativity, 99; and object-relations theory, 12–13; and other, 81; as philosophical category, 85; philosophy of, 93–95; and postcolonial feminism, 78–85; and postmodernism, 18; and power, 5–6; scope of, 86–87; and standpoint theory, 10, 17, 24–25, 53; and value, 86–87; among women, 36, 72, 98, 106; and see sexual difference
dimorphism, sexual, 168, 172
discourse, and feminist standpoint theory, 20; and material reality, 14; politics of, 136; and power, 99; and social relations, 62; and standpoint theory, 13–14, 24
discrimination law, and legal equality, 115
displacement, politics of, 234–35
dissension, difference as, 78–85
dissent, and hybridity, 82; and identity politics, 260
diversity, and equality, 86; politics of, 81
Djerrkura, Gatjil, 133
dogma/doxa, 96